CW00829518

RAILWAY NATION

RAILWAY NATION

TALES OF CANADIAN PACIFIC

The World's Greatest Travel System

David Laurence Jones

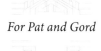

For Pat and Gord

Copyright © 2020 David Laurence Jones
Foreword copyright © 2020 Doug Cass

All rights reserved. No part of this publication may be reproduced, stored
in a retrieval system, or transmitted in any form or by any means—electronic,
mechanical, audio recording, or otherwise—without the written permission of
the publisher or a licence from Access Copyright, Toronto, Canada.

Heritage House Publishing Company Ltd.
heritagehouse.ca

Cataloguing information available from Library and Archives Canada

978-1-77203-349-6 (pbk)
978-1-77203-350-2 (ebook)

Edited by Warren Layberry
Proofread by Lara Kordic
Cover and interior design by Jacqui Thomas
Cover images: Jacqui Thomas (*front*) and High Level Bridge,
Lethbridge, Alberta (Author's Collection) (*back*)
Section opener illustrations by Jacqui Thomas. Illustration on page 72
is based on the photo on page 126 (Omer Lavallée in CPR steam
locomotive, Omer Lavallée Collection)

The interior of this book was produced on FSC®-certified, acid-free paper,
processed chlorine free and printed with vegetable-based inks.

Heritage House gratefully acknowledges that the land on which we live and
work is within the traditional territories of the Lkwungen (Esquimalt and
Songhees), Malahat, Pacheedaht, Scia'new, T'Sou-ke, and W̱SÁNEĆ
(Pauquachin, Tsartlip, Tsawout, Tseycum) Peoples.

We acknowledge the financial support of the Government of Canada through
the Canada Book Fund (CBF) and the Canada Council for the Arts, and
the Province of British Columbia through the British Columbia
Arts Council and the Book Publishing Tax Credit.

24 23 22 21 20   1 2 3 4 5

Printed in Canada

CONTENTS

FOREWORD

I t gives me great pleasure to write this foreword for David Laurence Jones's new book on the history of the Canadian Pacific Railway. My association with David began in 2012, when he and some of his colleagues from the National Dream Legacy Society approached the Glenbow Museum with an offer to volunteer in some way that could advance the preservation of CPR history. I was the director of the library and archives at the time and was happy to oblige. I am glad I did, for that began a seven-year association with David, Doug Phillips, and Don Heron, all three of whom brought immense knowledge of the history of Canadian railways to the museum and worked on a succession of projects benefiting Glenbow and future researchers.

The library and archives at Calgary's Glenbow Museum was a major regional collection of non-governmental publications and historical records documenting the development of southern Alberta and the Canadian West. A key priority from the beginning was the collection of company records, and as a result, for half a century, it has been one of the largest business archives in Canada. Among the earliest major acquisitions were the files of the Canadian Pacific Railway Department of Natural Resources, which was established in Calgary in 1912 and dealt with a host of company undertakings other than the actual operation of the railway, such as land sales, irrigation development, coal mining, and the promotion of immigration to the Canadian West. Over the years, the archives acquired nearly three hundred other archival collections dealing with the railway, and the library accumulated strong holdings of CPR publications, including the library of former CPR president D'Alton Coleman. All of this material is now available through the Glenbow Western Research Centre at the University of Calgary.

Through its work on a number of major exhibitions, Glenbow has had a long association with the railway. In the early 1980s, archivists Bill McKee and Georgeen Barrass developed a major exhibition on the history of the CPR in Western Canada and received extensive assistance from Omer Lavallée and the staff of the CPR archives. That exhibition ultimately resulted in a book *Trail of Iron* (Douglas & McIntyre, 1983) as well as a major conference on CPR history that led to the book *The CPR West: The Iron Road and the Making of a Nation* (Douglas & McIntyre, 1984). Portions of the *Trail of Iron* show were also on permanent display in the museum until 2007, when Glenbow re-developed all of the history galleries with the show *Mavericks: An Incorrigible History of Alberta*. That exhibition included a gallery on railway history focusing on several individuals, including William Van Horne, William Pearce, and Mary Schaeffer. Glenbow returned to the analysis of the impact of the railway in the 2009 exhibition *Vistas*, curated by prominent art historian Roger Boulet. That exhibit also resulted in book, this one put out by the archive itself in 2010 entitled *Vistas: Artists on the Canadian Pacific Railway*.

David and his colleagues noticed early on that the photograph identification in Glenbow's online photo catalogue was incomplete or erroneous, so their first project was to update the information for several thousand images, some of which appear in this book. They also encouraged others to donate a number of archival collections—including Floyd Yeats and Ray Matthews—and worked diligently to catalogue these photos, which spanned the whole history of the railway. Glenbow also received a number of large donations of plans and drawings of CPR structures and equipment, many saved by Doug Phillips, which led to several other arrangement and description efforts. Their unique knowledge of railway history also helped Glenbow staff answer dozens of research inquiries over the years.

It is only fitting that *Railway Nation* is able to draw as heavily as it does from the photographic archives of the Glenbow Museum after the excellent contributions of David Laurence Jones and his colleagues helped make the collection what it is today. ✣

Doug Cass
Director, Library and Archives at Glenbow Museum

PREFACE

The stories in *Railway Nation: Tales of Canadian Pacific, the World's Greatest Travel System* were largely inspired by my early years at Canadian Pacific, when I worked in the company's Corporate Archives, which was part of the department of Public Relations & Advertising (later Communications & Public Affairs).

The Canadian Pacific Corporate Archives collection was established in 1974, more than ninety years after the incorporation of the company—so we had a lot of catching up to do.

At the time, a number of factors contributed to the decision to start a formal archival program. The primary function of the company's Windsor Station headquarters building was on the wane, with fewer and fewer train arrivals and departures using the Montreal terminal facility. Much of the vault space below the station was being refurbished for uses other than storage. While many records were being microfilmed and then discarded, some original materials were retained for their intrinsic and historic value. The CPR president's vault, as well as those assigned to the company secretary and the legal department, was "rediscovered" to contain letters, engineering plans, advertising items and other materials of great historic interest, dating back to the railway's formative years in the 1880s.

With the approaching centennial of CPR's incorporation, public interest in the company's history was on the rise. The most overt example of this renewed fascination was the enthusiastic reception of popular historian Pierre Berton's bestselling histories of the company—*The National Dream* and *The Last Spike*, as well as the airing of an accompanying CBC television series.

Around the same time, CP was exiting several business ventures that were no longer viable, among them passenger rail service and passenger steamship service. Before long, the company would systematically divest of other assets, including its airline, much of its trucking interests and several hotels, to concentrate on core railway operations. Many of the closed businesses would forward their critical bookkeeping and ephemera to the head office.

For the next several decades, the staff of Canadian Pacific Corporate Archives, under the guiding hand of highly respected and knowledgeable historian and archivist Omer Lavallée, would accept and organize new acquisitions of legal and potentially historic significance. While the vast xi

majority of these records came from a variety of company departments, additional material was acquired, where appropriate, from individual employees, collectors, and private dealers.

Although the corporate archives was a private collection, with the primary function of serving the business requirements of Canadian Pacific, members of the public could make special arrangements to consult the archives for research or commercial purposes. Upon submission of a written request, access was provided at the discretion of the company. And, indeed, over the years hundreds of people took advantage of the opportunity to produce research papers, magazine articles, books, and movies from the information contained within the various records groups that were made available to them.

It was during my fourteen-year tenure with the archives that I encountered most of the stories and images that are presented in this compilation, while organizing, preserving, and cataloguing boxes full of letters, accounting records, engineering plans, advertising brochures, promotional posters, photographic negatives and prints, and much more. Though my father had been a CPR employee, and I grew up in a family that often took train trips to visit relatives during the summer months, I had not been aware of the full extent of Canadian Pacific's enormous contributions to the settlement and development of Canada.

But I did know that I liked tales about the golden age of passenger trains, luxury steamships, fancy hotels, and the people who were lucky enough to frequent them. The more I discovered about the endless connections between the transportation activities of Canadian Pacific and the vast army of immigrants, travellers, tourists, and others who have been guests of the "World's Greatest Travel System," the more I though others would like these tales, too. ⁙

NOTE: Canada did not adopt the metric system until 1970. As the lion's share of the stories in this book take place prior to that date, imperial measurements have been left in place. Due to the nature of the material explored, units of measurement come into play quite often. Rather than belabour the narrative with scores of parenthetical conversions throughout, miles, feet, pounds, and tons have been allowed to stand on their own.

1

RIBBONS OF STEEL

WHEN THE CANADIAN PACIFIC RAILWAY WAS COMPLETED in 1885, it was the country's first transcontinental, and the longest railway in the world under one management. Built in an era when railways were often constructed and exploited for political gain, the CPR had literally ensured the survival of the fledgling Canadian confederation from sea to sea, as envisioned by the nation's founders.

The decision of the CPR syndicate members to build the line on a more southerly route than had long been anticipated by government surveyors and private land speculators alike established the pattern of settlement in the country's "Golden Northwest" for decades to come. It also rewarded the company's patrons with some of the most spectacular scenery on earth, as the railway made its way along the rugged shores of Lake Superior, across the wide-open expanses of the Prairies, and through the towering peaks of the Rocky and Selkirk Mountains.

Canadian Pacific would soon grow to be much more than just a profitable railway or an essential instrument of national unity. The ambitions of company management to establish its own hotel chain, launch its own steamship line, and invest in a host of other transportation and resource-based involvements insured that the future of the CPR would be inextricably linked with the future of the country.

Donald Smith drove two "last" spikes at Craigellachie on that fateful day. A third, ceremonial spike didn't even make it to the event.
PHOTO BY ALEXANDER ROSS, AUTHOR'S COLLECTION

THE SAGA OF THE THREE LAST SPIKES

A t 9:22 AM, Pacific Time, on November 7, 1885, Donald Smith drove a plain iron spike at Craigellachie, British Columbia, to complete the Canadian Pacific Railway's transcontinental main line linking Canada's populous Eastern centres with the country's more isolated communities on the West Coast.

The spike hammered down by the future Lord Strathcona was just like the countless others that had been used to hold in place the twin bands of steel from one end of the country to the other. CPR's general manager, William Van Horne, had seen too many failed railroads in the United States begin with elaborate ceremonies and gold spikes to mark their completion. Eschewing such conceits, he decreed that his railway would keep things simple. He told the Eastern press that anyone coming to see the last rails laid on the CPR main line would have to be "either connected to the railway in some way, or they could pay their own way."

Despite the attitude of the railway boss, however, in the months leading up to the line's completion Canada's governor general, Lord Lansdowne, had ordered a silver-plated spike be prepared, in anticipation of receiving the call to be present at the historic event. Ultimately, neither the governor general nor the fancy spike would be involved.

In the absence of CPR president George Stephen, who was in the UK negotiating a critical mail subsidy to keep alive the company's whole financially shaky endeavour, Smith was chosen to do the honours. Smith was the senior member of the founding CPR syndicate of investors and Stephen's cousin. The name for the location where the tracklayers from the East met those from the West had been predetermined by Van Horne to recognize the importance of Stephen and Smith's contributions to the national enterprise. Craigellachie, from the Gaelic, meaning "Rock of Alarm," was the location in Scotland where the two men's clan had traditionally kept vigil against all enemies. In the darkest hour of CPR's financial dilemma just a year earlier, a determined George Stephen, immersed in negotiations to stave off disaster, had cabled his cousin Donald Smith with the fateful words: "Stand fast, Craigellachie!"

Now with the grand project nearing completion, other notables such as Sir Sandford Fleming, A.B. Rogers, and several high-level railway officials looked on as Smith struck the spike that had been set up for the simple ceremony a glancing blow, bending it slightly and rendering it defective.

CPR roadmaster Frank Brothers twisted and pulled it from the tie and replaced it with another that was successfully driven home by Smith. Once the cheering had died down, Van Horne, called upon to make an impromptu speech, said simply: "All I can say is that the work has been well done in every way."

Arthur Piers, private secretary to the general manager, spotting the spike that had been bent by Smith lying beside the track after the ceremony, picked it up and put it in his pocket. But the ever observant elder statesman of CPR saw this and asked Piers to hand over the now significant trinket, from which he had pieces of the iron mounted alongside a row of diamonds in spike-shaped pins as souvenirs for ladies connected with the railway party who were not present at the historic occasion.

Frank Brothers then removed the successfully driven last spike from the roadbed to discourage others from seeking to acquire the ultimate nation-building keepsake. Many years later, it was presented to then CPR president Edward Beatty, who kept it in a special presentation box on his office desk in Montreal's Windsor Station.

Lord Lansdowne's silver spike was, in later years, given to members of Van Horne's family, who served as faithful custodians of the artifact before turning it over to the Canadian Museum of Civilization (now the Canadian Museum of History), in 2012, where it currently resides.

The bent and chopped up spike was donated by Lord Strathcona, the great grandson of the CPR director who bore the same title, to Canada's National Museum of Science & Technology (now Canada Science & Technology Museum) in 1985, one hundred years after the CPR's completion. It is now on long-term loan to the Canadian Museum of Immigration at Pier 21 in Halifax, Nova Scotia, as a tribute to immigrant railway workers.

The intact spike, considered by many to be the most authentic and significant "Last Spike" of the CPR, disappeared from Beatty's desk some time before the Second World War, never to be seen again. ⸸

THE BIG HILL

For railway builders, two considerations are top of mind when the steel hits the ground: lay it straight and lay it flat. Curvature not only adds distance between Point A and Point B but contributes mightily to wear and tear on both track and wheels. Gradients are even worse, requiring more horsepower to pull loads uphill, more brake action to go down, more fuel to get where you're going, and more skilful train-handling to prevent runaways, pull-aparts, and the potential damage that the continuous stretching and compressing of the slack between cars can cause.

When the builders of the Canadian Pacific Railway made the decision to take a direct route through the Rocky Mountains via the Kicking Horse Pass, rather than run the line by way of the more northerly and circuitous Yellowhead Pass, they heeded the first cardinal rule while sacrificing a strict adherence to the latter.

Following the standard that had been set for virtually all previous railway lines constructed in North America, the Canadian federal government had specified in CPR's contract a maximum gradient of 2.2 percent for the entire transcontinental line, from one end to the other. What that meant was that no section of track should rise or fall more than 2.2 feet for every 100 feet that it progressed across the country. However, the fateful decision to use the Kicking Horse led to a temporary relaxation of this standard for a distance of just over seven miles between Hector, at the summit of the Rocky Mountains, and Field, in the valley of the Kicking Horse River to the west, on what was soon to be known as the notorious Big Hill.

To avoid the slow and expensive tunnelling that would be required to maintain CPR's contractual obligations, the railway builders convinced the government to allow a grade of 4.5 percent—more than double the specified maximum—over this short stretch of track. To address the obvious safety concerns this would entail, a unique set of mitigating construction features and operating procedures was put in place.

Safety switches and runaway spurs were installed at three locations on the steep slope, each manned by a switch tender, or guard, who, in the case of a runaway train, could divert the movement off of the main line and onto an uphill section of track, in much the same way today's truckers use highway runoffs on mountain roads when they experience brake failures. The railway's operating rules required its employees to set the switches to divert all downhill movements onto the safety spurs.

If the grade became too much to handle, CPR switchmen could send runaway trains onto uphill safety spur lines like the one shown here on the main line west of Hector, BC. AUTHOR'S COLLECTION

As trains approached each switch, their engine crews were obliged to blow four short whistle blasts to indicate that their trains were under control. Only then would the men at their posts throw the switches to allow trains to bypass the safety spurs and proceed down the Big Hill. Passenger trains were required to make a full stop before reaching each safety switch on the way down, but still often arrived in Field with brake shoes smoking. Eight miles per hour was fixed as the maximum speed for passenger trains to descend.

Westbound train crews were instructed to conduct tests of their brakes and inspect track sanders before beginning their descent. Inexperienced engineers were not allowed to come down the Big Hill alone. For their first few trips, their engines were coupled in behind other locomotives operated by veterans of mountain operations until they got a feel for the precipitous downhill manoeuvre.

For eastbound, uphill movements, one or more pusher engines were added to the rear end of trains at Field, which became known for the small fleet of powerful locomotives stationed there and the cadre of intrepid operating employees who specialized in escorting both freight and passengers safely up and down the hill. The pusher engines were uncoupled at Hector before trains proceeded toward Lake Louise and Calgary.

Initially, two of these *Consolidation* locomotives were permitted to take no more than seventeen loaded freight cars in daylight or twelve at night. A single engine was limited to twelve cars by day or nine by night. As the size and weight of trains increased over the years, so too did the size and power of the locomotives used to negotiate this challenging stretch of track. Even under the best of conditions, it could take as long as an hour to move a train between Field and Hector.

Accidents on the Big Hill were inevitable; indeed, a couple occurred before the line was even completed, including one nasty incident before the safety switches were installed during which sixty-five men working on construction were injured while bailing from an out-of-control train. Another train—wrecked on New Year's Day in 1899 and dubbed the Eggnog Express by a present-day history buff—dumped whiskey and eggs all over the first runaway track. Other spills were not so amusing.

In the twenty-five years that the CPR operated over this perilous section of track, before it was finally eliminated by the construction of the world-famous Spiral Tunnels, many employees

General Manager Van Horne acquired powerful Consolidation locomotives to operate on the Big Hill. PHOTO BY ERNEST BROWN, AUTHOR'S COLLECTION

were injured or worse, and much railway equipment was reduced to splinters in various mishaps. However, fatalities were mercifully rare, and the CPR was fortunate enough to never lose a paying customer to the Big Hill. ✥

TAKING COVER FROM AVALANCHES

By the time the last spike was driven on the CPR main line on November 7, 1885, only a few trains were able to pass over the railway that year before the mountain sections were abandoned to the elements for the winter.

Without snow sheds to cover the sections of track most exposed to avalanches, regular operations were out of the question. Instead, to profit from the enforced delay, crews were stationed in the mountains—particularly on the western slope of the Selkirks—to observe the frequency of the snowfall, the depth to which it might accumulate, and the consequential occurrence of avalanches that could endanger the line.

It was well known that Rogers Pass—the elusive route through the Selkirk Mountains discovered by the irascible Major A.B. Rogers in 1881—was prone to snowfalls of up to fifty feet deep during any given winter, and also that the avalanches that began more than a mile above the railway's sinuous roadbed could roar down the slopes at more than a hundred miles per hour. The observation camps set up that winter confirmed the worst fears of the railway men.

Although the winter of 1885–86 was milder than the previous one, Division Engineer Granville C. Cunningham nevertheless observed nine avalanches of varying intensity during the season in one location alone. Some sections of track were buried multiple times, with up to forty feet of snow. A single slide was recorded to be 1,800 feet long, 60 feet wide, and 30 feet deep.

James Ross, the engineer in charge of construction in the West, wrote to railway general manager William Van Horne to express his concern that the threat of snow slides might be more than either man had anticipated.

You can imagine what the effect of one million tons of ice and snow passing through the air at the rate of 100 miles per hour in the width of a few hundred feet would be. Trees three feet in diameter are torn to pieces like so many matches; if one-tenth of a tree is left standing, this portion is stripped of every branch and limb and slivered and split to the snow line.

And along with the devastating effects of ice, snow, and ruinous debris came another potential menace.

Countless hours of work and continuous trainloads of wooden timbers went into snow shed construction during the winter of 1885–86, after the main line was completed through the mountains of Alberta and British Columbia. AUTHOR'S COLLECTION

The effect of the wind during the progress of the slide is something terrific, scattering small timber and bush for a height of three hundred feet up the opposite side of the mountain . . . no train would be safe if caught in such a tornado.

As a result of the winter's startling revelations, a total of thirty-one individual snow sheds were planned for Rogers Pass alone, some as long as two thousand feet, representing an aggregate length of more than five miles of track under cover. The additional work added more than $1,120,000 to the cost of putting the line in shape for the 1886 season and involved the cutting and shaping of millions of board feet of hewn and sawn wood.

Twelve-inch by twelve-inch timbers of solid cedar and Douglas fir, braced and bolted together, were used for the cribwork and heavy planking covered the roofs. Where it was necessary to protect large sections of track, the snow sheds were divided into several short sections with open spaces between, as potential fire breaks. Above the openings, the ground was cleared, if continual avalanches had not already done so, and massive V-shaped fences were constructed to deflect slides over the sheds built to withstand them.

Because the shelters for snow protection also obscured the best views of the Illecillewaet and Asulkan glaciers, Van Horne instructed his construction forces to lay sections of summer track outside the snow sheds, onto which the trains could be diverted so as not to deprive the railway's patrons of the magnificent scenery afforded by the stretch of track from Bear Creek to the CPR's mountain hotel at Glacier, BC.

Despite all of these precautions, avalanches could and did still occur in unexpected spots, sometimes with fatal results. In February 1887, a large slide buried the plow that had been sent to clear away an earlier deluge of snow, along with sixteen men who worked to clear the line. Six of the men died, including a locomotive crew.

The worst incident occurred in 1910, when a mammoth avalanche demolished Shed 17, turned a hundred-ton rotary snowplow on its side, deposited the tender six hundred feet away, and killed sixty-two men almost instantly. Locomotive engineer Bill Lachance defied fate when he was blown from the cab of his engine and suffered no more than a broken leg, after floating on top of the slide until it ran its course. The avalanche left so much debris and, tragically, so many bodies in its wake, the line had to be cleared by an army of shovellers rather than by plows.

In the first thirty years of operations, the CPR's death toll among snowfighters had reached more than two hundred, until the construction of the Connaught Tunnel enabled trains to run five miles under Mount Macdonald and pass beneath the most treacherous stretch of track in the Selkirks. With great care and no small amount of luck, the CPR had lost no passengers to the frequent avalanches

To guard the line against the prodigious snowfalls and frequent avalanches that occurred in the Rocky and Selkirk Mountains, CPR built miles of snow sheds. The two sheds pictured here are located at the base of Cheops Mountain, where the track loops through the Illecillewaet Valley. AUTHOR'S COLLECTION

that plagued Rogers Pass. The Great Northern Railroad, just south of the border in the United States, had not been so fortunate. In the winter of 1910, two of its passenger trains stranded by snow in Stevens Pass were swept away by an avalanche, taking with it the lives of forty-nine men.

Many of the worst spots for potential avalanches on railways around the world, including on the CPR, would over the years be covered with concrete snow sheds, which would take up the protective role played by their staunch, wooden predecessors. ⁜

THE EVOLVING PACIFIC TERMINUS

The CPR's first regularly scheduled transcontinental train steamed out of Montreal's Dalhousie Station on June 28, 1886, and five days later pulled into the railway's West Coast terminal station at Port Moody, BC. But there was little land available for yard construction at that location. The offshore tidal flats were not conducive to the envisioned deep-water steamship operations that would connect the country with far-flung markets across the Pacific. A move farther west was inevitable.

The railway company built a twelve-mile extension during the winter of 1886–87 to a more appropriate site on English Bay, under an agreement with the province, which gave CPR a generous land grant of more than six thousand acres in Granville on which to build all the facilities it would require, as well as to develop a new commercial centre in what would soon be renamed Vancouver. Future land sales would more than compensate for the cost of the extension.

CPR's first Vancouver station was built just below the bluff at the end of Howe Street, on a narrow strip of land that allowed for a small yard and an elevated rail line to connect with the company's large new steamship wharf. Over time there would be plenty of space to expand the yard and provide a more permanent system of piers. The railway company would also control the evolution of the town's streets and structures overlooking the harbour.

The arrival of the railway was the impetus for a commercial boom in Vancouver, accompanied by a corresponding population boom. From the few hundred who had been on hand to welcome the first Pacific Express in 1887, the town's list of citizens had grown to nearly fourteen thousand souls four years later. The time was ripe to replace what CPR management had always regarded as a functional but temporary station building with something much more in keeping with Vancouver's rising status as a great port city.

In 1898, the original, modest station that had witnessed this rapid transformation was moved about a mile east to an empty lot at the foot of Heatley Avenue, beside a small CPR overflow yard. William Alberts, a CPR switchman who had been injured in the service of the railway, was allowed to live there rent-free for the next fifty years.

Its replacement would be built "up the hill" to fulfill its role as a vibrant commercial centre, side by side with the prominent banks, department stores, and substantial residences lining the bustling streets of Vancouver's downtown. Architect Edward Colonna, an art nouveau practitioner favoured

CPR's second Vancouver terminus rises like a castle on the escarpment above the original railway depot and steamship piers.
PHOTO BY JOSEPH HECKMAN, AUTHOR'S COLLECTION

by railway builder William Van Horne, was commissioned to design the unique structure that would arise one street east of Howe on Cordova, at the foot of Granville Street. The design was tweaked somewhat during its development by prominent Montreal architect Edward Maxwell, who was also a favourite of CPR. Built in the French chateau style, in keeping with other CPR buildings going up across the country, the station's eight-storey central pavilion was flanked by two towers, one circular and one octagonal. Its somewhat whimsical look became a favourite with the locals.

Local contractor C. Osborn Wickenden superintended the construction of what would become one of the town's most unique and admired structures. Sixty-five carloads of sandstone were imported from quarries in Calgary for the first floor and more than two million bricks from Victoria, BC, of a mottled buff colour were brought over to the mainland for upper floors of the superstructure. The bricks themselves were said by industry journal *Railway & Shipping World* to be "impervious to water and therefore particularly suitable for a building in a climate such as is experienced in Vancouver."

Several firms vied for the job of erecting the station, before it was awarded to the team of Thomas Tompkins, a builder from Brockville, Ontario, with a good reputation and solid connections to the CPR. Completed at a cost of about $130,000 and opened in 1899, the building's appearance from the harbour was particularly striking, with the north face dropping an additional thirty feet from the level of the southern station entrance on Cordova to the trackside platforms below.

The new building was designed to serve multiple purposes, providing appropriate space for the railway's dining car department, a Dominion Express office, and several showrooms for travelling salesmen.

In 1901, the entire street-side facade was illuminated by 1,585 electric lights for the cross-Canada royal tour of the Duke and Duchess of Cornwall and York.

However, within a dozen years, the castle-like terminus building, despite its imposing design, would be deemed inadequate by CPR management. "Vancouver will have a new and splendid depot from the CPR that will surpass the expectations of the most sanguine," President Thomas Shaughnessy informed the newspapers. By 1912, the architectural firm Barrott, Blackader & Webster of Montreal, and the engineering concern Westinghouse, Church, Kerr & Company of Montreal and New York, were already at work on a new, expansive, six-storey, steel-frame terminus building that would go on to serve as the city's busiest transportation hub well into the twenty-first century.

The site chosen for the new Beaux-Arts, neoclassical station was one block east of the Colonna building, which was torn down, making way for an extension of Granville to cross the CPR rail yard on a wide viaduct to a new pier on which extensive new freight sheds and an imposing steamship passenger terminal would serve the company's Trans-Pacific traffic, as well as its coastal steamship business.

The million-dollar price tag for the ultimate terminus building allowed for an imposing redbrick finish, with stone cornices and trim, and fourteen massive Corinthian columns along Cordova Street. It would take a full two years to install the station's many public facilities: general and women's waiting rooms, lunchroom and counter, barber shop, newsstand and restrooms. From the huge baggage area, a small army of workers ferried luggage, freight and express parcels between the arriving and departing trains and the holds of the company's stately *Empress* and *Princess* steamships.

The railway's ultimate Pacific terminal building, shown here shortly after completion, is still a major Vancouver landmark and a transportation hub for a variety of travel options. AUTHOR'S COLLECTION

Of special interest to the thousands of travellers who moved through the station's cavernous concourse were the sixteen landscape oil paintings executed by Mrs. Langford, the sister-in-law of CPR regional superintendent F.W. Peters. They were mounted on the walls high above the daily throngs. During the 1920s, the station newsstand rented out opera glasses to those awaiting their connections who wished to obtain a better view of the art pieces.

In 1974, the city declared the CPR Pacific terminus to be an official Heritage Building, ensuring its future preservation. The arrival of the SeaBus from North Vancouver and the inauguration of regular ferry service across Burrard Inlet in 1977, along with extensive renovations the following year, solidified the building's status as a downtown transportation hub, soon to be augmented by connections with commuter trains, SkyTrain, and VIA Rail intercity passengers services. It would also provide accommodations for buses, float planes, and helicopters.

Known now as the Waterfront Station, it is still a jewel in Vancouver's downtown cityscape. ✢

MAIL BY RAIL

For most of CPR's first century of operations, sorting, carrying, and delivering government mail was one of the most secure and lucrative sources of income.

The idea to sort mail on trains, while they were on route to their various destinations, originated in Britain on the Liverpool to Manchester Railway, in 1830. In North America, it was another thirty-four years before the first railway post offices were operated on the Chicago & North Western Railway, between Chicago and Clinton, Ohio. Soon thereafter, the service had expanded to virtually every railway on the continent.

Before the CPR transcontinental line was even completed, the Canadian postmaster general's reports show payments to the C.P. Construction Company for mail transportation between various points in the East and the *end of track*, which was, of course, a moving target as construction progressed westward across the country. Initially, the agreement didn't even require the railway builders to use the rails as the means of delivery. The contractual requirement was for a minimum of one trip per week and the mode of conveyance optional.

For much of the distance across the Prairies, the postal service was conducted from a railway car roughly fitted out for the purpose, moving westward a few miles each day with the progress of tracklaying. Rare, collectable envelopes from the period bear the stamp:

Care of the C.P. Mail Company, End of Canadian Pacific Track West, Via Winnipeg, Manitoba

After the rails arrived in Calgary, in 1883, scheduled trains, complete with specially built, customized railway cars staffed with government postal clerks, handled both westbound and eastbound mail. Over the winter, ahead of regular train service, work trains, wagon teams, and sled dogs conveyed the mails as far west as Laggan, now Lake Louise.

At the summit of the Rockies, construction headquarters was run by Tom Holt, brother of CPR engineer-contractor Herbert Holt, who would go on to become one of the country's wealthiest and most successful entrepreneurs. As the construction crews moved through the mountains, mail offices were established in several of the fledgling communities along the line, often in the same buildings such as Holt's store from which the railway obtained food and other supplies for the men.

After the last spike was driven on November 7, 1885, end of track ceased to exist. Permanent post offices began to appear across the CPR system, and the amount of mail moving by the railway grew exponentially. Along with letters and packages, newspapers were an important part of the railway mail service, particularly to smaller towns and rural areas. The loss of a mail contract would often mean the discontinuation of local train service, especially on secondary or branch lines.

To meet the large demand for the service, CPR built dedicated mail cars for the busiest runs, and for many years combination mail and express cars were on the head end of nearly every passenger train in the country. As many as five men worked and lived on each of these cars, which were equipped with stoves, cooking facilities, sinks, and toilets. Ingenious hooked arms on the sides of the mail cars enabled the clerks to pick up mail on the fly from trackside hangers, while sacks of mail could be handed down when the trains came to a stop or kicked off while in motion.

By the 1950s, railway mail service reached its peak, with as many as fourteen hundred mail clerks in mobile post offices onboard CPR trains, sorting, bagging, and labelling millions of letters and packages annually. But after the Second World War, trucking companies with their ability to serve locations from door to door were, increasingly, making serious inroads, while the national airlines were vying for the long-distance hauls. The railway mail clerks themselves contributed to their own demise during prolonged railway worker strikes in the postwar years.

For many years, mail contracts maintained the economic viability of railway passenger service. Special arms on the side of mail cars could grab mailbags while the trains were in motion, and letters were sorted en route between cities. GLENBOW ARCHIVES, ARCHIVES AND SPECIAL COLLECTIONS, UNIVERSITY OF CALGARY NA-67-29

"We started to carry the mail by truck," said David Calderwood, a former mail clerk for CPR and New York Central for seventeen years, describing the fallout of the disruptive labour actions.

"Of course, the truck drivers didn't know all of the connecting mail routes," he remembered in later years, "so we travelled with them and told them where to go. When we did that, we showed the post office that the trucks were not tied to train schedules and could get the mail through a lot faster."

By 1971, the last railway post office on the CPR would be gone, most of the business taken over by trucking companies and airlines. Over the next fifteen years or so, mail service would completely vanish from the rails. ⁜

RECORD STATISTICS FOR THE BIG BRIDGE

One of CPR's most spectacular engineering features is a steel trestle bridge that spans the Oldman River at Lethbridge, in southern Alberta. While it is neither the world's highest nor longest railway span, the High Level Bridge is often described as the largest of its type in the world.

It was built between 1907 and 1909 at a cost of $1,334,525 as part of a major diversion of the railway's Crowsnest Pass route that gave CPR easy access to the mining regions of southern British Columbia. The line that it replaced had been strung together through extensive steep-banked cuts and across twenty rickety, wooden bridges prone to washouts in the spring and during high-water conditions.

The new alignment, based on detailed surveys carried out through 1904 and 1905, eliminated 1,735 degrees of curvature, or nearly five complete circles, while reducing the old railway grade by as much as 1.2 percent.

The two largest and most expensive features on the new line would be the High Level Bridge—also known as the Lethbridge Viaduct or simply the Big Bridge—and the smaller Monarch Trestle, both of which crossed the Oldman River. (The High Level Bridge originally crossed a section of the river called the Belly, but its name was later changed to the Oldman.)

The High Level Bridge was the brainchild of CPR's renowned assistant chief engineer, John Edward Schwitzer, who was also the driving force behind the railway's world-famous Spiral Tunnels. Just to be on the safe side, Schwitzer recruited Charles Conrad Schneider to be the consulting engineer for the project. Schneider already had an impressive track record. He had been hired to help erect the Statue of Liberty in 1886. He had also served as president of the American Society of Civil Engineers and headed up the team that investigated the 1907 collapse of the Quebec Bridge.

The detailed drawings for the High Level Bridge were produced by Canadian Pacific's bridge department in Montreal, while the manufacture and erection of the steelwork was entrusted to the Canadian Bridge Company of Walkerville, Ontario. The groundwork, carried out by a gang of about a hundred men, was the direct responsibility of the bridge company's C.F. Prettie.

Arriving first on the construction site, in October of 1907, were the men from J. Gunn & Sons of Winnipeg, who would do the initial excavations. They would also build the concrete pedestals for the thirty-three riveted-steel towers that were to support the bridges' sixty-seven spans. To do so, they drove huge eleven-inch-diameter fir piles to a depth of twenty-four feet and applied thirty tons of pressure to them to ensure they were fully settled. In the vicinity of the tower designated Pier 23, the piles struck some old mine workings. Two workers died from exposure to accumulated underground gases, while trying to save a young boy, who, despite repeated warnings, had played in the exposed shaft.

The substructures for the towers that would be built in the river were the hardest to stabilize. Underlying layers of gravel and shale made it hard for the workers to form tight cofferdams in which to pour the concrete piles and pedestals. However, it wasn't until

As sturdy today as it was when this train crossed over in the mid-1920s, the High Level Bridge at Lethbridge is still viewed as a spectacular engineering achievement. AUTHOR'S COLLECTION

Not even repeated warnings from the spirit world could save the doomed railwaymen when death rode the rails. PHOTO COLLAGE BY NICHOLAS MORANT, AUTHOR'S COLLECTION

Eleven people perished in the head-on collision. GLENBOW ARCHIVES,
ARCHIVES AND SPECIAL COLLECTIONS, UNIVERSITY OF CALGARY NA-1313-7

Within days, as luck would have it, fireman Day was again in the locomotive cab—this time with engineer James Nicholson—when the exact same scenario was played out. Their train was rounding a curve on the line to Dunmore Junction, when a locomotive whistle sounded where none should have been. Again, a phantom train passed on a nonexistent track, with crew and passengers clearly visible, before disappearing as mysteriously as it had arrived.

After two close encounters with the phantom train, Gus Day was likely relieved when he was assigned to yard work the following day, rather than take his usual place as the fireman on the run to Dunmore. Instead fireman Harry Thompson would join engineer Nicholson on the next trip.

Sure enough, as their train approached the site of the previous ghostly train appearances, a whistle once again shrieked a warning that another train was just ahead. This time, however, rounding the curve on that single piece of track was a very real passenger train—the #514 from Lethbridge—with Robert Twohey freshly returned to work and at the throttle.

The cause of the ensuing catastrophic collision was determined by the railway to be a mix up in the interpretation and handling of train orders by the two locomotive crews. Whatever the official explanation, engineer Twohey perished alongside his firemen in the fiery confines of their demolished locomotive cab, just a few days after the time frame foreseen by the fortune teller.

Although his fireman escaped with severe injuries by jumping from their locomotive at the last minute before impact, engineer Nicholson died in the wreckage. Gus Day, who had been fortunate enough to work the yard that day, was left alone with phantom trains to haunt his dreams. ⁜

SCHWITZER'S RAILWAY PRETZEL

One of the most popular roadside attractions along the Trans-Canada Highway is the impressive engineering feature known as the Spiral Tunnels.

Built by CPR in the first decade of the twentieth century to reduce one of North America's steepest railway gradients, it is said that more tourists stop their vehicles to view this distinctive railway focal point than they do for any other scenic opportunity from coast to coast.

The Spiral Tunnels opened to railway traffic on September 1, 1909, eliminating the most notorious stretch of track—and the most accident-prone one—on Canadian Pacific's transcontinental system, the infamous Big Hill. A true railroader's nightmare, the Big Hill plunged from an elevation of 5,250 feet at Hector, BC, a few miles from the Alberta–British Columbia border to 4,121 feet at Field, BC.

The problematic stretch of track just seven miles long had been built as temporary concession to getting the line open for business in 1886, with the railway builders' agreement to remedy the situation as soon as possible. Twenty-five years would pass before CPR solved the dilemma that the Big Hill presented.

For safe and efficient operations, it's best to keep railway tracks not only as straight as possible, but as flat as possible, too. With that in mind, the federal government had specified a maximum gradient of 2.2 percent along the entire route of the transcontinental. However, while surveying the section of line through Kicking Horse Pass from the Continental Divide to the valley floor just a few miles west, CPR's engineering staff realized they would have to find a way to extend the track between the two points if they were to maintain the desired gradient. Inevitably, that would mean a great deal of tunnelling, which would have set back the completion time for the line by a year or more.

Finally, nearly twenty years later, the demands of the increased traffic became too great to ignore. Several schemes were contemplated to lower the grade by lengthening the line between Hector and Field. Some thought was given to building a large loop up the Yoho River Valley and back again, but that would only create additional problems, including the need to shelter nearly all of the track with expensive and vulnerable snow sheds. Because Kicking Horse Pass was so

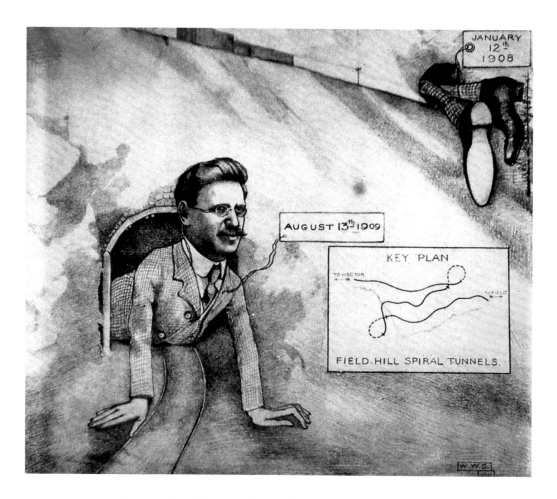

A promotional illustration featured a line drawing of CPR's newest roadside attraction, and a cartoon of engineer Schwitzer squeezing through one of the two Spiral Tunnels. AUTHOR'S COLLECTION

When the curved tunnels were opened to traffic, trains were not long enough to cross over themselves while passing through them. But that didn't stop CPR publicists from posing them as if they were. AUTHOR'S COLLECTION

crooked and narrow, a number of more practicable plans involving various combinations of tunnels and bridges were also considered.

Ultimately, CPR's senior engineer in the West, John E. Schwitzer, conceived and presented to CPR management an ingenious design for a pair of tunnels that would loop under Cathedral and Ogden Mountains on either side of the Kicking Horse River. Modelled on a similar engineering feat successfully completed for Switzerland's Gotthard Railway, the dual bores would allow the CPR to twice double the line back on itself and add more than four miles of track to the original configuration, allowing the track to descend from east to west by easy stages.

Steam shovels working from both ends simultaneously would dig each of Schwitzer's Spiral Tunnels. The Vancouver firm of Macdonell, Gzowski and Co. carried out the work, at a cost of about $1.5 million. In a time long before lasers and satellite imagery were used to aid engineering projects, the tunnel diggers missed meeting in the middle by mere inches.

Over a period of twenty months, from October 1907 to July 1909, more than 650 thousand cubic yards of rock were removed from the work site, nearly a quarter of which had to be blasted from the twin tunnels. Seventy-five carloads, or upwards of 750 tons, of dynamite were used by the contractor to complete the work.

For CPR, the end result was—and has since been—a much easier stretch of track over which to operate. For the motoring public, it is a marvel to see long freight trains looping over themselves as they pass through each of the tunnels in a long drawn out figure eight. Parks Canada has provided two official parking areas and lookouts for just such a purpose: one on the Trans-Canada, where the lower Spiral Tunnel can be viewed, and one a couple of kilometres up the Yoho Valley Road, where the upper Spiral Tunnel is clearly visible.

Curious anecdotes abound from the railway employees assigned to maintain the line or to operate trains over this unique section of track. The tale is told of Hughie Reid, a onetime signal maintainer at Field who used to patrol the area on a track speeder (a small motorized vehicle) with his faithful dog, Bud. Because Hughie's skittish companion didn't care to go through the dark tunnels, his four-footed friend would invariably jump off the vehicle at each tunnel mouth, run up the embankment, and wait for Hughie to emerge on the next level, before jumping back up to his side. Another story maintains that a CPR sectionman discovered a moose wandering through one of the tunnels and was painstakingly leading the animal out when a train came along. According to sworn testimony from railroaders then living in the area, that quick thinking railroader took the animal by its ear and held it against the side wall of the tunnel until the danger had passed and he could lead it to safety.

How's that for a storied piece of track? ⊹

FACE-OFF WITH THE MONTREAL CANADIENS

Given that Canadian Pacific was headquartered in Montreal from the railway's founding in 1881, until the conglomerate's corporate move to Calgary in 1996, it's perhaps no surprise the iconic Canadian business enterprise had occasion to cross paths with the premier Canadian sports organization that cohabited its hometown: The Montreal Canadiens, a.k.a. the Habs or Nos Glorieux.

For twenty-five years, before the expansion of the National Hockey League in several stages to the current thirty-one teams, it was just the Original Six teams from Montreal, Toronto, Boston, New York, Chicago, and Detroit that vied for Lord Stanley's cherished silver mug. The competing venues were close enough that train travel made a lot of sense and, having ready access to Montreal's Windsor Station, the Canadiens embraced the opportunity to ride the CPR on many occasions.

"That kept them all together and it was good for morale," said coach Toe Blake in later years. "They could relax by playing cards, talking, reading, or just resting. It gave them a chance to concentrate on the game coming up. They could discuss the playing habits of the guys on the opposing team and the best way to handle them."

In 1942, CPR had provided employment to Maurice "Rocket" Richard, the man who would go on to become the biggest on-ice star of his era. In the off-season, Richard earned forty dollars a week as a machinist in the munitions department at the railway's Angus Shops, in east end Montreal, one or two buildings away from where his carpenter father, Onesime Richard, was building freight cars. Maurice would resign his CPR job during the 1944–45 NHL season, as he was electrifying his fans by scoring fifty goals in fifty games, a record that went unsurpassed for decades. His father would complete a forty-year career with Canadian Pacific a few years later.

There were other low-key employees, too, such as locomotive engineer Harry "Mum" Mummery and auditor Dickie "Digger" Moore, who put in many workaday hours with CPR before signing up for more glamourous shifts with the Montreal Canadiens organization.

As early as 1889, the CPR had whisked Lord Frederick Stanley in dark, wood-panelled, lush-upholstered luxury on a whirlwind tour across Canada on its pioneer transcontinental rail line, just a few months after the governor general had witnessed his first ice hockey game at the Montreal Winter Carnival. Four years later, Lord Stanley would lend his name to the fifty-dollar silver bowl that would be awarded to the winner of what was then the Dominion Hockey Challenge Cup. The first

Maurice "Rocket" Richard, the Canadiens' most popular player, was often greeted by his wife and son upon arriving home at Montreal's Windsor Station. AUTHOR'S COLLECTION

team to hoist the trophy in victory—foreshadowing the soon to be unchallenged success of its hometown successor—was the Montreal Amateur Athletic Association, when it defeated the Ottawa Generals 3–2.

The president of CPR, Edward Wentworth Beatty, was the driving force behind the building of the original Montreal Forum in 1924. Home to the Montreal Maroons and, after 1926, the Canadiens, it was a veritable temple for the next seventy years of hockey fandom. From 1946 until the mid-1950s, CPR's president and chairman, D'Alton Coleman, was vice-president of the Club de Hockey Canadien Inc.

During the glory years of the Original Six, throughout the 1940s to the 1960s, CPR often arranged private sleeping cars for the Habs and their families to shuttle between games. It was not unusual after a Montreal game for a train carrying the team to pull out of Windsor Station around midnight for the sixteen-hour run to Chicago for a match-up with the Black Hawks. Sometimes, if the trains were late arriving, a police escort would be waiting to speed the team to the on-ice joust.

"One memorable moment came with our arrival into Windsor Station in 1966, after winning the Stanley Cup in Detroit," Habs star Jean Beliveau explained to the uninitiated. "We were greeted by hundreds of fans; the station was full of warm-hearted people," he said in understated fashion.

"If you were a hockey writer travelling with the Canadiens during the playoffs, you prayed that they'd win the final game that meant the Stanley Cup at home," reporter Dink Carroll related in the 1970s. "If they won it on the road, you knew you were in for a bad night on the train. The long season was over, and the celebration would start early and go on most of the night. The horseplay was rough and sometimes would get out of control. The writers were in another car, and the wise ones remained there and locked the doors of their chamberettes."

The current Montreal hockey arena, the Bell Centre, was built on Canadian Pacific land, adjacent to the company's former headquarters building and well-known landmark, Windsor Station. Alas, the team now travels almost entirely by air. ✠

THE "OTHER ROUTE" GETS A GREAT EXPRESS

f CPR had stuck with its original transcontinental route as surveyed by Sandford Fleming—from Winnipeg to Edmonton through the North Saskatchewan Valley and westward via the Yellowhead Pass to the West Coast—the railway's Great West Express might have become the most renowned train in Canada. But it would be another twenty-five years, after the last spike was driven in the Canadian Pacific main line farther south, before the company would piece together a regular service through the country's most productive and valuable agricultural lands.

By June 4, 1911, when the Great West Express (GWE) was inaugurated as a daily train service between Winnipeg and Edmonton on a two-nights-and-one-day schedule, the Canadian Northern Railway was already operating its twice daily Capital Cities Express between the two cities. Its other chief competitor, the Grand Trunk Pacific, was also offering a schedule for the same route on board its Daily Express that was four hours faster than CPR westbound Train 51 and three hours faster than eastbound Train 52, as the GWE was listed on Canadian Pacific timetables.

Nevertheless, CPR made a good showing with a solid, reliable service on what, for the company, was a secondary route. The consist of the Great West Express, which is to say its lineup or sequence of cars, typically included baggage-mail car, first- and second-class coaches, a dining car, and a sleeping car; and Canadian Pacific enjoyed a monopoly on traffic from Eastern Canada—making daily connections with CPR's transcontinental Imperial Limited at Winnipeg—until the federal government began a competitive service from Toronto to Winnipeg, in 1915, with the creation of its fledgling National Transcontinental Railway.

Westbound, the Great West Express left the CPR main line at Portage la Prairie and connected with the railway's Calgary-to-Edmonton line at Wetaskiwin, Alberta, before carrying on to Strathcona. In June 1913, Canadian Pacific opened the High Level Bridge, which brought its line across the North Saskatchewan River to a new Edmonton station on Jasper Avenue. The same year, service on the Great West was enhanced with new platform observation cars that included sleeping compartments and buffet facilities.

During the 1920s, through service on CPR Trains 51 and 52 was introduced between Edmonton and Toronto, as well as between Edmonton and Saint John, New Brunswick, in connection with CP Steamships transatlantic passenger liners. By 1926, steady traffic levels justified a year-round

CPR locomotive 2317 was at the head end of the Great West Express when it pulled into Sutherland, Saskatchewan, on October 18, 1939. GLENBOW ARCHIVES, ARCHIVES AND SPECIAL COLLECTIONS, UNIVERSITY OF CALGARY PA-4013-494

through sleeping car service to Montreal. All of these extended runs were made possible by switching GWE cars onto the Imperial Limited at Winnipeg. Schedules were arranged wherever possible to provide short waits and good connections with branch lines to remote Saskatchewan towns like Nipawin and Gronlid.

However, the thirties were not kind to the Great West Express. The severe depression in the national economy was reflected in a downturn in demand for both freight and passenger service on all CPR lines. The GWE began to remove sleeping cars from its consists; dining cars followed shortly after. Beginning in 1933, daily train service was reduced to six round trips per week, with no departures from Winnipeg or Edmonton on Saturdays.

Despite the setbacks, in 1938, passengers on the Great West Express were among the first to experience the luxury of new streamlined, air-conditioned coaches, alongside CPR patrons of the transcontinental Dominion and its Montreal-to-Chicago run. After the Second World War, the GWE was again equipped with the most modern equipment available to the travelling public. Still, traffic continued to decline.

By the 1950s, most communities along the line had good road service, and competition from the family car had relegated the now-dieselized Great West Express to little more than a glorified mail and express train. By the time it was withdrawn, on May 31, 1960, one year short of its fiftieth anniversary, Canadian National's Super Continental passenger train was making the run between Winnipeg and Edmonton eighteen hours faster than CPR's once great express.

Though its passing received scant attention from the press in the major centres of the Prairie provinces, the Great West Express is remembered fondly by those who took full advantage of the train and its vast network of feeder lines to move around freely and to distribute goods and services throughout the West. Without this vital community of wheels, settlers in places such as Wilkie, Saskatoon, Colonsay, and Yorkton would not have had the same access to markets in the East, nor would they have been energized by the regular and dependable arrival of newspapers, mail and express packages, and out of town visitors.

Nothing contributed quite so much to the social life of Prairie denizens as the chatter of the telegraph keys and the comings and goings of the local train on the CPR's *other* main line. ⚜

ODD OCCURRENCES IN THE CONNAUGHT TUNNEL

t was the ultimate solution to the CPR's snow problems in the Selkirk Mountains, when the railway engineers decided to bore a five-mile-long hole under Mount Macdonald, thereby bypassing the deadliest section of track in Canadian Pacific's entire transcontinental line.

The audacious initiative, which would be named the Connaught Tunnel in honour of Canada's then governor general, was celebrated around the world for the engineering marvel that it was. At the time, it was the longest tunnel in North America, and it included a few features that were highly innovative for 1916.

Ventilation was always going to be a big consideration in what employees called the Big Hole, given the length of the bore and the number of locomotives that would operate through it on a daily basis. To quickly remove the build-up of dense exhaust every time a train passed through, two fans thirteen feet in diameter were installed over the tracks at the west end. They were powered by mammoth, four-cylinder, five-hundred-horsepower diesel engines and could be activated at the flick of a switch. A team of four engineers would supervise the operation from their base in the nearby railway town of Glacier, BC, when not on duty in the tunnel's fan house itself.

No matter which direction trains were bound, the air was always blown down grade, from west to east. The ten-mile-per-hour breeze generated by the fans could completely clear the tunnel of fumes in less than forty minutes. A man could not stand directly in the air stream without being bowled over.

Daily patrols through the tunnel in both directions were a familiar feature of the engineering team's responsibilities. Inside the dark confines of the underground corridor, nine telephones were installed at regular intervals to allow for quick reporting of any obstacles to safe operations or other emergency situations.

At any time, items could fall from passing trains. During the winter, ice might build up on the walls of the tunnel. Not infrequently, animals would wander in through one of the tunnel portals, endangering themselves as well as railway operations. Rabbits, wolves, and even deer have been known to venture through the hole in search of food or shelter. Bears have been killed indulging their curiosity while a train was in transit. A good many rodents have taken up residence over the years within the tunnel's confines, though there is no evidence to

The blind mice may have been a myth, but other critters besides the iron horse were known to make their way through the giant bore. PHOTO BY NICHOLAS MORANT, AUTHOR'S COLLECTION

confirm the rumours that, after generations in the dark, a new breed of mouse has developed without eyes.

The Connaught Tunnel is so straight one can stand in the middle and see both portals outlined in daylight, but the effects of being deep inside the long, dark corridor are often disconcerting. A horse belonging to a Glacier National Park warden once managed to wander some distance into the Big Hole, before nearly trampling a tunnel patrolman in its haste to escape the clatter of an oncoming train. On another occasion, a domestic steer that somehow fell from a stock car landed in the darkness of the tunnel and went berserk, giving everybody plenty of trouble and severely injuring a railway worker before it could be recaptured. A hitchhiker, or railway stowaway, once surprisingly popped out of the tunnel mouth at Glacier, declaring that he had fallen from a train halfway through the tunnel.

Even the first engineer to negotiate the tunnel after its completion had a tale of misadventure to tell.

"The superintendent of construction gave me the okay to go ahead, but some overhead scaffolding had not been cleared," the hogger liked to tell people. "It knocked the smokestack off Engine 506 and damaged the caboose cupola. I worked the engine for about a week with a barrel tied on for a smokestack."

And not one but two babies came into this world while their mothers laboured in the darkness of the Connaught's famous bore hole. Records show that one such blessed event occurred in January 1939. On that occasion, CPR porter Conrad Pinder assisted with the birth of a little baby girl aboard the transcontinental train.

The other time the stork landed in a CPR passenger car while en route through that storied tunnel occurred a decade earlier. In 1928, another girl entered the world while her train passed under Mount Macdonald. The parents named her Constance Patricia Rosamond, giving her the initials C.P.R.

THE GREENING OF THE PRAIRIES

The Canadian Forestry Association (CFA) is Canada's oldest conservation organization. When it was established, in 1900, the CFA's mission statement clearly stated its focus: "Soil conservation and the importance of trees in this work." In the years immediately following the First World War, that objective dovetailed nicely with Canadian Pacific's own efforts to transform the prairies into a settler's paradise. The association's ambitious tree-planting campaign inspired CPR to donate a customized railway car in support of that noble effort.

In 1919, Canadian Pacific car builder Stan Harbord and apprentice George Beakley supervised the transformation of a steel passenger coach into a combined movie theatre and lecture hall. Representatives of the Forestry Association would be invited to travel in the refurbished railway car, while teaching farmers and ranchers across Manitoba, Saskatchewan, and Alberta about the care and feeding of trees. By the time the CPR men and their team at Winnipeg's Weston Shops were through, the unique railcar would be capable of hosting audiences of as many as a hundred people. It would also provide full accommodation for two members of the conservation group to travel on board.

The car's first lecturer was Archibald Mitchell, a supervisor at the Dominion Forest Nursery Station at Indian Head, Saskatchewan. Born in Scotland, Mitchell worked as a forester in Wales, before immigrating to Fort Macleod, Alberta, in 1899.

Mitchell and the Forestry Association had a fourfold message to deliver to Prairie settlers from the comfort of CPR's fully equipped tree-planting car, which could be coupled to any passenger or freight train heading in the direction of its ambitious itinerary. Foremost were tips on how to prevent fires and other forms of forest destruction. Secondly, plans were outlined for reforestation in areas where tree cutting was necessary for the support of both industry and livelihoods. Farmers were also taught the importance of soil conservation to sustain the value of their land holdings.

The sponsors of the tree-planting car and the employees that accompanied it were some of the country's earliest stewards of the environment.
LIBRARY AND ARCHIVES CANADA MIKAN 3842156

43

And lastly, they received guidance on how to protect their buildings and fields from the ravages of the Prairie winter with the aid of protective barriers.

Within two years, CPR had made an outright donation of the tree-planting car to the association. The two-man conservation crew appeared annually at sixty to eighty-five communities across the Prairies. The car was maintained and hauled free of charge by Canadian Pacific and, along with its usual stops in the three Western Canadian provinces between the Great Lakes and the Rocky Mountains, it made occasional forays to stations along the Great Northern, New York Central, and Vermont Central Railroads in the United States. More frequently, it was handled by Canadian National Railway (CN), over that company's network.

For the next fifty years, the Tree Planting Campaign of the National Forestry Association and its provincial affiliates used their trusty railway car to negotiate more than a quarter of a million miles of track, hosting better than 1.5 million visitors, and acting as a catalyst for the planting of 500 million trees on the Prairies, on 110,000 farms in Alberta, Saskatchewan, and Manitoba.

For nearly half that time, Alan Beaven, manager of the Forestry Association, was the organization's primary lecturer, becoming a more familiar face to western farmers than any other man in Canada. By 1924, the CFA had already grown to become the largest forestry association in the world. They would also become a formidable educator for future farmers. Spotted on railway sidings in small communities and Indigenous reserves across the West, Beaven and film projectionist R.H. Murray Pratt would show their audiences of school children educational films, interspersed with

In many small towns across the Prairies, more school children turned out in one afternoon than could be accommodated for a single lecture or movie showing. GLENBOW ARCHIVES, ARCHIVES AND SPECIAL COLLECTIONS, UNIVERSITY OF CALGARY NA-1889-3

comedies and cartoons to keep their attention. Servings of ice cream were also helpful in that regard. On one occasion in Taber, Alberta, 223 young children were squeezed on board for a single movie viewing.

In the evenings there were lectures and film showings for their parents. The presentations were so popular that at some stops there were often as many as forty or fifty people standing outside the car and peering through the open windows. In 1931 at Rosemary, Alberta, an entire lecture was translated into German by one of the settlers for the benefit of his Mennonite relatives and neighbours. In 1946, a nun in Lasalle, Manitoba, rendered the entire night's lessons into French for the 120 young people in attendance. On another occasion, a small boy was said to have ridden a horse seven miles with ten cents in his pocket to see the show at Halkirk, Alberta. Of course, he was welcomed to join the goings-on free of charge.

In 1949, two trucks—one from General Motors and the other from the Ford Motor Company—were also employed to take the message of soil conservation to towns where there were no railway tracks. The most remote communities were accessed by plane. But the Forestry Association's railway car remained the centrepiece of its communications strategy.

Pamphlets were handed out by the thousands to instruct the farming community on how to plant shelterbelts of trees, and how those same trees could restore depleted water tables and help to preserve the ground moisture essential to the growth of all types of vegetables. Films such as *Nature's Neighbours* and *Wonders of Plant Growth* revealed the necessity of good conservation stewardship to maintain healthy bird and animal populations in prairie marshes. They also, playfully, taught the kids why plant stems grow up, while their root systems grow down.

The only ambassador more effective at getting the message out than the CFA representatives who rode the rolling lecture hall was the association's famous spokesperson, Smokey the Bear, who told radio and television audiences alike, "Only you can prevent forest fires." What better front man to alert people to the benefits of soil conservation, and to let folks know when the tree-planting car was coming to a railway siding near them? ⊹

RIDING THE SIDE-DOOR PULLMAN

For as long as railway patrons have been climbing aboard trains to get from one point to another, their four-legged servants have been riding the rails right alongside them, in mixed consists or in dedicated bovine or equine specials.

Horses, in particular, have enjoyed increasingly comfortable accommodations for their intercity and cross-country excursions and have long since abandoned makeshift stalls in modified railway boxcars for the specially designed, custom-built interiors of the Palace horse cars, which have had nearly as many upgrades over the years as their human equivalents.

From CPR's earliest years, a variety of horses were shipped west from breeders in Eastern Canada and the US to perform various tasks on the burgeoning number of pioneer farms and ranches, while the best of their progeny were shipped back to demonstrate to the easterners the Northwest's great potential for raising championship stock. By the 1920s, horseflesh from across the West was converging once a year on the Royal Agricultural Winter Fair in Toronto, which was setting national standards for judging the quality of these majestic domestic animals.

Initially, only eight or nine cars were required to handle the entries from CPR's demonstration farms around Brooks and Strathmore, the Prince of Wales's own E.P. Ranch, and the various provincial government lands in the West, but the traffic volumes increased exponentially as herds grew and matured. The demand for special railway cars was also increased by the growth in the popularity and frequency of horse races.

Beginning in the mid-1920s, CPR operated Prairie Racehorse Specials in a circuit between Winnipeg and Calgary, Calgary and Edmonton, Edmonton and Saskatoon, and Saskatoon and Regina, usually in July and early August. Travelling with the horses in their rolling palaces were owners, trainers, grooms, walkers, and stable boys. It was not uncommon for four or five of these handlers to bed down at night in each car on well-worn mattresses, hammocks, or piled up straw, alongside their four-legged charges. A sleeping car would normally be attached to the trains, but that was mostly for the use of the women in the entourage. The men, ranging in age from sixteen to sixty, rode in the horse cars and attended to all of the necessary chores en route.

Typically, two 40-gallon drums were loaded onto each car to hold the onboard refreshments for all of the riders, one containing fresh water for the horses and the other ice and beer for

In later years, the railway's four-legged guests travelled in grand style aboard CPR's Palace Horse Cars.
DOUG PHILLIPS COLLECTION

the equestrian set. A few rickety chairs, some pinup girls, and a dog or two rounded out the ambience.

In 1946, as many as three hundred racehorses came to Calgary from Winnipeg for the annual Stampede competitions. In addition, eastbound trains moved unprecedented numbers of workhorses to meet the urgent need for rebuilding infrastructure in war-ravaged Europe. Twice weekly, CPR shipped more than eight hundred draft horses from the West to the CP Steamships freight shed on the Montreal waterfront. More than 90 percent of them were mares. At dockside, they were inspected, inoculated, and given a clean bill of health, before being walked onto ships bound for the Netherlands, France, the Balkans, and other Eastern European destinations. The lighter horses were loaded into the holds with slings around their midsections. More than eighteen thousand horses were sent overseas.

By the 1950s, the railway had provided the ultimate in steel-sided Palace cars for its thoroughbred passengers. The cars, now referred to as side-door Pullmans by the horse handlers, were eighty feet long and had a new and improved arrangement of stalls, which included built-in bins for hay and grain. They were said to ride the rails as smoothly as a passenger car. And, often as not, they were attractive enough to be coupled into regular CPR passenger service.

In the 1960s, several of the Palace horse cars were sold to Assiniboia Downs, a popular racetrack in Winnipeg; and during the 1970s, when CPR was called upon to help celebrate the centennials of many Prairie communities, historical displays were installed in two of the hollowed out, commodious railcars to tour the country in much the same way they had during their heyday (or *hay day* if you will). ⚓

ROLLING SCHOOLHOUSES

Engineer Bill McAdam liked to chat with the kids who ran up to his train while he waited on a siding north of Lake Superior for the CPR main line to clear. In remote Northern Ontario, many of his energetic visitors were children of railway employees, though some were the offspring of the trappers, prospectors, and woodsmen who eked out a living in the Canadian hinterland. But shouldn't they be in school?

McAdam couldn't stop thinking about his new wilderness friends, nor could he abandon them to an uneducated life of illiteracy and lack of opportunity. Between rail assignments, he petitioned the Ontario premier and the minister of education to consider the welfare and the wasted potential of these accidental truants who had fallen between the cracks of the public-school system. As a result of McAdam's entreaties, school inspector Dr. J.B. McDougall was dispatched to investigate the situation, and an innovative scheme was hatched. If the children did not have access to a permanent schoolhouse, the Ontario School Board would bring mobile classrooms to the children.

Although initially skeptical about the prospects for success, Canada's two major railway companies—Canadian Pacific and Canadian National—agreed to outfit first-class railway coaches as school cars. The first of these cars on CPR's system operated out of Chapleau, Ontario, during the 1926–27 school year. Walter NcNally was headmaster of School Car No. 50, attending to the academic needs of children from age six to their late teens, who arrived for classes via snowshoes and skis, by canoe and on foot.

Typically, the school car would uncouple from a passing freight train and sit on a siding in the various northern communities along the CPR main line: Flourite Forks, Ramsey, Nemegos, Eureka, and Lochalsh to name but a handful. For the next five days, the children would be subjected to an intense regimen of studies that mirrored the Ontario school curriculum for Grades 1 through 8. In conjunction with the daily lessons and the home assignments doled out by McNally during his scheduled visits, the students were expected to cover six weeks of material on their own while awaiting the return of the school car.

Some of the children came from such great distances that they had to spend the entire week eating and sleeping on the school car, as well as taking their lessons there. Others camped beside the car, weather permitting, or were billeted temporarily with CPR families in the area.

The Ontario Department of Education supplied all textbooks, pencils, pens, and scribblers at no cost to the students or their parents. The teachers, fully qualified under Ontario regulations, in many cases also acted as interpreters, letter writers, legal advisors, and friends to their northern charges.

The classrooms in the railway school cars were fully outfitted with desks, chalkboards, charts, maps, and library books. In each car, the instructors' quarters included a complete kitchen, a sitting room with easy chairs and a chesterfield, sleeping berths, and a full-size bathtub and toilet facilities.

By all reports the program was a great success. The scholastic marks of the children in the remote communities rivalled the results of kids in major urban centres to the south. By 1934, McNally could report: "Throughout the year all pupils worked exceptionally well . . . The most of them covered the regular course as set out for the full Public School year . . . I consider this a very fine achievement."

As early as 1928, a formal agreement had been signed between the province, and the two railway companies to continue the rolling classroom program for the foreseeable future. CPR added School Car No. 51 on its Northern Ontario route. One car then operated from Chapleau to Cartier, while the other plied the line in the opposite direction, from Chapleau to White River.

Parents and other, older members of the communities benefited from the school car visits as well, particularly immigrants with limited language skills. Evening classes for adults were held and the cars served as social centres, where students of all ages could find and borrow reading materials, play bingo and other games, or listen to recorded music.

According to McNally,

On many occasions, one notices that the children's education reflects in the parent's home life. Homes are kept neater and cleaner, rules of health are better observed, and parents evince a keener interest in life about them. Newspapers and periodicals are common where the English language was scarcely spoken when the school car first came here.

Over the years, several other instructors put in stints of varying lengths in the remote northern communities, before moving on to teaching posts in more urban settings, among them William Wright, Cecil Corps, William Colcock, and husband-and-wife team Florence and Cameron Bell.

Children hiked in from the wilderness to benefit from a learning experience that, in many ways, mirrored what they would have found in more populated areas of the country. AUTHOR'S COLLECTION

By the late 1950s there were permanent schools in most northern communities previously served by the school cars, though the mobile classrooms did make sporadic appearances, as required, into the mid-1960s.

CPR School Car No. 50 was eventually removed from service and scrapped. CPR donated School Car No. 51 to the Canadian Railway Historical Association and delivered it to the Canadian Railway Museum (now Exporail), in Delson, Quebec, where one can still climb aboard and take a seat at a small wooden desk, complete with armrest and inkwell hole. ✛

KIDS KNEW THE DRILL IN THE DENTAL CAR

For people in small railway towns across Canada, two thin bands of steel were often the only link with the outside world. Most of the necessities of life, including food and clothing, arrived on the local train along with just about everything and everybody new in town.

Medical supplies and medical professionals, in particular, were scarce commodities in the sparsely settled hinterland of Northern Ontario, perhaps none more so than the men and women concerned with dental care. Not unlike their big city counterparts, few looked forward to a visit with the dentist. Nevertheless, the citizens of those isolated communities were full of smiles when the railway dental car rolled into town for the first time in 1931.

Well aware of the urgent need for dental care in those lonely railway outposts, the Rosedale chapter of the Imperial Order Daughters of Empire (IODE), from Toronto, had approached the Government of Ontario and the Canadian Pacific Railway to outfit a custom-built, rolling clinic. Equipped with living quarters for two dental practitioners, the specially outfitted railway cars would bring oral hygiene to the suffering children of the North, many of whom had never had a cavity filled or a rotten tooth extracted.

To begin the quest, CPR contributed a former 1904 wooden sleeping car named Welsford. To make the best use of it, the IODE had raised more than $5,000 to refurbish the interior with the necessary dentist's chair, cabinets, sterilizers, drills, operating lights, and mandatory spit bowl.

To reach its clientele, the railcar would simply hook up to any freight or local mixed train and be pulled to each inhabited spot along the route. For more than forty years, that old wooden dental car, and later its steel successor, would run back and forth between Cartier, about thirty-three miles west of Sudbury, and Ingolf, on the border between Manitoba and Ontario. Once every two years or so, the rolling oral hygienists would spend between three days and two weeks in each of the remote communities.

Patients of all nationalities arrived trackside. Many, of course, were the children of railway workers, while others were from one of the many Indigenous settlements along the shores of Lake Superior. It was not uncommon for parents to shepherd their kids several miles through harsh conditions to have their teeth examined by the itinerant frontier dentists. Poor conditions and malnutrition in many small settlements ensured that more than one child was in need of urgent dental care.

Sometimes the adults, too, were in dire need, and the railway dentists attended to the more pressing cases. The *Toronto Mail & Empire*, covering the launch ceremony of the mobile tooth care facility at CPR's North Toronto Station, cited a letter from one young woman in Northern Ontario who had enquired whether she should have her teeth taken care of right away, or whether she should wait until after marriage.

The unfortunate soul was only twenty-six years old, but every tooth in her head was decayed.

While CPR handled all the maintenance and servicing of the dental cars at its Montreal Angus Shops, as well as covering the costs of hauling them around the province, the Ontario Department of Health paid the salaries of the oral care specialists and took care of day-to-day operating expenses. In later years, both the Canadian Red Cross and the Royal College of Dental Surgeons were involved with staffing the cars and ensuring their widest possible use.

Upon arrival at each town, the railway dentist would give the local schoolteacher a stack of consent cards for students aged three to sixteen to take home to their parents. Given that the service was essentially free, it's no surprise that nearly all of them returned with the necessary signatures, and the children were soon being escorted in small, anxious groups to the dental car.

Although the railway dentists could not offer the same kind of plush waiting rooms that city kids enjoyed, they no doubt provided similar outdated reading material to their young patients and engendered sufficient confidence among the children that they all wanted to be the first to open wide in the examination room each morning. ⚜

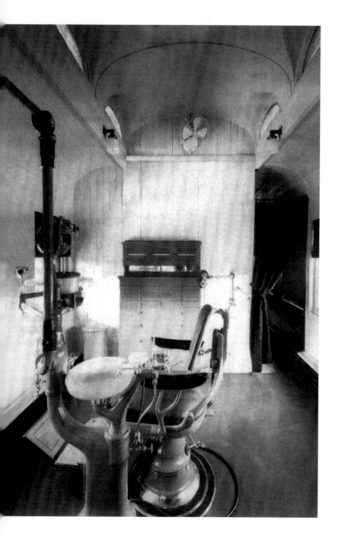

It may have been viewed with dread, but the dentist car managed to draw line-ups of willing patrons when it came to a nearby siding. DOUG PHILLIPS COLLECTION

ANOTHER CHINOOK BLOWS DOWN THE TRACKS

Shoppers in the Eaton's toy department in downtown Montreal were among the first to view what some train fanciers consider to be Canadian Pacific's finest achievement in engine design. The 1935 Christmas season was in full swing and a scaled down prototype of the railway's newest locomotive was a magnet for little kids and big kids alike.

Responding to the need to reduce operating costs, while providing high-speed local passenger service, the CPR was about to launch a train with a new look. To introduce it to the public, the railway's chief of motive power and rolling stock, in partnership with the T. Eaton Company, offered rides through the department store on a miniature version of what was to come.

The five full-size, stylish, streamlined engines under construction at the Montreal Locomotive Works were to be known as Jubilee-type locomotives, to commemorate the fifty years of transcontinental service CPR had provided prior to the launch of the new fast service, beginning early in 1936. The engines were designed with a rare 4-4-4 wheel arrangement that incorporated four oversized eighty-inch driving wheels for maximum speed, along with their four leading and four trailing wheels. In addition, the locomotive's front end and general appearance were engineered to give a smooth, uncluttered appearance, with the headlight set into the smokebox door and the bell, whistle and sand box hidden under the engine cowling.

Completing the service were three new car types that, when coupled to one of the Jubilee locomotives, would create a unified look and constitute a fleet of four complete passenger train sets. The new equipment was designed by CPR's mechanical department. The frames were built by the National Steel Car Company of Hamilton, Ontario, and the interiors were finished by the railway's own employees at Montreal's Angus Shops.

One of the principal objectives of their design was to reduce weigh, so the cars were light on ornamentation and employed such materials as aluminum, where possible. Four mail and express cars, four combination baggage and buffet coaches, and eight first-class coaches rolled out of Angus in CPR's familiar Tuscan red and black paint scheme. "Canadian Pacific" was stenciled on the black letter-board panels in gold letters.

Passengers in the large men's and women's lounges would gaze in awe at the splendour of their surroundings. The interiors of the first-class coaches were painted a cream colour down to the

Travel by train

SAFETY
COMFORT
ECONOMY

CANADIAN
PACIFIC

RAILWAY
LINES

WORLD'S
GREATEST
TRAVEL
SYSTEM

The thoroughly modern Jubilee-type locomotive, launched by
CPR to coincide with the company's fiftieth anniversary, was the
primary ambassador of a reinvigorated marketing campaign.
POSTER BY NORMAN FRASER, AUTHOR'S COLLECTION

brown wainscoting, with marbleized brown linoleum on the floors. The walls in the buffet coaches
were done in green to the wainscoting, and the floors were a marbleized green to match. To help
keep the overall weight down, most of the seats had tubular stainless-steel frames. The one excep-
tion was in the men's lounge of the first-class coaches, where brown leather upholstery created the
desired rich and luxurious effect. Separate men's and women's washrooms were located at either
end of the buffet coaches. All of the cars were equipped with ice-activated air-conditioning systems.

Two of the modern, eye-catching train sets were placed in service between Montreal and
Quebec, on a four-and-a-half-hour schedule in each direction for the 173-mile run, which included
thirty-two intermediate stops. Another streamlined train was assigned to the Toronto-to-Detroit
run, making the 229-mile trip in five hours and thirty-five minutes. That train was christened the
Royal York, the same name as CPR's landmark Toronto Hotel. It made nineteen intermediate stops
between the two terminal cities.

A fourth train, pulled by a Jubilee locomotive dubbed the Chinook, blew up and down the
track in the Calgary-to-Edmonton service. Twenty-two intermediate stops were made in the five
hours and fifteen minutes required to cover the 194-mile distance. As a nod to the intense football
rivalry between the two cities, the train to Calgary was referred to as the Stampeder, while the
Edmonton train became the Eskimo.

The travelling public loved the new trains and the quick and efficient service they provided;
but larger forces were at play. With the outbreak of the Second World War, in 1939, the concept
of the high-speed unit train was shelved. In the East, the war caused traffic patterns to change.
With heavier loads to haul, the Jubilees were assigned to local runs between Toronto and London,
Ontario, and between London and Windsor.

The equipment on the Montreal-to-Quebec trains was reassigned, in favour of heavier locomotives that could haul more war supplies. Older, wooden coaches returned to service, and the
schedules became slower and longer. Only the trains in the West that were pulled by the locomotive
with the Chinook nameplate retained their former glory, but even in Alberta the sleek train sets
were often reassigned to less important runs.

The Chinook nameplate on the side of the locomotive was a unique feature of the speedy, streamlined passenger service between Calgary and Edmonton.
IMAGE C-08520 COURTESY OF THE ROYAL BC MUSEUM AND ARCHIVES

After the war, the stylish Jubilee locomotives faced the final indignity, losing their speed supremacy to a new usurper. The Budd Company's rail diesel cars, known on the CPR as Dayliners, were now setting records and garnering all of the attention. Beginning in 1953, these self-propelled, stainless steel vehicles replaced conventional train equipment on most inter-city runs, and soon consigned the railway's remaining steam locomotives to the scrap-cutter's torch.

In 2009, the Royal Canadian Mint produced a twenty-dollar silver coin in homage to the sleek locomotives with the oversized driving wheels, which had once streaked along CPR tracks with such panache. To represent the well-loved Jubilees on this commemorative collector's item, the engraver chose to illustrate none other than the locomotive that carried the name Chinook throughout its career. ⊹

STAMPEDER SPECIAL CHANGED THE GAME

I n the years immediately before and after the Second World War, it was de rigueur for sports teams to travel by rail back and forth between cities in their respective leagues; but the special train that brought the Calgary Stampeders football squad and its most loyal fans to the 1948 Grey Cup game in Toronto set a new standard for exuberance and team branding that would rarely be matched in the mythologizing of Canadian sport.

All of the planets were aligned that year when a group of Calgary businessmen approached CPR a little more than a week ahead of the big game to forego the usual arrangements of adding a few sleeping cars to its regular Toronto-bound transcontinental passenger train. What they wanted was something more in keeping with the delirious excitement the local team had generated when they defeated the Regina Roughriders to win the Canadian Football League's Western Conference. The Stamps were on the way to the Big One, and the CPR joined in the spirit as readily as the locals who were determined to make the pilgrimage to the Queen City for the final gridiron showdown.

Support for the excursion built quickly. "First there were thirty-four definitely prepared to make the trip," Reg West, CPR's passenger agent in Calgary, told press members eager for details. "Then we had enough to fill three cars," he enthused. "I had just finished arranging for these when the figure jumped to ten cars, enough to run a special, and by the time we were ready to go we had fifteen cars sewed up."

Two dining cars to handle the hungry entourage and a horse car to house the mounts that would bring a little western culture to the city slickers in the East were added to the train, but it was the custom-built rumpus car that played the largest role in keeping the Calgary rooters amused on their cross-country odyssey. A baggage car, emptied out and painted at CPR's Ogden Shops—and outfitted with a dance floor, piano, and bar on Calgary's Stampede grounds—provided the appropriate en-route venue for the four-piece country and western band and the square dancers that accompanied the travelling party.

Between the players, the fans, and the onboard entertainers, 198 passengers rode the eastbound Stampeder Special. From all reports, much revelry was engaged in, but there were no untoward incidents.

"They were a marvelous bunch to travel with," sleeping car conductors S. Todd and J. Doody said, after the event. "They never gave us any trouble at all. It was like a pleasure cruise. Everybody knew everybody else and first names were the order of the day."

61

Along the route, football fans and Grey Cup enthusiasts turned out in droves. In Winnipeg, keen members of the crowd sang cowboy songs and kicked up their heels on the station platform. In Fort William (now part of Thunder Bay), nearly the whole town came down to the station, though the festive train only arrived in town at an ungodly 1:30 A M; and the same scenario was repeated later that day when Chapleau's entire population of about a hundred arrived trackside to hoot and holler.

At every railway division point where the train was stopped for ten minutes or more, the coach hustled his men off the train and had them jog around the train until departure time, creating lots of opportunity for interaction and light-hearted banter with the public. At dinner, the players were expected to wear jackets and ties and dine in a civilized manner.

"Not a single breakage," dining car stewards J.R. Armitage and William Donaghue reported. "The players were gentlemen at all times."

Arriving in Toronto, the trainload of wild westerners proceeded to create a legendary chapter in Grey Cup history. Sporting flamboyant cowboy fashions and Stetson hats, they rode horses through the Union Station concourse and set up rustic chuck wagons downtown to serve the Stampede's trademark flapjack breakfasts. Before the festivities were over, they would witness the triumph of their beloved squad over the Ottawa Rough Riders, 12 to 7.

Back in Calgary four days later, an unofficial civic holiday was declared to enable an ecstatic citizenry to pack the streets, sidewalks, and parking lots surrounding the CPR station. Railway and city police officers assigned to keep things under control were unable to prevent the estimated crowd of forty thousand from spilling onto the railway station platform and mobbing the team members as they disembarked

Players and fans show their enthusiasm on the 1948 Grey Cup train. Stampeder star and future lieutenant governor of Alberta, Norman "Normie" Kwong, is leaning against the window on the right. GLENBOW ARCHIVES, ARCHIVES AND SPECIAL COLLECTIONS, UNIVERSITY OF CALGARY PA-2453-378

Despite having lost the big game to Ottawa in 1949, the Stampeders were met back home by a crowd of fans as they disembarked their CPR Special, where a parade of cars awaited.

GLENBOW ARCHIVES, ARCHIVES AND SPECIAL COLLECTIONS, UNIVERSITY OF CALGARY NA-3354-1

with their wives and girlfriends, who had been allowed to board and greet the conquering heroes in the town of Shepard, just east of the city. Four private planes buzzed the celebrations in Calgary, and an RCAF jet gave an official overhead salute, before the Stampeders were loaded into open cars for an impromptu parade through downtown.

The very next year, another train would again carry Calgary football fans to the championship in Toronto; and in subsequent years, others would be organized for hundreds of followers of the game from Regina and Winnipeg. A tradition had been born, and over the years many more special trains would whistle down the tracks to Grey Cup games in Toronto, Vancouver, and elsewhere, but none would be as celebrated or as well-remembered as the 1948 Stampeder Special. ⊹

RUNNING OUT OF STEAM

One of the most dramatic transformations in railroading began to emerge in the years leading up to the Second World War. It affected a wholesale revolution within a decade of the cessation of hostilities. The triumphant ascension of the more efficient diesel locomotive and the corresponding demise of the temperamental steam locomotive profoundly changed the nature of railway operations not just for those men and women who worked in the running trades, but for the trainspotting public and all those who had grown up with the smoky plumes that had previously swirled around the industry. The workhorse had replaced the iron horse.

In 1949, CPR accepted delivery of Selkirk locomotive No. 5935, one of a class of the largest and heaviest steam locomotives in the British Commonwealth and the last standard-gauge steam locomotive built for a Canadian railway. That same year, Canadian Pacific acquired its first diesel-electric road locomotive, a 2,250-horsepower unit, numbered 1800 and built by General Motors at LaGrange, Illinois.

The first diesel-electric locomotive owned by the company had been a switcher, numbered 7000, purchased in 1937 from the National Steel Car Corporation of Hamilton. The 550-horsepower unit served on CPR lines for five years, before being sold in 1943 to an industrial plant.

By the mid-1950s, diesel-electric locomotives were pulling 30 percent of the CPR's passenger trains, handling 35 percent of the railway's road freight, and performing 55 percent of its switching services. In 1956 alone, Canadian Pacific scrapped 195 steam engines, 92 of them at Angus Shops, the railway's huge locomotive plant in East Montreal. Workers, who for years had toiled to keep these great lumbering beasts in working order, now took acetylene torches in hand. In just a few days, a once proud but now sombre grey, mechanical hulk could be reduced to a pile of nuts, bolts, springs, boiler tubes, and scrap metal.

Many in the railway business, and not a few of the general public, missed the old steamers, each of which had exhibited its own personality while in service. "Each had its own quirks, and you had to know how to nurse and coax them along," said CPR engineer Charlie Klein, who spent nearly forty years operating steam locomotives. But there was no denying that the new breed of locomotive was cleaner, easier to maintain, and ultimately could produce more power more economically. While some shed a tear for the demise of their beloved engines, others took a more pragmatic view.

Within a very short period of time, all of these once-loved engines awaiting the cutting torch at the railway's Weston Shops, in Winnipeg, would be nothing but scrap metal.

PHOTO BY NICHOLAS MORANT, AUTHOR'S COLLECTION

"Steam had its day, that's all," veteran CPR locomotive engineer J. Benzy told a reporter from the company's *Spanner* magazine, in January 1961. "To be sorry to see steam go, would be sorry to see progress made," he said. "All I ever got out of steam was a lot of hard work."

Sentiment aside, what was not to like about diesels? Unlike working in a steam locomotive, where the conditions were semi-outdoors, dirty, and either too hot or too cold depending on the season, the cabs in the new diesel engines were like riding in a modern automobile, with comfortable foam-rubber seats, heaters and defrosters, and wide safety-glass windshields with windshield wipers, not to mention on-board lavatory facilities.

Diesel-powered dynamic braking, not friction braking or brake shoe against wheel, would keep trains under control. When an engineer flipped a switch in the diesel cab to set a speed at the top of a hill, the locomotive's traction motors became generators and the resulting resistance would hold back the train and precisely control the speed of its descent. For extra safety, there was even a *dead-man pedal*, which the locomotive engineer had to press down with his foot at all times when his train was running. If for any reason the engineer became incapacitated and removed his foot from the pedal, the air brakes would be instantly applied and bring the train to a halt.

Unlike steam locomotives, diesels could be coupled together to haul heavy trains and controlled by a single crew at the head end. There was no longer a need to tend the fires and watch the boiler pressures in each engine. Three or four diesel units could easily be linked electrically to a control panel in the lead locomotive.

More than any man at Canadian Pacific, Senior Vice-president N.R. "Buck" Crump had been responsible for shepherding the company's transformation from a steam to a diesel-driven one. As early as 1928, Crump had obtained a bachelor of science degree from Purdue University, in Lafayette, Indiana, while studying mechanical engineering. The subject of the young railroader's thesis was "Internal Combustion Engines in the Railroad Field."

Crump's conversion of CPR motive power to a full roster of diesel locomotives took twelve years to complete. The steam engines that had powered the railway for more than seven decades were now scrapped or relegated to museum showrooms. And there was nobody in the business that defended the diesel revolution like the true believer who went on to serve as president, chairman, and chief executive officer of Canadian Pacific.

"When people talk to me about the lonely cry of the steam whistle in the middle of the night on the Prairie," Crump was reported to have said at the time, "I say bullshit!" ✠

VAMOOSE CABOOSE

Roadside trainspotters might have done a double take when CP Extra East 348-049-14 took to the rails between Winnipeg to Thunder Bay on November 14, 1989. In place of the proverbial little red caboose at the tail end of the hundred-car grain train, a small metal box variously known as an ETIS, an ETU, an SBU, or a FRED had usurped its traditional, near-sacred role as safety watch keeper. It was the first fully cabooseless train operated over CP tracks, and life in the running trades would never be the same.

Approval from the Canadian Transport Commission to eliminate cabooses from everyday operations had come nearly two years earlier, after several years of public hearings and many apocalyptic predictions about the safety implications of such a drastic makeover of the face of railroading. Who would apply the brakes? Who would watch for shifting loads or overheated wheel bearings? Who would know if a train was blocking a crossing, or whether a nasty level-crossing incident had occurred?

FRED, that's who.

Since the first piece of track was spiked down to a wooden tie more than a century and a half earlier, the railway industry has embraced innovation in all aspects of its operations, and increasingly so with the advent of modern technologies during the late twentieth century. Centralized traffic control and other automated signalling systems eliminated the need for walking back from a stationary train to leave a flag warning for a following train. The installation of remotely controlled power switches and spring switches that restore themselves to their normal position after trains have passed eliminated the need to jump down from a train to throw your back into it. Electronic trackside scanners eliminated the need for constant visual inspections to detect dragging equipment and hotboxes, the overheating of the ubiquitous and heat-sensitive journal boxes that housed the lubrication of every railcar wheel and axle assembly. Technology and FRED had eliminated the need for a crewmember in a caboose at the end of a train.

FRED is an acronym for flashing rear-end device. Earlier protypes for essentially the same tail-end metal box were known as an ETIS (end of train information system), an ETU (end of train unit), or an SBU (sensitive braking unit). Not very sexy, perhaps, but reasonably descriptive of their basic function and utterly unambiguous about where they were to be employed.

Some early vans, or cabooses, lacked the iconic cupolas that came to epitomize the cars that were coupled to the end of every freight train. AUTHOR'S COLLECTION

FRED gave the new technology a personality. FRED could monitor air brake pressure *and* tell the head-end crew when the last car on the train was in motion, or whether or not the train had cleared the last level crossing. FRED was unaffected by unfavourable weather conditions and could perform equally well with poor visibility or in extreme temperatures. And similar devices had already proven their worth, and notably their safety *bona fides*, over the last decade in the US: on the Norfolk Southern, Florida East Coast Railway, Conrail, Southern Pacific, and other roads.

Other developments, including continuous welded rail and the introduction of roller bearings on freight cars, lessened the need for constant human monitoring and hastened the demise of the caboose; but FRED eliminated the home away from home for conductors and train workers, and opened new portals to the summer cottages, restaurants, tourist information offices, and motel units that some of these familiar railroading icons would some become.

In North America, the first railcars for tail-end crewmembers began to appear in the 1850s, modelled after British-style *guard* vans or *brake* vans that featured huge brake wheels in the middle of the floor, designed to create enormous drag on a train when applied. The added box on the roof, with the sliding windows and seats facing front and back, is said to have originated in the 1860s after a conductor rigged up a seat to stick his head through a hole in the roof of his caboose to get a better view of his train. From this rooftop perch, conductors could see along the car sides and watch for hot boxes (overheated bearings on the wheel axles) or dragging equipment. This was particularly effective on curved track. By the 1870s, in response to the demands of fledgling railroad labour unions for better working conditions, the caboose, as we know it, had become a standard fixture on most freight trains.

From the modest confines of their tail-end office and home, conductors and crew could perform their duties in relative comfort. With time, the workers would customize the cabooses to their own tastes with such amenities as linoleum floors and curtains in the windows to go with the standard pull-out bunks, eating areas, caboose stoves, and those dog-house-shaped observation quarters on the roof known as cupolas. Some crewmembers took to erecting sheet-metal embellishments on the top of their cabooses in the form of animals, crosses, crescent moons, and geometric shapes, to make them more readily identifiable in rail yards in and among other rolling stock.

Railway conductors installed distinctive embellishments on the
roofs of the rolling bunkhouses to which they were assigned.
PHOTO BY NICHOLAS MORANT, AUTHOR'S COLLECTION

Early on, cabooses—or vans—were also referred to variously as cabin cars, shanty cars, way cars, and saloons, but railway workers christened then with less conventional monikers like bone-breakers, monkey houses, bird cages, brain boxes, and crummies, taking a dig at both the living conditions aboard and the company one might keep.

Modern cabooses constructed in the early 1980s, shortly before reaching their past due date, represented an investment to CP of $100,000 for each one that rolled out of the shop. By then, they included two-burner stoves and seven-cubic-foot refrigerators, as well as cutlery, dishes, cooking utensils, foam insulation, and toilet facilities. No longer would it be necessary to hang off the rear platform to answer the call of nature. And no longer were CPR cabooses painted red; indeed, the rolling symbol of railroading domesticity would now sport a bright yellow jacket, tempered-glass windows, and captain's chairs with headrests in the cupola.

In the end, the most compelling factor for retiring the caboose was the need for railways to control expenses and remain competitive with other transportation modes. The joint annual savings CPR and its rival CN would enjoy was cited at $60 million. "Vamoose caboose," wrote one reporter in a flurry of articles that both lamented the passing of the venerable tail-end vehicle and recognized the inevitability of that watershed moment in railway labour history. ⚜

2

RAILROADERS, REBELS, AND ROYALTY

THE PEOPLE WHO BUILT AND NURTURED THE Canadian Pacific Railway were truly lords of the line. They made sweeping decisions that influenced the broad economic development of the country, and they created worldwide networks that trumpeted their many services and enticed immigration to Canada from the far-flung reaches of the globe. They curried favour with politicians, the influential, and the rich and famous from all walks of life, keeping their hands on the reins of power, in the boardrooms of the nation, and the ballrooms of society's most fashionable social centres. They were elite members of the Canadian who's who.

As the company expanded its investments in the Canadian economy and diversified its holdings in a multitude of directions, nationally and internationally, its workforce grew to as many as a hundred thousand people by the Second World War. Some of them achieved a measure of fame or notoriety performing their tasks with grace and élan, while many others laboured in relative obscurity to keep the engines of the economy well oiled and running smoothly.

Contractors, politicians, freight-forwarders, business travellers, tourists, and investors sought and maintained ties with the globe-spanning corporation that wielded influence on a massive scale. It would become somewhat of a rarity to find a Canadian or somebody closely associated with the country that did not eventually have some close encounter with the Canadian Pacific Railway or one of its affiliates.

Taking a cue from the California railway builders, Andrew Onderdonk was the primary employer of Chinese labourers in Canada. IMAGE A-01321 COURTESY OF THE ROYAL BC MUSEUM AND ARCHIVES

CHINESE NAVVIES

Labourers from the Guangdong Hong Kong region of China built what was arguably the most difficult section of the CPR transcontinental main line, through the picturesque but treacherous canyons of the Fraser and Thompson Rivers.

Before the Canadian Pacific Railway Company was incorporated in 1881, the federal government had undertaken to build the transcontinental as a crown enterprise. The government had made a promise to British Columbia a decade earlier to connect the remote West Coast colony with the more populous eastern provinces and form one viable country from sea to sea. In the absence of a sufficient labour market in BC, the administration of John A. Macdonald had authorized the recruitment of Chinese workers, or navvies, as all railway construction labourers were referred to at the time.

In 1879, the Dominion government gave the contract to Andrew Onderdonk to begin the railway line at Port Moody on the coast and push through the mountains to Savona's Ferry on Kamloops Lake, a distance of 212 miles. Onderdonk was a New York engineer with experience in a number of public works projects in the East. He had been instrumental in building a seawall in San Francisco, where large numbers of Chinese workers had been employed.

The mass influx of Chinese workers to work on Onderdonk's contract began in 1881. Some men were brought up from California, where their previous railway and mining jobs had begun to taper off. The majority, though, were shipped over from China by Chinese merchants already active in Canada. The two main firms engaged in the recruitment campaign were Kwong Lee & Company and the Tai Soog Company, both of which owned their own ships on the Pacific. The merchants acted as labour brokers. They took care of all of the details of the men's employment, including transport, the provision of food supplies and other living needs, and the paying of wages.

At the time, BC had a population of around 49,500, more than half of which were Indigenous People. Another 19,500 were of European ancestry, mostly located in Port Moody, New Westminster, and Victoria. There were also a little more than 4,500 Chinese in the province. Some had arrived during the 1858 gold rush on the Fraser River. Others came to construct the Cariboo Wagon Road through the treacherous mountains, from Fort Yale to the BC Interior.

Over the next four years, Onderdonk would bring an additional seventeen thousand unskilled Chinese workmen into the province to work as cheap labour on the westernmost end of the transcontinental railway. Working alongside them would be a couple of thousand white workers, who were also employed by the contractor. The Chinese men were paid $1 to $1.25 a day, just half of the $2 to $2.50 their white counterparts were earning.

Regrettably, though not surprisingly, given the language barriers and the complete social isolation of the foreign workers imposed on them by their paternalistic labour brokers, none of the men from China were ever interviewed by the local or itinerant newspaper reporters who keep tabs on the slow but steady progress of the railway.

As the main line passed through the towering mountains, clung to the sheer canyon walls, and spanned the raging rivers on spidery trestles, safety concerns were not always top of mind. It was dangerous work, and many Chinese workers were killed on the job, but not out of proportion to overall numbers in the workforce as a whole.

More Chinese than white workers did die, however, from illness and disease while building the CPR through BC. Malnutrition, combined with the Chinese workers' rejection of Western medicines and remedies, rudimentary as they were, took their toll.

For the most part, those who died on the job were shipped back to China for burial in accordance with the agreements that brought them across the ocean in the first place. This was necessary to show the men's relatives that the ill-fated workers had not been sold into slavery while they were overseas. It also showed respect for the strong belief among the Chinese workers that the souls of the deceased could only rest at peace if they were buried in their homeland.

In 1884, Onderdonk was awarded an additional contract by CPR to continue construction of the main line eastward from Savona's Ferry to a spot in Eagle Pass that would come to be known as Craigellachie, where the Last Spike would ultimately be driven.

Onderdonk's grading crews ran out of rails in September 1885 and could go no farther. Accordingly, the contractor laid off all of his workers, Chinese and whites, and provided them with free transportation back to the Pacific Coast, where they had been hired. Virtually all of the workers left for the season. Two months later, when CPR's construction forces arrived from the East to lay the last rail in the transcontinental line, none of Onderdonk's workers were present.

When photographer Alexander Ross recorded one of the most famous scenes in Canadian history, as Donald Smith (soon to be Lord Strathcona) drove home the last linchpin in the National Dream, not one of the Chinese workers who had contributed so much to the project's success would appear in the picture. ⁌

RAILWAY BOSS DEFENDS CHINESE LABOUR

Prime Minister John A. Macdonald was a ready proponent of importing labourers from China, when it seemed there was no other option available to his government if the national transcontinental was to be built as promised in 1871.

Both the Anglo-European, white population in British Columbia and the provincial government had opposed the scheme from the beginning. Railway construction had languished for nearly a decade, in part due to the extreme shortage of workers on the Pacific Coast needed to build the line eastward. Chinese workers had succeeded in the United States under similar circumstances, so the proposal to employ them for this massive new undertaking in Canada was pushed through, despite the general misgivings.

Four years later, the public hue and cry against this imported work force would grow to such an extent that the federal government would feel compelled to levy a $50 head tax on each new Chinese worker entering the country. The racist Chinese Immigration Act of 1885 was the first Canadian law to exclude, or severely restrict, immigration on the basis of ethnic origin. Before the legislation was repealed, in 1923, the head tax would be raised first to $100 and then $500.

Though the Chinese had worked hard and behaved well while on the job for CPR's contractor in British Columbia, the company never again had the occasion to employ them in large numbers. However, many Chinese workers did travel by CPR during the ensuing decades to work on large public works projects in Cuba and the United States. Thousands of Chinese labourers were also sent to the European theatre during the First World War. Throughout the years, they were subjected to many prejudiced and discriminatory attacks from the public and from the media. CPR president Sir William Van Horne publicly condemned the irrational fears and blatant hostilities directed at these men who had benefited the nation's development to no small extent.

As early as September 24, 1896, in a letter to the editor of the Toronto *Globe*, the railway boss was more than forthright about his views, while chastising the paper for fanning the flames of discontent. In his view, the Chinese workforce was undervalued relative to other groups of labourers who were coming to North America in equally large numbers.

Past experience has shown that there is no ground for your fear of a large movement of Chinese to any part of Canada. The lines of occupation open to the Chinese are very limited, comprising

Without Chinese workers, the railway builders would have been hard pressed to get the job done as quickly as the federal government had promised. GLENBOW ARCHIVES, ARCHIVES AND SPECIAL COLLECTIONS, UNIVERSITY OF CALGARY NA-387-27

ordinary labour with pick and shovel, cooking or other household work, laundry work, fruit and hop picking, salmon canning, and a few things of lesser importance.

The railway chief opined that the Chinese held all people but their own in contempt, but he was of the opinion that their general lack of involvement in North American affairs was

. . . decidedly in their favour as against the Sicilians, Danubian Jews and other worthless European people, who are let in without a word of objection, and who have, in the United States, created festering sores on the body politic to an extent which has now become most serious, especially in the large cities.

The Chinese who come to us are simply labour-saving machines, and, as a rule, they are confined to a class of work which our people will not do except from the most extreme necessity, but work which absolutely must be done by something or somebody.

Van Horne went on to implore the reporter to examine the origins of anti-Chinese agitation.

It is in British Columbia, as it was in San Francisco, instigated largely by the saloon-keepers and such like. They know that if they had a white man for every Chinese, they would sell more whiskey: but as was the case with their kind in San Francisco, they fail to see that if they had no Chinese at all, they would not have so many white men.

If the paper was to send a reporter to British Columbia to interview the "businessmen and the better class of people generally," said the railway president, "everyone will tell you, confidentially, that they cannot get along without the Chinese, but that it will not do for them to say so, because of probable boycotting and other unpleasantness."

Unfortunately, it would be another quarter century before the views of what Van Horne called the "insignificant minority, embracing the very worst elements in British Columbia" were brushed aside with the repeal of the discriminatory Chinese Immigration Act. For the moment, the agitators would continue to "influence our Dominion legislation, and inflict incalculable damage upon the Province of British Columbia and upon the Dominion at large," he maintained. ✣

THE PIONEER GUIDE AND THE PUBLIC RELATIONS MAN

n 1882, Tom Wilson was the first white man to lay eyes upon the enchanting vision of Lake Louise and the Victoria Glacier, while on a break from working with railway surveyors in the Rocky Mountains. Wilson was beholding a scene that would become the most well-known and popular attraction along the entire main line of the Canadian Pacific Railway. Though Wilson would never be a salaried employee of CPR or any of its many subsidiaries, the intrepid mountain man and entrepreneurial outfitter and guide would be one of the company's greatest public relations assets during its formative years.

Wilson's second "discovery" later that year of another lovely little gem would be named Emerald Lake. It would also become a star destination for CPR, underlining the value of the pioneer guide to the company that hoped to "capitalize the scenery." While the railway builders moved quickly to build mountain hotels, bungalow camps, and teahouses throughout one of the most picturesque regions of the world, Wilson would be the one to clear tourist trails between the various attractions and alert the company's public relations men to such newly exposed wonders as the spectacularly cascading Takakkaw Falls and the monumental 11,860-foot Mount Assiniboine.

Wilson's friendly relationship with local Indigenous People served CPR well when the guide was informed about a disturbance near the Blackfoot Reserve on the Bow River. While prairie surveyor Charles Shaw and his men were approaching Calgary with their transits, a party of Blackfoot had been pulling up survey stakes in their frustration at the slowness of the federal government to make good on promises of food and other supplies. Wilson's reputation among the Blackfoot, and his reassuring words, calmed the situation. Within days, CPR general manager William Van Horne sent large amounts of supplies to the surveyor's camp, with instructions that the Blackfoot were to be treated generously. No expense was to be spared in gaining and maintaining their goodwill.

Wilson soon established an outfitting company in the Town of Banff, complete with a corral and stable of riding ponies. The railway was his regular patron. In 1902, he was granted the privilege of advertising himself as a CPR guide and, as such, was often called upon to attend to the adventuring and touring needs of the railway's guests at the Banff Springs Hotel, the Lake Louise Chalet, Mount Stephen House in Field, and elsewhere.

From left, John Murray Gibbon, Dr. Charles Walcott of the Smithsonian Institute, and Tom Wilson pose in Yoho Valley with Takakkaw Falls in the background. GLENBOW ARCHIVES, ARCHIVES AND SPECIAL COLLECTIONS, UNIVERSITY OF CALGARY NA-1263-1

With the substantial floods experienced in the West during the spring runoff, in June 1894, the railway's main line was closed for a number of days, leaving many passengers stranded at various mountain resorts, including a large number at Banff. Wilson convinced his friends at the Stoney Reserve at Morley, just west of Calgary, to come to the mountains in full ceremonial regalia and entertain the tourists. The ensuing public relations coup, which would soon be formalized as "Indian Days," would be staged on an annual basis with the help of the resourceful mountain man for the next seven years, and carried on for decades under the control of a committee consisting of railway employees and townspeople.

Wilson left his beloved mountains just after the First World War. While living for a short time in Vancouver and the small BC town of Enderby, he was lured back on occasion by CPR to guide guests of the Alpine Club. During this period, Wilson became well acquainted with CPR's general publicity agent, John Murray Gibbon. Together, the two men went on to even greater heights, promoting both the railway and the surrounding mountains.

In 1924, Gibbon was caught in a summer snowstorm on Wolverine Plateau. While hunkering down, he came up with the idea for an organization to celebrate everything he loved about horseback riding and outdoor western culture—a hallowed order that continues to hold annual rides to this day.

To inaugurate the Trail Riders of the Canadian Rockies, a unique institution that would go a long way toward preserving the legacy of the pioneer mountain guides and outfitters, Gibbon arranged to pay tribute to Tom Wilson. He had a bronze plaque mounted on a large boulder at the mouth of the Yoho Valley, at the very spot from which the Trail Riders' first expedition would set forth. In the days leading up to the first ride, Wilson recruited all of his old clients, buddies, and riding companions to join the order. He would himself become one of its most active and loyal members.

Two years later, Gibbon invited Wilson to travel to Montreal with him. There, they stayed a couple of days at CPR's Place Viger Hotel, at the company's expense. On a weekend visit to Gibbon's home in suburban St. Anne de Bellevue, the railway's publicity agent managed to convince the pioneer guide to accept a long-term contract with CPR, beginning in 1927. All he would be required to do was spend time with the guests at the company's tourist hotels in Banff and Lake Louise

Railroaders, Rebels and Royalty

and regale them with stories of the good old days on the trail. Gibbon also encouraged the crusty raconteur to submit regular written pieces about his past exploits to liven up the copy in company promotional materials. From all reports, Wilson took on both duties with great panache, mixing historical facts with tall tales from the early days of packhorses.

Soon afterward, the Trail Riders of the Canadian Rockies even wrote a campfire song about old Tom, which included the following lines:

> *And when he told a fishing tale, you saw the fishes grow*
> *From mountain trout to giant whales, all swimming in a row;*
> *And if at times you thought he had a tendency to blow,*
> *He said he caught the habit from those whales of long ago.*

Six years on, just months before Wilson died, Gibbon was still engaged in a lively and good-natured correspondence with his old friend and business associate.

"Thank you very much for your letter of June 7th," he wrote, "with the very interesting record of some of your work in the Mountains. I see nothing in this of your adventurous trip in a motor car to Vermillion Pass, where you were stopped by an unmelted snowdrift and witnessed the tragedy of the accidental destruction of a bottle of Scotch whisky." ⚜

NOT JUST A MAN'S WORLD

Like most heavy industries, railroading has traditionally been a man's world, many of the jobs requiring considerable physical strength, not to mention the near impossibility of an employee pursuing a family life for at least the junior years in the running trades. Of course, there have always been exceptions, and increasingly, women have shown their mettle from trackside to the executive suite.

Before the First World War, it was extremely rare to find female railroaders, but not completely unknown. CPR's pioneer railway hotels in the mountains of Alberta and British Columbia provided the first opportunities for enterprising women. As early as 1888, the Mollison sisters, Annie and Jean, left their home in the Scottish Highlands to find employment as housekeepers in the Banff Springs Hotel. Jean went on to manage the railway's Fraser Canyon House, in North Bend, as well as the chalet at Lake Louise, earning a reputation as a respectable singer and pianist while entertaining guests in the evening.

On occasion, practicality and unique circumstance made it quite logical for women to fill the position of their husband or father, at least temporarily, in remote locations. Station agents and telegraph operators played an essential role in railway communities across the country. Their family members, male and female, learned the language, discipline, and rulebook of the railway as a matter of course, by virtue of their proximity to the action.

Wilderness stations in Northern Ontario had more than a dozen of these accidental female railroaders, dating back to at least 1891. A yardmaster by the name of Sullivan had three competent operators in his family, one of whom was his daughter. At one time or other, there was a Maggie Seibert at Pearl, Mary Morrow at Hurkett, and Mrs. Laferte at Hemlo, whose husband was a station agent. Etta D'Arcy of Mizzoukama, now Kama, learned about railway culture and the duties of an operator from her brother-in-law Alex Ward. On occasion husband and wife teams spelled each other off, with the full approval of CPR, as with Mr. and Mrs. McQuon and Mr. and Mrs. MacIsaac, long-time station agents on the Schreiber Division.

Beatrice Pigeon of Montreal was the first women to break through the male bastion at Windsor Station, as a secretary, in 1912. It would be several more years before railway vice-presidents and other senior executives would give up their male secretaries, who typically travelled with their bosses and were essentially manservants.

More than any other factor, it was the two world wars that presented opportunities for women to break down the barriers to employment with the railways, in much the way they had filled roles in government departments and served in the nation's arms industries when male workers left in droves for the armed forces. Men too young or unfit for service moved up the ranks from call boy— alerting train crews when they were needed for a shift—to positions with more responsibility, such as fireman or trainman, allowing women to fill in as a different sort of *call girl*. The routine jobs of an engine wiper, car cleaner, and baggage handler would as often as not be filled quite adequately by women.

For the first time, women reported for work in railway engine houses and freight sheds across the country. They stood in as station agents, ticket clerks, telegraph operators and janitors, as gardeners and maintenance of way workers. In some cases, the cultural shift was so unprecedented that the ladies felt the need to sneak to work along the back streets and alleys in their respective towns so that the neighbours would not see them in their coveralls.

Beginning in the 1920s, increasing numbers of women could be found working in administrative roles in city and yard offices, though they were subjected to a fair amount of condescension. They were stenographers, typists, office clerks, and switchboard operators. Each morning in the larger centres, the women would be lined up two-by-two in the halls, before being escorted by a supervisory matron to the various departments in which they were employed. Their motherly overseer would remind them not to talk while on the job and check their work periodically for accuracy and neatness. Acceptable office dress was limited to navy-blue or black skirts and long-sleeved blouses. If they got married, the women were expected to resign and let their husbands support them.

During the Second World War, Mary McCarthy was one of four women to be schooled as a train telegrapher, tapping out the day-to-day messages required to keep the railway running, as opposed to the commercial operators who were concerned only with sending public telegrams.

Margaret Wilde, a graduate of the University of Manitoba, became CPR's first female architect, designing railway stations and other structures based on rough sketches and plans sent

During the two world wars, women took over many railway jobs while the men went to war. At the end of the hostilities, some stayed on. AUTHOR'S COLLECTION

to headquarters by roadmasters and district engineers in the West. Eleanor Georgina Luxton had an arts degree from the University of Alberta and a science degree from Montreal's Sir George Williams. She also studied civil engineering at McGill, worked as a draftsman on CPR's locomotive design team, and helped to develop G5, 4-6-2 Pacific-type engines, the first to be built at the company's Angus Shops since 1931.

By November 1943, with more than sixteen thousand CPR men gone off to war, there were 675 women filling traditionally male roles.

After the war, many of the female employees left the ranks to make way for returning soldiers, but others stayed on. With the growth and popularity of business and administrative courses, their numbers continued to increase. Women were hired by the finance and marketing departments, worked in public relations, and served as solicitors with the railway's legal staff. Breaking new ground in 1974, Joanne Peggie, daughter of CPR master mechanic Bob Peggie, was the first female dispatcher, coordinating and sending messages to operators throughout Alberta.

Women were now being accepted as locomotive engineer trainees, as well as potential employees in any operating role for which they could qualify, head to head with their male counterparts. They would continue to level the playing field, successfully executing their responsibilities in most of the critical railway positions historically filled by men, up to and including the vice-presidencies of many key departments.

The only remaining challenge is for a woman to become chief executive officer of a national railway like the CPR. ✣

VAN HORNE'S GARDEN OF EDEN

S t. Andrews, New Brunswick, became a CPR town when Canada's newly built transcontinental railway completed the International Railway of Maine, during the years 1886–88. Known as the Short Line, the new rail connection delivered on the promise of the Macdonald Conservative government, re-elected in 1878, to build a link between Montreal and McAdam, New Brunswick, connecting the CPR with the New Brunswick Railway, which had fallen under Canadian Pacific's sway by 1890.

Though the charming, little maritime town could never rival Saint John as an Atlantic deep-water shipping port for the World's Greatest Travel System, as CPR would later style itself, it did become a very popular tourist resort and a favourite getaway for railway builder Sir William Van Horne and several of his business colleagues.

When Van Horne first came to St. Andrews to inspect CPR's new franchise in the Maritimes, he soon discovered the natural beauty of the area and, in particular, the merits of a small five-hundred-acre island in nearby Passamaquoddy Bay, which was only accessible while the tide was out, when a curved gravel bar on the seafloor would provide a temporary bridge.

Over the years, ownership of the island had passed through the hands of several United Empire loyalists. For a period, it had also been home to a local ship's captain. It had been named Minister's Island after St. Andrews' first Anglican reverend, Thomas Andrews, who was the place's oldest resident in living memory.

Almost immediately, Van Horne began to transform the island into his own family retreat, complete with a large working farm that showcased the potential of the area and incorporated a number of features that were as typically innovative and successful as their entrepreneurial owner.

Sir William designed the initial farmhouse himself, with a few suggestions from his architect friend, Edward Colonna. It was a modest eighty-four- by sixty-foot structure, which he named Covenhoven after his father, Cornelius Covenhoven Van Horne. Edward Colonna, North America's foremost practitioner of the art nouveau style, had been employed by CPR to fit out railway passenger car interiors. He had also been kept busy doing interior design work for the railway president's Montreal home on the northwest corner of Sherbrooke and Stanley Streets. A few years later, another noted CPR architect, Edward Maxwell, would more than double the size of the house

The main house at Covenhoven was designed to Van Horne's exactly specifications by his favourite architect and art nouveau designer, Edward Colonna. AUTHOR'S COLLECTION

and, in addition, design and supervise the construction of an enormous stone and wood barn, as well as several smaller buildings on the property.

Ultimately, Covenhoven grew to incorporate more than fifty rooms and eleven fireplaces. A large covered veranda, running its full length, added a graceful touch. Van Horne himself laid out an extensive network of roads, paths, orchards, and gardens. Telephone and telegraph wires connected the island to the mainland. Self-sufficiency was the ultimate goal.

A spectacular, three-storey barn housed the railway baron's prized collection of Clydesdale horses, as well as his herd of Dutch Belted cattle, a rare and valuable breed, along with an ever-expanding assortment of pigs, sheep, chickens, geese, turkeys, and ducks. It

All of the structures on the estate, including the barn and silo, were solidly constructed and kept in an impeccably clean and orderly condition. AUTHOR'S COLLECTION

included two silos and a freight elevator and was kept immaculately clean by Van Horne's groundskeepers.

Just a short walk from the house stood the gardener's cottage, and close by were two expansive greenhouses, which provided an ideal environment for growing grapes, cucumbers, peaches, pears, plums, nectarines and cherries. All three buildings were equipped with an early solar heating system.

Equally impressive was the stone windmill, which the railway president built to pump water from his own artesian well to the house and other buildings on the island, using a system of hydrants. An adjoining plant produced gas for lighting and cooking, by means of carbide pellets dropped into a tank of water.

For twenty-five years, until Sir William's death in 1915, the family would arrive in late spring and stay at Covenhoven until November. Over time, his entourage of more than thirty staff members would grow to serve not just himself and Lady Van Horne, but also his children and extended family.

When not entertaining prominent townsfolk or hosting famous politicians, businessmen, and celebrities, Van Horne occupied his time with projects like building the round, stone tower on Passamaquoddy Bay that housed an observation deck, a painting studio, and a swimming pool carved from the rock at the sea's edge. In later years, he added an equally impressive stone garage to shelter his collection of automobiles, among them a Rolls Royce, a Pierce-Arrow, and a Ford Model-T.

Van Horne was such an outspoken advocate of St. Andrews's charms and advantages that a number of his CPR associates also chose to make the town their summer haven. Van Horne's successor as CPR president, Sir Thomas Shaughnessy, built a grand summer residence he dubbed Fort Tipperary in honour of the British garrison that once stood there.

Edward Maxwell fell in love with the maritime scenery and the climate while working on Minister's Island and was soon constructing himself a stately home on the mainland. Hayter Reed, who for many years managed CPR's hotel properties along with his wife, Kate, erected a lovely cottage, which they called Pansy Patch. The railway's hotel department went so far as to acquire St. Andrews's finest hostelry, the Algonquin, in its quest to lure tourists to Canada's newest summer playground.

The Van Horne family retained ownership of Minister's Island, regularly referred to by the locals as Van Horne's Island, until 1961. At that time, it was bought by an American syndicate that planned to build an exclusive club there for golfing, fishing, and skeet shooting. Despite the grand designs of the group, nothing ever came of it. In 1977, the Province of New Brunswick purchased the island to preserve it as a National Historic Site. By then, many of the original furnishings and other elaborations had long been sold.

Fortunately, though, a newly created, non-profit Canadian charity, the Van Horne Estate on Minister's Island Inc., has completed restorations on some of Covenhoven's buildings in recent years, and continues to work toward preserving the essence and the spirit of Van Horne's maritime paradise. ✛

THE TRAGIC BC ARCHITECT

Mention to someone that Victoria's Empress Hotel was designed by the same man who drew the plans for the impressive BC provincial legislature, which stands next to the famous CPR landmark in the city's Inner Harbour, and you might pique their interest. Tell them that same architect was murdered by his wife's drug-crazed boyfriend, and you will surely get their attention.

It was 1892 when Francis Mawson Rattenbury, fresh off the boat from Bradford, England, competed for the contract to design the Legislative Assembly in Victoria. The "Notice to Architects" that ran in the *Vancouver Daily World* specified that proposals should be submitted anonymously to avoid any sort of bias. The capital city was where the young immigrant intended to live and do business, so Rattenbury entered his drawings under the nom de plume "BC Architect," hoping that the local association might play in his favour.

There was intense competition from architects based in Toronto, Chicago, and Boston. Thomas Sorby was among the five finalists. Sorby had made his name by designing CPR's first hotels in Field, Glacier, and North Bend, in the mountains of British Columbia. He was also responsible for the railway's seminal Hotel Vancouver. Despite the credentials of his competitors, Rattenbury secured the contract for what would be one of his most renowned creations.

By the time the Legislature opened, complete with a fireworks show, on February 10, 1898, the now-celebrated Rattenbury was too busy with his latest business interests to attend the festivities. The discovery of gold in the Canadian north had opened his mind to other opportunities. In partnership with pioneer meat merchant Pat Burns, the two men would satisfy the insatiable hunger of the ballooning population in the mining towns. Rattenbury also founded the Lake Bennett and Klondike Navigation Company, to ship both people and cattle to Dawson City. Within a year, he had also jump-started the Arctic Express Company, using sled dogs to relay packages between Dawson and Skagway.

Although he now tended to describe his architectural work as a "leisure activity," he managed to find time to design small hotels and offices for the Bank of Montreal in the BC towns of Rossland and Greenwood, office blocks in Vancouver and New Westminster, and a handful of residences, including his own in the Victoria suburb of Oak Bay. Notably, he also designed an eighteen-room mansion for Burns in Calgary.

By the turn of the century, Rattenbury was the most accomplished architect in the Canadian West. He had no problem winning a number of further, lucrative contracts from Canadian Pacific. He designed a new wing with a fresh look for the Hotel Vancouver, and greatly expanded the capacity of the previously modest chalet at Lake Louise, using a number of Tudor elements that characterized his developing style.

In January 1901, CPR bought a controlling interest in the Canadian Pacific Navigation Company, updating its fleet and paying special attention to the Vancouver-to-Victoria run. Rattenbury was given the job of designing the interior of the *Princess Victoria*, the first ship to be built for the railway's new service.

Above all, the creation of CPR's iconic Empress Hotel, in Victoria, would do for that town what the company's Chateau Frontenac had done for Quebec City—make it instantly recognizable internationally. The famous structure would cement Rattenbury's legacy as an accomplished architect, but not without controversy. Ironically, while crowning his status as CPR's go-to hotel designer, the Empress would also be the cause of a major falling out with his steady sponsor.

When CPR allowed Montreal architect Walter Painter to make changes to the arrangement of rooms on the first floor, Rattenbury was upset. When the railway company then assigned the task of interior decoration to Kate Reed, the wife of hotel superintendent Hayter Reed, Rattenbury left Canadian Pacific's employ in a snit. He had wanted to handle both tasks himself.

Turning his attention to the north once again, Rattenbury became heavily involved with CPR's competitor, the Grand Trunk Pacific (GTP), designing a huge transportation complex in Prince Rupert, which included a large Chateau-style hotel and a steamship terminal. He also prepared drawings for mountain hotels in Jasper, Miette, and Mount Robson to rival CPR's successful resorts.

If all had gone well, his work for the GTP might have surpassed his previous achievements, but it was not to be. In 1912, the death of his chief sponsor and Grand Trunk president, Charles Hays, with the sinking of the *Titanic* also scuttled Rattenbury's plans. The bankruptcy of the GTP, which followed immediately after the First World War, put an end to virtually all of the projects with which Rattenbury was involved.

There would be one last revival of the architect's relationship with Canadian Pacific, when the company and the City of Victoria hired Rattenbury and Percy L. James to design an enormous glass-covered swimming pool and amusement centre, adjacent to the Empress Hotel. The unique structure, which incorporated exotic gardens, dance floors, and a large saltwater pool, soon became one of the city's most popular social centres. In 1925, at the celebratory dinner for the newly named

Crystal Garden, Rattenbury was to meet Alma Pakenham, a beautiful and fashionable wartime nurse, piano teacher, and flapper.

Within the year, the BC Architect would divorce his first wife to marry the much younger Pakenham. Rattenbury flaunted his relationship with the woman, who was thirty years his junior, causing tongues to wag among the more prominent members of their community.

"The man's bewitched," they said, while whispering among themselves of the couple's dalliances with morphine and cocaine.

The Rattenburys tried their best to fit into polite society, but rumoured drug use tainted their reputations beyond repair. Four years later, they sailed for England and settled in Bournemouth, where they lived in relative obscurity on the architect's former earnings. Before long, they were mostly living separate lives under the same roof.

In 1934, the family chauffeur and handyman, who had become his wife's lover, murdered Rattenbury. At the ensuing trial, the jury concluded that the man may have been maddened by cocaine usage at the time of the deed. It was a tragic end for the creator of some of Canada's and CPR's most well-known and well-loved landmarks. ⁜

Rattenbury's hubris led to a downfall of mythic proportions. IMAGE F-02163 COURTESY OF BC MUSEUM AND ARCHIVES

PRINCE FUSHIMI'S DIPLOMATIC VOYAGE

The early twentieth century was not a welcoming time in Canada for people of Asian descent. British Columbia, in particular, had become a breeding ground for resentment as a result of the large number of low-wage Chinese workers recruited to build the CPR and to work in labour-intensive industries such as mining. The backlash led to various discriminatory measures, including the head taxes that were imposed upon each "Oriental" or "Celestial," as their detractors dismissively referred to them, just to enter the country.

In 1907, the BC government had gone so far as to pass legislation intended to completely curtail the immigration of all Asians into the province, though the federal government quickly ruled that the province was overstepping its authority. Later that year, both levels of government would be called upon to roll out the red carpet for a very auspicious visitor from Japan, a country that, despite Western xenophobia, was a staunch ally of the British Empire.

The year before, Prince Arthur, Duke of Connaught, the third son of Queen Victoria and Prince Albert, had travelled to Japan to present Emperor Meiji with the Order of the Garter on behalf of his uncle King Edward VII. Britain and Japan had formed an alliance in 1902 based on their mutual distrust of the Russian Empire. In the wake of Japan's successful conduct in the Russo-Japanese War of 1904–5, Britain had agreed to renew the treaty with Japan for ten more years, calling for each of the signatories to come to the aid of one another in the event of an attack by a third party. In 1907, the emperor dispatched his emissary to thank the king for his grand gesture and to negotiate the terms of the new agreement.

Accordingly, His Imperial Highness, Prince Fushimi Sadanaru—first cousin to Emperor Meiji, and second in line to the throne after the crown prince—was sent as a special envoy to the court of St. James, on what the international press dubbed the Garter Mission. He was to meet personally with His Majesty King Edward VII. Boarding a Peninsular & Oriental steamer along with the prince, for the westbound voyage to Britain, would be Admiral Yamamoto, General Nishi, and other high-ranking officers of the Japanese Imperial Navy and Army. Also on the passenger list was the prince's personal aide de camp, the comptroller of his household, the councillor of the Imperial Court, and a medical man who carried the title "physician extraordinary."

Every effort was made to ensure the desired outcome of the negotiations between Fushimi and Yamamoto, representing of the Japanese delegation, and Sir Edward Grey of the British Foreign Office, representing the United Kingdom. As an added precaution, so as not to offend His Imperial Highness, a London performance of Gilbert & Sullivan's *The Mikado* was suspended for the duration of the visit. On a more official note, Fushimi was made a Knight Commander of the Order of the Bath.

To ensure the Prince's return trip would be every bit as satisfactory as his stay in England, the Brits looked to Canadian Pacific to provide the necessary deluxe accommodations.

"He and his Mission must return to Japan with their hearts overflowing with gratitude to Canada and her people," Canadian governor general Albert Grey advised CPR president Thomas Shaughnessy on May 8, 1907.

The prince's royal treatment began with an enthusiastic formal welcome from Captain H.G. Kendall. To take up residence for the transatlantic crossing, he would be given the best suite available aboard one of Canadian Pacific's newly launched transatlantic greyhounds, the *Empress of Ireland*.

Because the timing of the royal trip across Canada did not coincide well with the scheduled departure from Vancouver of Canadian Pacific's luxurious Pacific *Empress* steamships, a rumour arose that Fushimi's entourage might have to traverse the Pacific on the US Northern Pacific's steamship *Minnesota*.

Sir Grey once again fired off a message to the CPR president.

"I called to Lord Elgin [Secretary of State for the Colonies] the moment I heard of this abominable arrangement," he wrote, "pointing out how undesirable it is that the Japanese Mission should return to Japan in any other than a British Ship." As a result, the diplomatic scrambling went into overdrive. The Americans would ultimately be left out of the arrangements.

For Canadian Pacific's part, the Atlantic voyage went splendidly. After a short rail trip from Halifax to North Bay, Ontario, courtesy of the Intercolonial Railway and the Grand Trunk, Fushimi's private car Cornwall—on loan from the federal government—was handed over to Canadian Pacific for the rest of the trans-Canada tour to the West Coast.

Underlining CPR's ability to fulfill all of the political entreaties, the royal train was reported in the international press as "a marvel of luxury in the manner of its appointments."

Three government special service men were dispatched to provide security, and Joseph Pope, Canada's undersecretary of state, accompanied the prince's party to ensure nothing went amiss.

An illustration by Charles Wyllie of Prince Fushimi departing for Canada on the *Empress of Ireland* was printed in a 1907 edition of British newspaper *The Sphere*. AUTHOR'S COLLECTION

Fushimi's train included federal government private cars York and Cornwall and CPR sleeping car Canada. Before his cross-country odyssey, as a special nod to the prince, CPR dining car Dunsany was renamed Yodogawa for one of the twenty-four wards in Osaka, Japan, and the sleeping car Cartier was renamed Kagashima after a neighbourhood in the City of Gifu. Private car Cornwall, where Fushimi slept and received visitors, was embellished on its exterior with the Japanese royal coat of arms.

After a fairly uneventful cross-country railway tour, highlighted by a polo match and fireworks display at Calgary's Mewata Park, the prince was treated to a visit at the CPR's ever-enlarging chateau at Lake Louise. For the hotel stay, five large wagons were needed to haul the prince's extensive effects from his palace-on-wheels to his specially decorated royal suite.

The whole diplomatic show culminated with a grand reception in Vancouver. A monumental, evergreen welcome arch in front of CPR's Vancouver railway station featured a *Banzai* banner. As the prince and his delegation arrived at the railway's Hotel Vancouver for a luncheon and overnight stay, they were greeted by a guard of honour consisting of the Duke of Connaught's Own Rifles and a band belting out the Japanese national anthem. A large contingent from Vancouver's not inconsiderable Japanese community had turned out to welcome the distinguished guest, in separate groups of men, women, and children, as was their custom.

Eighteen cases of various spirits, plus two barrels of wine had been rushed from the East by Dominion Express at the request of the Canadian government, to add a festive touch to the ceremonies at the hotel. The next day would feature a whirlwind tour of the city and Stanley Park.

Prince Fushimi expressed his great satisfaction with the City of Vancouver and with CPR by presenting the manager of the Hotel Vancouver with a gold cigarette case, embossed with the Japanese imperial crest. He also made a generous donation of one thousand yen to a local Japanese school.

The royal entourage was ferried to the provincial capital of Victoria aboard CPR's *Princess Victoria*, which was lavishly festooned with colourful flags and bunting for the occasion. Along with the party's prodigious amount of baggage went the head of a moose, as a prized souvenir of the great Canadian hinterland. In the preceding days, the UK authorities and the British Admiralty would work overtime to prevent any untoward involvement of the Americans. As a result of their efforts, the British warship HMS *Monmouth*, a China-based battle cruiser, would be waiting in Victoria harbour for the honour of carrying the prince back home to Japan.

For their service to the emperor, Joseph Pope; Captain D.O. Newton, aide de camp to Earl Grey; and W.R. Baker, assistant to CPR's President Shaughnessy, all received Japanese honorifics. The Order of the Sacred Treasure, Third Class, was bestowed upon Baker, while Shaughnessy did him one better and was bestowed with a Second Class medal.

Before the year was out, CPR officials had named a railway siding Fushimi, between Regina and Pilot Butte, to commemorate the company's historic association with the prince. Ironically, seven weeks after Fushimi's heralded visit to Canada, the country's most vociferous anti-Asian riots broke out on the streets of Vancouver, fomented by the rabid racism of the city's Asiatic Exclusion League. ⚓

THE UNSINKABLE CAPTAIN KENDALL

Canadian Pacific's legacy is enlivened by a long list of personalities who have added colour to the company's globe-spanning saga, and the story of Captain Henry George Kendall puts him front and centre with the most storied characters in that historical pantheon.

Born in the UK on January 30, 1874, Kendall went to sea at the tender age of fourteen on the Blue Funnel liner *Agamemnon*, getting an early start to his adventurous career while ferrying troops during the fifth Anglo-Ashanti War and the British campaign against the West African kingdom of Benin. By 1898, he was sailing with the Elder Dempster Company's Canadian service, better known as the Beaver Line. By the time Canadian Pacific Railway acquired that line's fourteen ships on the North Atlantic run, five years later, he had worked his way up to second officer on the *Lake Champlain*.

Two years as chief officer earned Kendall a command post on four CPR steamships between the years 1908 and 1912: *Milwaukee, Monmouth, Lake Champlain,* and *Montrose*. It was aboard the *Montrose* that Captain Kendall made a name for himself when he became a pivotal figure in the international hunt for the notorious Edwardian wife killer Dr. Hawley Harvey Crippen.

After the police had discovered the body of Dr. Crippen's wife buried beneath the floor of his home in Holloway, an inner-city district of London, a disguised Crippen had boarded the *Montrose* in Antwerp with his mistress, Ethel le Neve, in a bid to escape to America. An astute Captain Kendall had seen through the doctor's subterfuge and transmitted a wireless message to Scotland Yard that led to the murderer's arrest. Boarding the White Star's swift ocean-going greyhound, SS *Laurentic*, Detective-Inspector Walter Dew had been able to overtake the *Montrose* at Father Point, Quebec. Dressed in a pilot's uniform, Dew came aboard the CPR ship and nabbed Crippen unawares. It was the first time that a ship's radio had been used to catch a criminal, and the story in all of its scandalous detail was an international sensation. Crippen was subsequently hanged. Kendall received a cheque for 250 pounds for helping to bring the infamous doctor to justice.

Four years later, Captain Kendall was back in the news—this time in a somewhat more negative light. While master of CPR's luxurious Atlantic steamship *Empress of Ireland*, he had the great misfortune of having his vessel sunk beneath his feet on May 29, 1914, when the Norwegian coal carrier *Storstad* rammed the passenger liner on a foggy night in the St. Lawrence River.

The *Empress* went down in fourteen minutes with the loss of more than one thousand lives. Kendall himself was thrown from the bridge. A half hour later, some of his crewmembers rescued him from the water, where he was floating in the wreckage. He immediately took command of the lifeboat and made several trips back and forth to the *Storstad* with rescued passengers, until no more survivors could be found.

"You have sunk my ship," were the first words Kendall uttered to the *Storstad*'s captain when brought aboard. He was exonerated after a formal inquiry, while the collier's chief officer was blamed for wrongfully and negligently altering his vessel's course prior to the fatal collision. Nonetheless, Kendall never commanded another ship while in Canadian Pacific service.

That's not to say, however, that Kendall's career at sea came to a sudden end, for very shortly after he was in the service of the British Admiralty and the Royal Navy, and once again became intimately involved with CPR's ships, many of which were requisitioned for war duties. At the outbreak of the First World War, he had been given command of his old steamship, *Montrose*, and oversaw the escape from Antwerp of some six hundred refugees during the German invasion of the Low Countries, and the towing of CPR's SS *Montreal* across the channel from that port. The *Montrose* was one of several ships chosen shortly thereafter by Winston Churchill, First Lord of the Admiralty, to be sunk at the western entrance of the harbour for the British High Seas Fleet at Scapa Flow to prevent U-boat penetration.

For much of the time between September 1914 and November 1918, Kendall served as commodore of convoys, shepherding 197 ships safely across the Atlantic in groups of as many as forty ships without a mishap, a worthy accomplishment for which the Admiralty expressed its deep appreciation after the war. Luck was with the fated seaman when he arrived with the armed merchant cruiser HMS *Calgarian* mere hours after the disastrous Halifax Explosion on December 6, 1917, but failed him less than three months later when the *Calgarian* was sent to the bottom by a torpedo from a German submarine, seven miles off Rathlin Island on the coast of Northern Ireland. Fortunately, Kendall was plucked from the water by a fast patrol boat operating in the area.

Kendall's career was cursed with misfortune, but he lived to tell the tale. AUTHOR'S COLLECTION

After the war, Kendall was appointed marine superintendent for Canadian Pacific Ocean Services dock staff, in Southampton and London, a post he held until his retirement in April 1939. He lived out his later years in the Brighton Sea Front Home for officers, where he was frequently sought out for media interviews as a former legendary figure on the Seven Seas. ⁜

THE EMPIRE'S PRINCE CHARMING

George VI and Queen Elizabeth's 1939 royal tour of Canada was an occasion for which Canadian Pacific rallied its full array of expertise. The company ferried their majesties across the Atlantic, outfitting and running an extravagant, custom-designed train to whisk the royal couple across the country, and employing a virtual army of public relations, operations, maintenance, and security personnel to handle the critical details to make the event a success.

But despite the wide publicity and the cascade of souvenirs and mementoes that resulted from that most famous of royal visits, it was another, less remembered and now somewhat infamous member of the Windsor Dynasty—Edward, the Prince of Wales—who was CPR's favourite royal figure, a close friend to two presidents of the globe-spanning corporation and a familiar face to hundreds of its steamship, railway, and hotel employees. In 1919, he would arrive in Canada to considerable fanfare, as part of a whirlwind tour of the British Empire to thank the colonials for the solid support and supreme sacrifices they had made to the successful outcome of the First World War. He would return five more times in various guises, before and after sitting on the throne, at the peak of his popularity, and in the wake of his fall from grace, but he would never fail to get the royal treatment from CPR.

Considerable effort was expended to convey the Prince of Wales across Canada in the manner to which he was accustomed on that first three-month tour of the country, mostly by rail. Canadian Pacific provided his Highness with the private railway car Killarney for his personal fiefdom, a rolling castle complete with private bedroom, dining room and bathroom, and equipped with all the latest conveniences: onboard telephone service, bath and shower, and thermostatically controlled temperature. The railway also arranged for a twice-daily bulletin of world events to be telegraphed to the royal train.

Coupled to his railcar was the Cromarty, to house his personal staff, the Carnarvon, filled with the inevitable entourage of newspaper and magazine correspondents and ever-present photographers, and the Renown—named by CPR for the battle cruiser on which the Prince of Wales had sailed to Canada—to keep a small contingent of CP police officers comfortable while they provided security for the royal tour.

The prince was received on the platforms and grounds of the major stations across the CPR system by uniformed bands, dignitaries in top hats, and wildly enthusiastic crowds of citizens. Between stops he occasionally indulged himself by accompanying the engineer in the cab of the locomotive, taking the throttle with great delight when he had the opportunity. Despite generally accepted operating practices and the mild admonitions of the train crew, Edward was not averse to pulling the emergency brake when he spotted ducks in the air or wood pigeons flitting through the bush along the right of way. On these occasions, he would blast away with his shotgun from the back platform of the Killarney and jump down from the car to retrieve the spoils.

More officially, CPR stopped the royal procession for three days of fishing in Nipigon, a site in Northern Ontario where the railway operated one of its popular bungalow camps. The prince was reported to have had terrible luck with rod and reel and, in a fit of petulance, pronounced the activity boring, when the railway's official photographer was the only member of the fishing party to land a decent catch.

It was not until the royal train reached the Canadian West that the prince would really put aside ceremony to enjoy himself. For three days, he was a guest at George Lane's Bar U Ranch, twenty-six miles southwest of High River, on CPR's Calgary-to-Macleod railway line, where he rode horses, adopted western dress, participated in various ranching chores and chewed the fat with his cowboy neighbours. Before continuing by the CPR to Banff, Lake Louise, the Rockies, and the West Coast, the prince had expressed a wistful desire to become an Alberta rancher. By the time he reached Winnipeg on the return leg, he had announced his purchase of what he would dub his E.P. Ranch—the letters for Edward Prince—right next door to Lane's spread.

By the end of his tour, Edward had a strong attachment to CPR and its employees, including the railway police officers who joined his entourage. He had formed a particularly strong bond with the CPR's chief of police, Rufus Chamberlin. "Canada is populated by seven million people," the prince commented to the press, "mainly friends of the Chief."

Before the year was over, Canadian Pacific had handled all the details of shipping twenty-six shorthorn cattle, three thoroughbred mares, eleven Dartmoor ponies and sixty Shropshire sheep from Great Britain to southern Alberta to begin what would be a very respectable breeding program at the E.P. Ranch. The prince himself was most anxious that local children should have access to the very solid and compliant ponies, which he imported to supplant what he deemed were the sorry looking nags on which they previously rode to school

The ranch would be the main reason for the Prince of Wales's return trips to Canada in 1923 and 1924. Travelling aboard the Canadian Pacific Ocean Services steamship *Empress of Scotland* as the Baron Renfrew, he had notified CPR president Edward Beatty in advance that he would be

The prince, seen here at Calgary's Palliser Hotel, became a very familiar figure to CPR staff members, on the trains and off. GLENBOW ARCHIVES, ARCHIVES AND SPECIAL COLLECTIONS, UNIVERSITY OF CALGARY NB-16-42

incognito as a private citizen, and that no particular fuss was to be made during his visit. That said, the world's most famous member of royalty could not go unnoticed.

Hardly a wallflower, while staying at CPR's Chateau Frontenac in Quebec City, Edward danced until the wee hours with an endless stream of young women who waited none too patiently to glide across the ballroom floor in the arms of Prince Charming. Menus and match packs were grabbed up as keepsakes. In Calgary's Palliser Hotel, the waiters and room staff had to watch that overzealous fans were not running off with the linens and cutlery. The busboy at the company's Banff Springs even went so far as to save the cigarette butts from the royal entourage, while clearing tables. Grateful female guests of the hotel eagerly received the filter tips, each imprinted with "H.R.H. Prince of Wales" as souvenirs.

In 1927, Edward came back to Canada aboard the *Empress of Australia* in the company of British prime minister Stanley Baldwin and his wife, who were on an official visit to the Dominion. He also brought along his little brother, the Duke of Kent, to show off his Alberta homestead and to once again take full advantage of Canadian Pacific's hospitality.

Throughout the years leading up to Edward's coronation in January 1936 and his abdication in December that same year, CPR took an active interest in helping the prince keep his ranch well stocked

The Prince of Wales, left, travelled to Canada with his brother, the Duke of Kent, in 1927. GLENBOW ARCHIVES, ARCHIVES AND SPECIAL COLLECTIONS, UNIVERSITY OF CALGARY NA-4399-1

with various desirable breeds of cattle and sheep, as well as Arabian, Percheron, and Clydesdale horses. The E.P. Ranch's manager, W.L. Carlyle, sailed to England on the company's SS *Minnedosa* on more than one occasion to personally supervise the acquisition of prize stock to be shipped back home.

After his abdication, the man officially known as Albert Christian George Andrew Patrick David, the Duke of Windsor, would only return to his ranch in Alberta for two very brief visits: in 1941, as the governor of the Bahamas, and in 1950 as a retiree now living in Paris. On both occasions, he travelled with his wife, the American divorcée Wallis Simpson, for whom he had given up the throne. By this time, his popularity had waned, in light of revelations of the royal couple's fraternizations with high-level Nazis in the years leading up to the Second World War, and he travelled on CPR private cars Mount Stephen and Strathcona, simply as David Windsor. Both the duke and his wife expressed an interest in spending more time at their Alberta residence in future years, but many press people detected a distinct lack of enthusiasm on the part of Wallis for the wild west. The couple never returned to Canada.

For the next six years, CPR's Department of Immigration and Colonization was hired to supervise the operations of the E.P. Ranch and the Duke's remaining herd of Hereford cattle. In 1956, a Canadian company was formed to take over the task, but by 1962 the entire property and all of its buildings and livestock—such as they now were—had been sold to neighbouring rancher Jim Cartwright.

After six cross-country tours by rail, several steamship voyages, and numerous nights in company hotels, CPR's royal patron, the man of many names who once sat on the throne of the British Empire, would forever be the Prince of the CPR. ✢

LAST OF THE OPERATING GIANTS

From engine wiper to chairman, president, and chief executive officer of Canadian Pacific, Norris R. "Buck" Crump was the last of the railway barons to work his way up through the ranks to the very apex of the company's command structure.

Crump was reared in the railway life. His father, Tom Crump, signed on as a section hand with CPR at Winnipeg in 1890, less than a month after his arrival in Canada from England. Born at Revelstoke, BC, in 1904, Buck was already hard at work for the railway by age sixteen.

His thirst for knowledge and his drive to succeed were apparent from a young age. While working full-time, he attended classes five nights a week, finishing three grades of high school in two years. In 1925, at age twenty-one, he attended Purdue University in Indiana, earning a bachelor of science degree. While working as a night foreman in the roundhouse at Wilkie, Saskatchewan, he completed a master's degree with a thesis on diesel locomotives.

His hard work and natural ability did not escape the attention of his superiors, and he rose quickly to prominence under CPR president William Mather. He is remembered chiefly for the system-wide dieselization of the railway's motive power, but he also made significant contributions to controlling operating costs and improving the railway's profit margin in an era of falling revenues. He accomplished those goals partly through introducing efficiencies and partly through pursuing business diversification.

When Crump became president, CPR faced enormous challenges from competing transportation options such as planes, trucks, and the ubiquitous family car. In the *Financial Post*, May 14, 1955, he commented that "railways are still regulated on the same basis as when there was little competition. Management needs more freedom to deal with the relatively new situation." In *Railway Age*, one month later, he elaborated:

> Railroads are more needed today than ever before. Their basic strength is low-cost movement of large volumes in all terrains and in all weather. Their main job now is to obtain the freedom with which to exploit those advantages. Meanwhile they must continue to find new ways to move traffic and maintain plant so as to cut their costs still further.

It was a call to action that would ultimately propel the railroad industry to a new golden age as a humming engine of the modern economy, and a very profitable one at that.

When Crump took his seat in the president's office in 1955, the company had been without firm leadership since the death of Edward Beatty more than twenty years earlier. Suffering mightily from a rapidly changing operating environment and having withstood the ravages of the Second World War, CPR was teetering on the edge of bankruptcy. On top of that, Crump was faced with a distinct bias, as a result of his outsider status. "We are accustomed to wise men from the East," he was informed by the Montreal boardroom establishment.

"This company is a tankful of sharks, and I'm just going to have to learn to swim with them," Crump replied. And, indeed, he did more than just tread water.

While working sixteen- or eighteen-hour days, he remained approachable. Those who worked with him admired his great courage and determination. He earned the respect of the rank and file, as well as the union negotiators with whom he jousted. When negotiations were particularly tough, he was purported to have removed his jacket and given his suspenders a good snap. "I was working for this railway before you were born," he informed his adversaries. "Now what is it you want to tell me?"

opposite: Crump rose to the president's office from modest beginnings as an engine wiper. AUTHOR'S COLLECTION

above: The railway boss had the respect of employees across the property, both management and union members. AUTHOR'S COLLECTION

Many a reporter or government official tried to trip him up on questions about engineering or financial matters. Invariably, Crump demonstrated a thorough knowledge of all aspects of railroading that left his audience in awe and earned him near universal respect and loyalty among railway workers.

During his fifty-two years with the company, the country grew from a pioneering land to become one of the world's major trading nations. Under Crump's guidance, Canadian Pacific expanded into a dynamic and diversified transportation and natural resource development company. Two of his most cherished accomplishments, though not his most financially successful ones, were the creation of the iconic streamlined passenger train, dubbed The Canadian, and the reintroduction of the White Empress line of steamships on the North Atlantic.

Despite working long hours, Crump found time for skiing and the occasional round of golf. He was also an avid collector of historical firearms and other antique weapons, many of which he restored in his home workshop in Calgary.

In later life, he served in the Senate of the University of Alberta. He was also appointed Companion of the Order of Canada, the highest civilian honour our country can bestow. His life was impressive in its accomplishments and made a lasting contribution to both the Canadian public and business communities.

When he died in 1989, Crump's ashes were scattered by his wife and family on CPR's famous Big Hill, not far from Field, BC, where his long and successful career had begun. ✛

ICE GANGS KEPT PASSENGERS COOL

Until mechanical refrigeration was perfected in the early 1950s, millions of pounds of ice were harvested every year from Canadian rivers and lakes to protect perishable freight goods while in transit and to keep passenger car interiors comfortable during the summer months.

On the frozen waterways, work crews with giant buzz saws cut eighteen inches down into the ice. Following close behind were their cold-weather coworkers with crowbar-like tools tapered at one end into two sharp prongs. Those men would wedge out blocks of ice along the slices made by the saws. Once the blocks floated free, a winter-clad gondolier would hop aboard each ice flow and pole it to a nearby conveyor belt that carried the blocks to shore. From there they were loaded onto railway flatcars for transport to ice houses at stations across the railway system.

One of the first outfits to supply CPR with large quantities of ice was the Brewster Company of Banff, which harvested nearly all of the frozen blocks used by the railway in Western Canada from the Bow River.

Later, most of Canadian Pacific's supply would come from Lake Superior, St. Boniface Lake near Winnipeg, Regina Beach on Last Mountain Lake, and Moose Jaw Creek. Several thousand tons of ice were hauled up the banks of these readily accessible sources every year after freeze-over. Large amounts to meet the needs of Alberta and British Columbia were also taken from the Bow River at Keith, just west of Calgary. In 1944, unexpectedly heavy volumes of meat moving to markets along the Eastern Seaboard prompted CP to expand their ice-gathering activities to Saint John, New Brunswick, and Buffalo, New York.

By 1947, one of the last years of massive ice consumption on the CPR, the railway was stacking more than 600 million pounds of it into icehouses throughout Canada. Were this much ice loaded into a single train, it would extend along the tracks for more than eighty miles.

The storage requirements were massive. The blocks of ice on the bottom level inside icehouses would often merge together from the weight of the massive load above and the slow melt, forming a solid ice floor. The resulting iceberg would help to maintain a low temperature in the buildings even during the warmest months.

One of the most desirable summer jobs for young men in railway towns across the CPR system was to secure a position with an ice gang. Schoolboys as young as sixteen could make a good

top: A giant circular saw was used to cut blocks of ice from the Bow River in Banff National Park. GLENBOW ARCHIVES, ARCHIVES AND SPECIAL COLLECTIONS, UNIVERSITY OF CALGARY NA-841-71

bottom: The ice blocks were floated down river to a nearby railway spur. GLENBOW ARCHIVES, ARCHIVES AND SPECIAL COLLECTIONS, UNIVERSITY OF CALGARY NA-841-67

wage, working with supervisors or charge hands as youthful as themselves. Outfitted with rubber gloves and steel-toed rubber safety boots, the gang members cut the ice blocks, loaded them onto push cars, and hauled them down track platforms to the awaiting trains. There, the well-travelled giant ice cubes were transferred to four-wheeled dollies and shuffled into bunkers beneath the passenger cars. Each air-conditioned car could consume up to 4,500 pounds of ice every thirty-six hours in the summer months, depending on outdoor temperatures.

As the ice melted, it was circulated through the car interiors by means of radiators, pumps, and electric fans. Electric motors and batteries were located beneath the cars.

The young men who strained every muscle to transfer the frozen blocks from icehouse to passenger car bunker draped themselves in canvas aprons, waterproofed with linseed oil to offer some protection from the water that inevitably sloshed out of the iceboxes.

Sometimes, the ice gangs would be called upon to assist carmen in icing and serving dining cars. This required the ice handlers to employ a special technique, similar to what riveters used on construction sites. The young men at trackside would chop the ice blocks into chunks as big as five or six pounds and toss them from the platform to workers on the roofs of the cars. Those on top would drop the ice through hatches, into shoots leading to the kitchens.

Even more ice was required for the protection of perishable goods in transit. Each refrigerated freight car consumed eight to fourteen thousand pounds of ice per trip, depending on the length of the haul and the degree of refrigeration required for the particular product. In 1947, CPR was operating 3,942 refrigerated cars. The largest of the perishable commodities were fish from both coasts; meat from western producers; and fruit from BC's Okanagan Valley, Ontario's Niagara Peninsula, and Nova Scotia's Annapolis Valley.

After the Second World War, Canadian Pacific was among the first industries to fully embrace new systems of mechanical refrigeration, not very different from what was then powering domestic refrigerators across the nation. To meet the challenge of large-scale refrigeration, the company's

Giant blocks of ice were cut from lakes and rivers and transported by rail to fill CPR icehouses across the country. PHOTO BY BYRON HARMON, GLENBOW ARCHIVES, ARCHIVES AND SPECIAL COLLECTIONS, UNIVERSITY OF CALGARY NA-841-80

engineers were able to boost the power of their axle-driven generators beneath railway cars from ten to thirty-three horsepower. Stationary generators were installed at major terminals to supply electrical power while trains were standing in the stations.

Most of the ice that the railway now consumed in day-to-day operations would go into the water and cocktail glasses of the CPR's patrons. ⚜

MAGNIFICENT MEN AND THEIR FLYING MACHINES

There was no better training ground for early aviators than flying a bush plane between isolated communities in the Canadian North, unless it was piloting a fighter plane in overseas service during the First World War. The legendary air crew that Canadian Pacific gained with the company's acquisition of ten pioneering airlines had plenty of schooling in both of those theatres—and then some.

Clennell Haggerston "Punch" Dickins flew for Western Canadian Airways and Canadian Airways, before helping to consolidate Canadian Pacific's air services. Born in Portage la Prairie, Manitoba, Dickens had enlisted with the Canadian Army at seventeen. Following his desire for adventure, he soon transferred to the British Royal Flying Corps and, within a year, had qualified as a bomber pilot. He flew seventy-three missions during the First World War, earning the Distinguished Flying Cross for shooting down seven enemy aircraft.

Back in Canada, Dickins served three years with the Royal Canadian Air Force (RCAF), before leaving the military for civil aviation. As a pilot with Western Canada Airways, he inaugurated airmail service on the prairie circuit between Winnipeg, Regina, Calgary, Edmonton, and Saskatoon. Dickins also delivered the first airmail in the Northwest Territories, flying more than a million miles in all kinds of weather. Across the uncharted North, he was known as Snow Eagle.

A Canadian Pacific employee by the early years of the Second World War, Dickins became general superintendent for the company's airline division. During the conflict, he was chosen to head up the Atlantic Ferry Command, which organized the delivery of combat aircraft to Britain.

After 1942, Dickins was a leading proponent of the British Commonwealth Air Training Plan. He was one of the key people who enabled Canada to train thousands of combat fliers, through a network of schools across the country. By the end of the war, he was vice-president of Canadian Pacific Air Lines (CPAL).

Wilfred R. "Wop" May was another Canadian boy, growing up in Carberry, Manitoba, before going overseas as an infantryman in the First World War. Like Dickins, he quickly made the leap to the Royal Flying Corp and was assigned to the British Naval Squadron. He was awarded the Distinguished Flying Cross for bringing down thirteen German aircraft. May was not just a skilled combat pilot; he was also lucky. Famously, he was the last Allied pilot to be pursued by Manfred von Richthofen, before the Red Baron was shot down on the Western Front, on April 21, 1918.

After the war, May and his brother founded May Airplanes Limited. The two daredevils toured rural Canada with one of the world's first barnstorming shows, flying used wartime JN4s or Jennies. May was also an intrepid bush pilot and airmail pioneer. In the late 1920s, he carried mail in all kinds of weather to Alberta communities north of Fort McMurray, while flying with Commercial Airways.

May also distinguished himself during the Second World War with the British Commonwealth Air Training Program. As Canadian Pacific's general manager, in charge of three air observation schools in the West, he was awarded the Order of the British Empire for developing a parachute training program for medical teams with the RCAF. In the postwar years, he served as director of development for CPAL and, in 1951, managed the RCAF's No. 10 repair depot at Calgary's Currie Field, along with his other company duties.

Joining "Punch" and "Wop" in the executive ranks at Canadian Pacific's ambitious new airline was Walter "Babe" Woollett, an Englishman who had flown for the British Royal Air Force from 1924 to 1929 before immigrating to Canada and signing on with Canadian Airways. Like his CPAL colleagues, he too put in time as an airborne postal worker, carrying the bags from Moncton and Saint John, New Brunswick, to Montreal, Toronto, Hamilton, London, Windsor, and Detroit.

In 1934, Woollett flew for Dominion Skyways. Five years later, he had racked up a career record of 5,600 hours in everything from fighter planes to flying boats.

When Canadian Pacific bought out his airline, Woollett's experience and general expertise made him an ideal candidate for the position of CPAL's eastern general manager in charge of air observation schools. In that role, he helped to set up the first and one of the busiest of the training facilities at Malton, Ontario. After the war, Woollett stayed on with Canadian Pacific, rising to district sales manager for the Hawaiian Islands.

Of all the assets that CP gained with their acquisition of Canada's pioneer airlines in the turbulent years of the Second World War, none served them so well as these colourful and legendary men, who stepped down from the cockpits of their ragtag fleet of vintage aircraft to take a seat in the company's executive suites—and continued to make aviation history. ✛

From left: "Wop" May, airline president Grant McConachie, and "Punch" Dickens. GLENBOW ARCHIVES, ARCHIVES AND SPECIAL COLLECTIONS, UNIVERSITY OF CALGARY NA-1258-11

NOT JUST "COFFEE, TEA, OR ME?"

By the time Canadian Pacific assembled its own airline in the early 1940s to compete with Trans-Canada Air Lines, stewardesses were already well-established members of the industry. The young women who pursued this relatively new profession had more on their minds than just giving the pre-flight safety demonstrations, making sure those sitting in emergency exit rows were if necessary willing to assist in evacuations, or ensuring that all seats were in an upright position prior to taking off.

Twenty years earlier, pioneer carriers such as Imperial Airways of the United Kingdom had employed cabin boys dressed like hotel bellboys to perform such tasks as carrying baggage and cleaning the interior of the planes between flights, but it wasn't long before the airlines realized the benefits of adding an onboard female presence. Ellen Church, who was both a licensed pilot and a registered nurse, was successful in convincing the executives at Boeing Air Transport, the predecessor of United Airlines, of the soothing effect of having women on staff.

"Don't you think that it would be good psychology to have women up in the air?" she is purported to have argued. "How is a man going to say he is afraid to fly when a woman is working the plane?"

On May 15, 1930, Church and seven other "stewardesses" began their first day of work—and other airlines were quick to recruit their own employees for a role that would initially be steeped in ageism and sexism.

Canadian Pacific Air Lines, falling in line with the across-the-board discriminatory standards of the major world airlines, required its onboard female hostesses to be between the ages of twenty-one and twenty-six, to stand between five foot one and five foot six, and to weigh in at a petite 100 to 120 pounds. In later years their height allowance was upped to between five foot three and five foot eight, with "weight in proportion to height," provided it fell between 105 and 135 pounds.

Along with the early requirement of being trained nurses, the stewardesses were expected to report to work in excellent health, with flawless hearing and vision. Oh, yes, and those who were deemed not pretty or were married, widowed, or divorced need not apply. Before too long, the education requirements would be relaxed and a high school diploma would prove to be sufficient, but the physical requirements remained stringent: good eyesight, without the use of glasses or contacts; even teeth, no dentures, full or partial; clear complexion, natural colour hair, and "erect carriage."

The want ads for onboard female staff members left no room for imperfection. "Natural charm and personality" were, of course, essential to the job, as well as "sufficient tact and good nature to handle passengers under all conceivable conditions." It was also specified that it would be helpful to have a "pleasant voice, good vocabulary and diction." There were never any spoken racial requirements, though early applicants were expected to be British subjects, who could read, write, and converse fluently in English. As well, a proficiency in French, Spanish, Italian, German, Dutch, or Portuguese was considered an asset.

The "girls" were trained under a chief stewardess and were schooled in the geography over which CP flew, the history of the settlements the airline served, and the people who lived in them, as well as the peculiarities of the various districts and any historical facts of interest. While in flight, the stewardesses were expected to keep the airplane's clocks wound and accurate, make sure that passengers didn't mistake the emergency exit

Stewardesses were expected to attend to the needs of everyday passengers and famous travellers alike . . . or reasonable facsimiles thereof. AUTHOR'S COLLECTION

for the door to the washroom, and—in the days when windows could still be opened—warn those onboard about the dangers of throwing garbage or lit cigarette butts out of the aircraft, particularly over populated areas.

Despite the strong emphasis on interpersonal skills, which could even include polishing passengers' shoes, many of the duties performed by the first stewardesses transcended the realm of public relations: helping to fuel the planes, cleaning the cabins, and dusting the cockpit, and sometimes tightening down passenger seats that had rattled loose during a flight, a task for which the ever-attentive women carried concealed screwdrivers.

Stewardesses working for Canadian Pacific were expected to know the basic principles of aerodynamics, to be conversant with meteorological reports, weather maps, and flight plans, and to have a thorough knowledge of the types of aircraft flown by their company and how CP handled mail and express packages, as well as passengers.

Should their plane be forced to land in some out of the way place, stewardesses were trained to access the airline's onboard emergency rations, which consisted largely of dried beans, rice, flour, dehydrated fruit, and a variety of other space-saving foods with high nutritional value. In addition, they were prepared to cook over an open fire, if necessary, with "a high degree of skill" and to ensure their stranded clients received a balanced diet while waiting to be rescued. They were even instructed to have a railway timetable handy, in case the passengers needed to be transferred to a train.

By the 1960s, many of the discriminatory practices in the airline industry had begun to ease off. In 1968, federal courts struck down the rules forbidding marriage and specifying stringent standards for the height, weight, and age of stewardesses. A few years later, the ruling came down that men could not be discriminated against when it came to onboard service positions, so the term *stewardess* fell out of favour and was replaced by the more gender-neutral *flight attendant*.

By the time CP Air merged with Nordair and Pacific Western Airlines in 1987, to form Canadian Airlines, the business of hosting and attending to airline passengers had evolved into the more-inclusive job that we know it to be today. ⚜

THE GURU OF RAILWAY HISTORIANS

He was more than just the dean of Canadian railway historians; to his many friends, colleagues, and admirers, he was the font of all knowledge, the Great One, the go-to person for all things related to Canadian Pacific Railway, its antecedents, and its competitors.

As a man who preferred to work mostly behind the scenes, Omer Lavallée would not have described himself that way, but his highly distinguished career as a writer, editor, lecturer, and archivist confirms his status as the country's most well-respected authority on railway lore. He is widely remembered for both his professional work and his engaging personality.

Things were never dull when Omer was around. He was interested in everything, and never failed to astonish his friends and associates with his encyclopedic knowledge on any number of topics—from history, philosophy, religion, and language to travel, music, wine, and the culinary arts.

Lavallée could be kind and congenial or cantankerous and crusty, but rarely was he condescending, judgmental, or unfair. Though he was a very conservative man, more a connoisseur of Gregorian chants than rock and roll, he welcomed change. Sometimes he wore a hard exterior, but children found him to be a magical figure, a 230-pound elf with a mischievous grin. He could be a relentless and fierce adversary in the pursuit of his goals, but he was always a staunch and loyal friend.

A descendent of paternal French forbearers who came to New France in 1618 and maternal ancestors from mid-nineteenth-century Ireland, Lavallée was a fourth-generation Canadian railroader. He honed his keen interest for all things railway related as a young boy who received deluxe, tin-plated toy trains for Christmas, and spent every spare moment watching full-size railway operations through the fence at Montreal's Outremont Yard.

CPR's former corporate archivist and historian is best known for his work as a prolific and talented author. In particular, *Van Horne's Road*, a lavishly illustrated history of CPR's construction years, and *Canadian Pacific Steam Locomotives*, an exhaustive study of pre-diesel-era CPR motive power, are considered classics, widely recognized as the most authoritative works in their field.

For many years, Lavallée was also the most prominent figure in the railway equipment preservation movement, which began in earnest just after the Second World War. The efforts of Lavallée and his history-minded colleagues resulted in the establishment of a number of fine collections,

Lavallée's status as both a respected employee of Canadian Pacific and a prominent member of the Canadian Railroad Historical Association enabled him to arrange for the preservation of several CPR steam locomotives. OMER LAVALLÉE COLLECTION

among them the representative assortment of freight and passenger equipment at the Canadian Railway Museum (now Exporail) at Delson, Quebec.

After a short stint at Canadian Pacific Air Lines, Lavallée spent twenty-four years working in Canadian Pacific's finance department, where he rode the rails on one of the last railway pay cars in North America. An ardent pacifist and no fan of firearms, he kept his service revolver locked in a safe while delivering cheques to CPR employees throughout the Maritime provinces.

Lavallée wrote definitive works about CPR steam locomotives and the construction of the CPR main line. Acolytes came from far and wide to consult with the master.
PHOTO BY CECIL HALSEY, AUTHOR'S COLLECTION

In 1966, Lavallée's lifelong interest in history ultimately landed him in the company's public relations and advertising department, where he served initially as a history specialist and public speaker. In 1973, he established the Canadian Pacific Corporate Archives department and collection, to preserve important legal and historical documents from the company's storied past and to celebrate CPR's key role in the settlement and development of the country.

Railroaders, Rebels and Royalty

Faced with the passing of several well-established Canadian Pacific services in the early 1970s, particularly the passenger train and steamship businesses, Omer was selected by the company to also head up a unique project that captured the imagination of the public.

Many Canadians—and others around the world—had cherished memories of their association with one or another of the operating arms of the "World's Greatest Travel System," as CP was known for many years. As the company divested itself of some key activities, there were literally warehouses full of surplus china, silverware, lamps, lanterns, signs, pamphlets, timetables, and a plethora of other potentially collectable items waiting to be written off for their scrap value, or simply discarded.

As a result, CPR launched a collectors' sales program known as CP Bygones, which for the next seven years would sell off the surplus memorabilia at very reasonable prices, while achieving somewhat of a public relations coup. At the same time, in a manner that would have done the original Scottish founders of the company proud, Bygones managed to show a better earnings-to-operating-cost ratio than every other profit centre in the Canadian Pacific family, a fact that was brought to the attention of the board of directors by then-chairman N.R. "Buck" Crump.

In addition to contributing hundreds of articles to professional and hobby publications in North America and Europe, Lavallée lent his vast expertise to a long list of museums and historical societies, as well as to government agencies such as the National Museums of Canada, Parks Canada, and Canada Post. He also served as a technical advisor to several high-profile television and movie productions for the National Film Board and the Canadian Broadcasting Corporation, notably the filming of *The National Dream*, an eight-part documentary on the building of the transcontinental railway, which was released on television in 1974.

Through his tireless efforts to promote the company's legacy, Lavallée earned his place in the pantheon of great CPR public relations men, alongside such worthies as noted raconteur Colonel George Henry Ham and prolific author John Murray Gibbon. Upon retiring from Canadian Pacific in 1985, Lavallée maintained an association with the company as its emeritus corporate historian and archivist. Four years later, Omer was officially recognized with the Order of Canada for his accomplishments during an outstanding career, and for his contributions to Canadian cultural life. ✠

FATEFUL RENDEZVOUS WITH A GHOSTLY MISTRESS

t's hard to imagine anyone wanting to be forty-five to fifty metres below the surface of the turbid waters of the St. Lawrence River, where the temperature is often as chilly as one degree Celsius and the visibility limited to two or three metres, at the best of times. But that's where one man chose to go on more than six hundred occasions, when he began his passionate love affair with a sunken ocean liner that had met its tragic demise while sailing from Quebec City to Liverpool.

In 1970, when Phillipe Beaudry took a break from his successful ten-year practice as an accountant to pursue more actively his favourite pastime of diving, he had at least a passing knowledge of the nation's worst marine disaster. The Norwegian coal-carrier *Storstad* had rammed Canadian Pacific's flagship the RMS *Empress of Ireland* in the dead of night, more than fifty-six years earlier. The collision occurred while the ships were far from shore in the St. Lawrence River. It had left a gaping hole in the 14,500-tonne luxury liner's hull, which allowed torrents of water to rush in, sending the ship to the bottom in a mere fourteen minutes, taking the lives of over a thousand passengers and crew.

In fact, in terms of passengers alone, more perished on the *Empress of Ireland* on May 29, 1914, than had been lost on the *Titanic* two years earlier—840 on the former versus 832 on the latter—but the outbreak of the First World War soon after the *Empress* disaster displaced the CPR liner in newspaper headlines around the world, and the story of the ship's doom slipped into relative obscurity.

It was during Labour Day weekend 1970 when Beaudry arrived for the first time at the colourful buoy placed by the Marine Institute of Quebec to mark the spot where the *Empress* rests at a precarious angle, forty metres below the surface. On the silted floor of the St. Lawrence, he would soon meet his mistress of the deep, up close and personal.

The *Empress of Ireland* and sister ship *Empress of Britain* had been launched in 1906 from the Fairfield Shipping Company's yard in Scotland, to ensure Canadian Pacific's pre-eminent position on the North Atlantic. For eight years, the two liners had served the company well, carrying Canadian goods and tourists to Europe and the continent's emigrants and dispossessed to the new world.

Within months of the *Empress of Ireland*'s sinking, hard-hatted divers were busy recovering the silver bullion from the purser's safe, as well as 319 bags of disinterred mail, 60 percent of which was then forwarded on to its intended recipients. One diver had died during these operations.

The *Empress of Ireland* rested in peace for a half century, until sports divers in the mid-1960s rediscovered the sunken ship. In the rush to bring salvaged artifacts to the surface, one massive propeller was melted down for scrap metal and many smaller items were spirited out of the country without authorization from the proper authorities.

After familiarizing himself with the significance of the wreck, Beaudry, too, began to retrieve items from the site, but he remained respectful of their historic value and became anxious about preserving the legacy of the *Empress of Ireland* and documenting its remaining contents for posterity.

Setting up a scuba shop in Rimouski to subsidize what would become hundreds of dives to the wreck site, Beaudry put his accountancy practice on hold. He began to pursue his new-found passion with a vengeance.

Canadian Pacific had long since given up its title to the wreck, so he was free to retain and display recovered items in his shop, after dutifully reporting them to the regional Receiver of Wrecks. Soon he had accumulated enough of a collection to attract the attention of local marine museum, Musée de la Mer, and he deposited a significant number of artifacts with that institute.

To his regret, however, he decided after two or three years that the storage conditions at the museum were not what he expected, and that he had maybe been a little careless in framing his agreement with that repository. After a trip to court and an additional outlay of $15,000, Beaudry had his precious artifacts back. He continued to seek an appropriate home, where the public could view them. In the meantime, of course, he could not tear himself away from making descents to the wreck every chance he could get, a compulsion he would indulge for many years to come.

Growing up on his family's dairy farm in Montreal's Eastern Townships, before spending long days going over figures in ledger books, is not the most obvious path to a career as a professional scuba diver; but once he put his mind to it, Beaudry was acknowledged by those in the business as a top-notch practitioner in the field of underwater exploration.

Donning a neoprene dry suit and over sixty kilograms of specialized equipment, he would spend many fair-weather days over the next two decades inside the dangerous confines of the *Empress of Ireland*. In short forty-five-minute descents, he would explore the many public galleries, staterooms and passageways, often in the company of other experienced diving companions.

Three times, the intrepid explorer came close to losing his life while diving to the ghostly hulk. On one occasion, Beaudry got lost in the ship's interior, before finding his way out as his air supply dwindled. Another time, the bag full of china that he had recovered from one of the dining rooms was too heavy to enable an easy, controlled ascent. The most serious event, however, occurred when Beaudry experienced a catastrophic failure in his breathing apparatus and had to make a quick swim to the surface from more than forty-five metres down. Fortunately, he did not suffer any lasting ill effects, and was able to resume diving as before.

Not content with what he could learn from his hands-on encounters with the *Empress of Ireland*, the man who would become the ship's most knowledgeable enthusiast made pilgrimages to every major marine museum and archives in Canada, the United States, and the United Kingdom in pursuit of his obsession. Scouring flea markets, second-hand stores, and online sites, Beaudry amassed an impressive collection of letters, telegrams, and photographs related to the *Empress of Ireland*, her thousands of passengers, and her distinguished career as a transatlantic greyhound. While adding to his growing gallery of artifacts recovered from the wreck, he founded the Empress of Ireland Historical Society to exchange and share information with shipping fans and other interested parties around the world.

In the 1980s, Beaudry was called upon to accompany Jean-Michel Cousteau and a National Film Board crew to the site of the historic wreck. On another occasion, Robert Ballard, the discoverer of the sunken *Titanic*, asked him to accompany his support team.

Beaudry also made it a point to seek out, befriend, and videotape individuals who had survived the tragedy and were still alive to tell the tale, including Ronald Fergusson, the wireless operator who issued the distress signal from the imperiled liner. The most memorable of these was Grace Martyn, the seven-year-old daughter of the Salvation Army bandmaster who lost his life along with most of his colleagues when the *Empress of Ireland* went down. For many years, on the anniversary of the sinking, Grace would lay a wreath in Toronto's Mount Pleasant Cemetery, at the memorial dedicated to the memory of the 150 Salvation Army victims of the sinking. When he could, Beaudry accompanied the grieving survivor, who was still haunted by that terrible night so long ago.

Inevitably, as the location of the wreck became common knowledge among members of the diving community, many other underwater explorers and salvagers arrived at the site to exploit the opportunities for obtaining rare and historic artifacts, or to harvest the vessel's vast number of brass fittings or teak deck planking for the considerable scrap value they held.

Often as not, the gleanings went unreported or, more seriously from a moral standpoint, disturbed the remains of those who had perished on the great ship, a breach of decorum that Beaudry had always studiously and unfailingly avoided. As a result, the more conscientious diver was driven

Beaudry made himself the world's foremost authority on the history of the *Empress of Ireland* and its sunken remains. PAINTING BY PIERRETTE MOLAISON, PHILLIP BEAUDRY COLLECTION

to lobby the authorities to declare the site of the sunken liner off limits to further salvage operations. For that, he almost paid a terrible price, when a bomb was discovered to have been planted under his porch, presumably by someone not pleased about his meddling with their licence to plunder. The perpetrator was never identified.

In 1999, the Government of Quebec declared the resting place of the *Empress of Ireland* an historic site, banning the removal of any more artifacts from the sunken liner, while continuing to allow divers to visit and film around the wreck. From Beaudry's perspective, one major problem had been resolved, but the now-aging diving enthusiast still needed to find a permanent home for the hundreds of artifacts he had acquired over the years and, hopefully, recover some of the costs he had expended in its accumulation.

Of the firm belief that the story of the *Empress of Ireland* was an integral and essential part of the country's history, Beaudry tried for many years to come to a mutually acceptable agreement with every appropriate museum in Canada. Surprisingly, given the intrinsic value of the material in question, and the enormous public interest in the fate of other doomed passenger vessels such as the *Titanic* and the *Lusitania*, he received no serious offers.

Finally, when it looked like Beaudry would have to look south of the border, where private collectors with deep pockets were making attractive offers, a group of concerned Canadian patriots hastily assembled an Empress of Ireland Artifacts Committee to purchase a representative selection of items from the diver's collection to ensure they would stay in the country. Those items were then donated to the Royal Alberta Museum, where they have been exhibited.

Ultimately, the remainder of Beaudry's invaluable archive of items from and about the ship was acquired by Ottawa's Museum of History (formerly the Museum of Civilization) in 2012. At long last, the steamship's main telegraph and steering wheel would go on public display, along with about five hundred other pieces of the ship's hardware and fittings, china, glassware, silverware, and the impressive brass ship's bell lettered *Empress of Ireland*. Surprisingly, the collection includes wine, beer, and champagne bottles from the ship's galleys that still retain their contents. Nearly one thousand photographs, documents, and other items related to the *Empress of Ireland* are also included.

As for Beaudry, he only received a small fraction of the precious artifacts' potential value when he divested himself of his treasures, relative to the tens of millions paid for comparable items recovered from the *Titanic*. Nevertheless, he is a happy man, for his life's work has been duly recognized, and the legacy of his beloved mistress of the sea has been preserved for all to experience and appreciate.

As of the writing of this book, Philippe Beaudry is seventy-five years old and living in Longueuil, Quebec—some five hundred kilometres upstream from Rimouski. Although his health no longer allows him to dive, he still feels a strong connection to the cold, dark waters of the St. Lawrence. ⊹

3

THEATRES OF WAR

WHEN THE BUILDERS OF THE CPR WERE tasked with creating an economic and political link between the isolated British colonies on the Pacific Coast and the more established communities in Eastern Canada, one of the justifications for the massive effort and expense was the railway line's potential as a strategic asset. While UK troops never made use of the company's network to reach and defend the empire's possessions in the Far East, CPR soon proved its military worth. Before the line was even completed, soldiers were rushed to the Northwest to successfully suppress a rebellion there, and not two decades later the railway was called upon to transport a contingent of Canadian horsemen to the East Coast, on its way to the Boer War in South Africa.

However, CPR's full military value, its industrial infrastructure, and its vast workforce was truly revealed during the two wars that embroiled most of the globe. During the First World War, fifty-two CPR ships would be requisitioned by the British Admiralty to carry more than a million troops and four million tons of cargo into battle. German U-boats and other hazards of war sank a dozen of them. Railway shops were converted to the manufacture of munitions, employing female workers to replace men who had gone off to the front. Ultimately, more than eleven thousand Canadian Pacific employees would enlist for duty, nearly 10 percent of whom would not survive the conflict.

Twenty years later, CPR was an industrial powerhouse that would contribute manpower, machinery, and morale on a scale unrivalled by any private corporation on the Allied side of the Second World War. Twenty-two more CPR ships would be pressed into service; CPR shops would manufacture hundreds of tanks and naval guns among the thousands of munitions that were produced; and the company's new airline would inaugurate a bomber delivery service to the UK while operating a number of flying schools at home. Before peace was restored, 21,787 CPR employees would enlist; 658 would pay the ultimate price.

THE FIRST WORLD WAR AFLOAT

n August 1914, not yet a month after the outbreak of open hostilities, the German army was overrunning Belgium. All ships of British nationality in or near the port of Antwerp, as well as those of other Allied countries, were pressed into service to evacuate refugees to the British Isles. Canadian Pacific's president, Thomas Shaughnessy, had pledged all of the resources of his company to the cause, even before his steamships *Montrose* and *Montreal* had boarded hundreds of evacuees. Across the Atlantic in Canada, plans were already being laid to ferry the first wave of the country's expeditionary force into the fray.

By the middle of August, Sir Sam Hughes, Canada's minister of militia, met with representatives of the country's larger shipping companies to assemble thirty staunch vessels to carry the tens of thousands of fighting men being assembled at Camp Valcartier, Quebec.

Twelve Canadian Pacific and Allan Line ships—those of the latter company purchased by CPR just five years earlier—would sail less than two months later with the first Canadian contingent of 36,000 men. Along with the soldiers, the convoy would carry on board 7,679 horses, 70 field guns, 110 motor vehicles, 705 horse-drawn vehicles, and 82 bicycles. The men would soon be serving on the front lines, as infantry, cavalry, engineers, signallers, artillerymen, and medics.

Thirty-one ships led by British cruisers HMS *Eclipse, Diana,* and *Talbot* sailed from Gaspé on October 3. Close astern was a fourth cruiser, *Charybdis,* to further protect against potential surface raiders or, as they neared the coast of Europe, the feared U-boats of the Imperial German Navy. Other capital ships of the British Grand Fleet patrolled continuously up and down the North Sea lanes.

On the morning of October 5, as the convoy steamed past St. Pierre Island, the heavy battle cruiser HMS *Glory* joined the procession, underscoring the importance the British Admiralty attached to this strategic force. A final transport ship, the *Canada,* requisitioned from the British and North Atlantic Navigation Company, would join the convoy with the 2nd battalion of the Lincolnshire Regiment (British regular army) on board, after steaming north from Bermuda.

The elaborate precautions paid off. The convoy reached Britain safely, despite the perils of the war at sea, which would only build throughout the next three years to its apex in 1917. Between

August and December of that year, more than 11 million gross tons of Allied shipping would be sent to the bottom. As many as 4,800 merchant ships were lost to submarine attacks alone, a monthly average of 95 vessels.

Many more Canadian Pacific steamships were soon requisitioned by the Admiralty or offered up by the company to fill the need for troop and cargo transport.

In October 1914, the British Grand Fleet left Scapa Flow, in the Orkneys, as a precaution against the high risk from U-boats and mines. Among several ruses to confuse German command as to the fleet's whereabouts, ten merchant ships were disguised to simulate battleships. The British Admiralty hoped the ploy would cause the enemy to overestimate the strength of the UK's naval resources. With the aid of false upper works, constructed from wood and canvas, and laden with heavy ballast to reduce their freeboard, CP steamships *Lake Champlain, Lake Erie, Montcalm, Montezuma,* and *Mount Royal* masqueraded as HMS *King George V, Centurion, Audacious, Iron Duke,* and *Marlborough*, respectively, to remarkable effect.

Among the thousands of Canadian Pacific employees who served the Allied cause as merchant navy crewmembers, more than three hundred company employees enlisted with the Royal Navy, as officers and engineers. One of those recruits, Ronald Neil Stuart, won the Distinguished Service Order and the Victoria Cross.

By the end of the war, fifty-two CP ships had been in active service as armed merchant cruisers, transports, and cargo carriers. Twelve were lost to enemy action; two sank in marine accidents. Between them, they boarded more than one million troops and transported four million tons of cargo.

CP ships in the Pacific service carried 450 thousand tons of war supplies to Russia, in support of the Eastern Front. Chinese workers came to France en masse to serve in labour battalions, in vessels transporting vast quantities of rice. Thousands of horses were ferried from North Africa, to back up the mechanized vehicles of the Allied expeditionary forces.

Canadian Pacific carried the war to China and Japan, Singapore, Bombay, Columbo, Suez, Gallipoli, Dar-es-Salaam, Durban and Mauritius, and a number of other ports in the Mediterranean and on the North and South American continents. In all of those voyages, only eight Allied troops were lost to enemy action. ⊹

The CPR steamship *Montezuma* was requisitioned by the British Admiralty and converted to a mock-up of the British Royal Navy battleship *Iron Duke*. AUTHOR'S COLLECTION

RAILWAY TROOPS SHOW STEELY RESOLVE

A fter nearly a year of highly destructive total warfare on the front lines of the First World War, vast tracts of land in Belgium and Northern France presented a nightmare vision of ravaged fields, denuded forests, and pockmarked roadways. It was late in coming when the Dominion government, on behalf of the country's besieged Allies, called upon Canadian Pacific to hastily assemble a force of five hundred men to engage in much-needed railway repair and reconstruction work on the hotly contested battlegrounds of Europe.

Given the green light to proceed, CPR president Thomas Shaughnessy wasted no time in granting a leave of absence to Colin Worthington Ramsey, the railway's thirty-two-year-old engineer of construction for eastern lines, and gave the newly appointed lieutenant-in-command the task of heading up the scheme. Ramsey had more than sixteen years' experience with general railway construction and previously held a captain's Class-A certificate from the Royal School of Infantry at St. John's, Quebec. In building the new railway construction force, Ramsey would not be confined to seconding men from CPR service but was authorized to recruit freely from railway companies and other industries across the country.

Shaughnessy called upon F.L. Wanklyn, Canadian Pacific's general executive assistant, to manage logistics on the home front. The federal government gave him the rank of an honorary lieutenant colonel with the corps. On March 13, 1915, Ramsey sent notices across the land by telegraph that men were required between the ages of eighteen and forty-five "with good ears, with good eyes, with good limbs and physically fit" to rebuild the railways of Belgium and France. Two weeks later, he had more than three thousand applications to fill the five hundred positions in the corps. Seventy-five men were from CPR, and many others came from government railways, along with a smattering of bank clerks, schoolteachers, and labourers from other industries.

All of the officers recruited for the corps, however, were qualified engineers and railway constructors, having special knowledge of building and repairing steel bridges, erecting emergency wooden bridges and trestles, laying and grading track, and all such operations as would normally be carried out by railway maintenance gangs.

The nascent construction corps was mobilized at a location known as Christopher's Pit, just outside of West Saint John, New Brunswick. Forty to fifty CPR colonist sleeping cars were placed on a railway siding to accommodate them. The Canadian Overseas Railway Construction Corps, as the group would be called, sailed on June 14, 1915, aboard SS *Herschel* with 21 officers and 505 non-commissioned officers and men, bound for Longmour Camp in England, about sixteen miles from the so-called Home of the British Army at Aldershot, roughly thirty miles southeast of London. A British destroyer escorted the lone troop carrier through the U-boat infested waters of the North Atlantic.

Before being deployed to the front lines on the continent, the corps took up the task of maintaining and repairing railway lines in and around their camp. Ramsey was briefed by Lord Kitchener, the British secretary of state for war, and toured the trenches from Ypres north.

By the end of 1915, the men had spiked down a narrow-gauge railway line behind the front line of trenches, extending the whole length of the Belgian front. The corps was also responsible for building concrete gun emplacements that could withstand heavy shelling from the Germans.

"Life is not all beer and skittles," Ramsey advised Wanklyn during the work. "There are some fairly severe hardships."

Not least among his concerns was the difficulty of moving and protecting heavy equipment so close to the battlefields. Along with the damage caused by shellfire came a new insidious threat from gas attacks. On occasion, death and destruction raining down from the skies.

"We had to move our camp a few days ago," Ramsey wrote early in the new year. "The German aeroplanes and Zeppelins got so unpleasant; bombed us four consecutive days, and then we considered discretion the better part of valor and sought a more sequestered spot."

By early summer in 1916, several other work groups had been deployed from Canada to the European theatre, including the Number 1 and Number 2 Construction battalions, charged with undertaking heavy work of almost any nature, and the Number 1 Section, Skilled Railway Employees, tasked with operating the more than 150 miles of railway track that had by then been completed in the northern part of France.

News of a successful naval engagement in the North Sea and the German defeat at Verdun, after months of gruelling hand-to-hand combat, buoyed the construction forces. But as the war progressed and dragged on far longer than initially anticipated, the overlapping responsibilities of the hastily assembled work battalions, coupled with the fierce competition for prize military postings, created an administrative nightmare.

More than a dozen railway construction companies were put into the field, attached to one army battalion or another, along with three sections of Skilled Railway Employees, a Broad Gauge Railway Operating Company, a Canadian Light Railway Operating Company, a (Canadian) Engine

With the aid of a mobile pile driver, CORCC (Canadian Overseas Railway Construction Corps) forces were able to replace this bridge in France that had been destroyed by the Germans in a mere twenty hours. CRHA/EXPORAIL, CANADIAN PACIFIC RAILWAY FONDS P170-A-4342

Crew Company, a Wagon Erecting Company, and a Canadian Bridging Company. Eventually, most of the construction forces were disbanded and folded into the Corps of Canadian Railway Troops under the command of Canadian Brigadier-General J.W. Stewart.

Over the course of the war, the displaced railway workers contributed to the ultimate victory of the Allies, far exceeding both their numbers and expectations. The original goal of building railway lines twenty miles from the trenches had been modified so that the track came within one thousand yards of no man's land. On average, the rail crews managed to install more than fifty miles of new track per week. Even the long-range, high-velocity guns of the German Army could not drive the railheads back.

"The Hun put a shell through the boiler of a locomotive the other day, which exploded between the front drivers and blew them off," Ramsey dutifully reported back to headquarters at one point. "And occasionally, he breaks the track or gets a man or so, but he is not keeping us back at all."

As the Germans began to retreat from France in late 1917, the construction battalions took over daily operations on many of the railway lines, in addition to handling the necessary maintenance and ongoing construction. Fortunately, their ranks included many former locomotive engineers from which they could draw.

During the early summer of 1918, when the Germans engaged in some of the most intense bombing campaigns of the war, a three-arch, double-track masonry viaduct on the Boulogne-Calais main line was in serious danger. Numerous attempts were made by the enemy to destroy it and cut off the main artery of supply to all of Belgium and the northern Allied front. To ensure its survival, the railway men shored up the arches with heavy hard pine timbers and constructed a solid steel floor across the entire viaduct. Later in the year, a six-hundred-foot wooden trestle forty feet high and containing more than 150,000 board feet of timber, was built by the First Railway Battalion on a strategic section of railway between Frevent and Hesdin in France.

Some of the heaviest work executed by the railway construction corps was on, or near, the most famous battle sites in Ypres, Flanders, Dunkirk, and the Somme, not only repairing and maintaining rail infrastructure, but also erecting water towers, pumping stations, and pipeline. ⚜

LOCOMOTIVE ENGINEER'S HEROIC SACRIFICE

His fellow railroaders in Alberta called him Singing Pete. His sunny disposition enlivened their hours together, and an upbeat song could often be heard emanating from the roundhouse or an engine cab whenever he was working. The popular CPR employee would go on to be a favourite among the Canadians who signed up for duty in the Great War. He was the first locomotive engineer to be awarded the Victoria Cross.

James Peter Robertson was one of ten children born to Presbyterian parents in Springhill, Nova Scotia. When he was sixteen, the family moved west to Medicine Hat, Alberta, and Pete hired on with the railway, where he rose to become an engineer. When the call came for recruits to join the Canadian Expeditionary Force that would go to Europe in support of the British troops who were already there, Robertson was working out of Lethbridge—not too far from home. He sent a letter to his mother telling her he intended to enlist with the Canadian Mounted Rifles.

"The Empire needs the very best that's in us," he told her.

By July 6, 1916, Robertson had arrived in England aboard the troop ship SS *Olympic.* He was immediately posted with the 27th Infantry Battalion, Manitoba Regiment, for final training before being shipped over to the front lines.

One of the most punishing battles Canadian forces took part in during the First World War took place at Passchendaele, in Belgium. When his platoon was held up by barbed wire and under heavy fire during the final assault on the village, Private Robertson leapt over the barriers and rushed the gun crew. He was able to kill four of the enemy and turn the weapon on his remaining foes. Inflicting numerous casualties, Robertson was said to have "used the machine gun to keep down the fire of enemy snipers, inspiring his comrades to their finest efforts and consolidating their position."

But the firefight was not over. When two of Robertson's comrades were wounded, he left the security of his trench to bring them back to safety. Carrying the first man, he staggered back to his own lines under heavy fire, but he would not be so lucky when he returned for the second wounded soldier. As Robertson pulled the man toward safety, an enemy shell exploded nearby, killing him instantly. He was just thirty-four years old.

The former CPR engineer who they called Singing Pete would not leave his wounded comrades to die alone in no man's land.
AUTHOR'S COLLECTION

Pete was buried in Belgium's Tyne Cot Cemetery, alongside many others who fell that day in the battle for the high ground near the village of Passchendaele. The victory of the Canadians and the Allied forces in that deadly confrontation is considered to be one of the most important and glorious events of the First World War.

For his outstanding devotion to duty and his extreme gallantry under fire, Robertson was awarded the Victoria Cross posthumously, in April 1918. Alberta lieutenant-governor R.G. Brett, travelled to Medicine Hat to present personally the empire's highest award for valour to Pete's mother, at a public ceremony.

In 1956, Branch Number 17 of the Royal Canadian Legion, in Medicine Hat, was dedicated to Private James Peter Robertson, V.C. in his memory. The townspeople also named a neighbourhood swimming pool after him and christened a local street Robertson Way. In addition, the local Kiwanis Club sponsored a 1967 centennial project, naming a beautiful memorial park near the centre of the city in honour of the fallen soldier.

A century after Peterson's heroic sacrifice, the honours bestowed upon the gallant locomotive engineer from the Prairies are still forthcoming. In 2012, the Canadian Coast Guard added nine new patrol boats to its fleet. The first of the Hero-class vessels to be launched was the CCGS *Private Robertson, V.C.* ⚓

IF YOU CAN'T HIDE FROM THEM, DAZZLE THEM

One of the bleakest periods of the First World War, in the early months of 1917, intensified with the decision of German High Command to fully implement a campaign of unrestricted submarine warfare.

As the land war in Europe ground to a virtual stalemate in a brutal series of back and forth advances and retreats across the front lines that expended human and material resources on both side to their limits, the devastating advances in German U-boat technology were exacting an equally deadly toll on Allied sea power. Fully one-fifth of merchant ships attempting to resupply the British Isles with urgently need war supplies had been sent to the bottom by the end of 1916. The explosion of the hospital ship HMHS *Lanfranc*, torpedoed in the English Channel on April 17, 1917, with the loss of forty people including eighteen wounded German prisoners, showed the world that nothing was safe from the "Hun savagery" that had been unleashed.

The constant threat to shipping and, indeed, to the eventual positive outcome of the Allied efforts in the worldwide conflict, brought an outpouring of ideas for making ships less vulnerable to the depredations of the roving underwater wolf packs. The problem was compounded by the vagaries of the weather, light conditions throughout the day, the angle of the sun and the resulting relative visibility of ships against a constantly changing background of sea and sky. Schemes were needed to render both merchant and naval vessels, if not invisible, at least more fully camouflaged than their drab grey coats of paint were achieving. Some of the suggestions were more bizarre than others, and some came from unexpected sources on both sides of the Atlantic.

One of the ideas was to cover the ships in mirrors; another was to somehow disguise them as giant whales, or to drape them in canvas painted to look like clouds. Renowned inventor Thomas Edison purportedly briefly outfitted one ship to appear like an island, complete with trees, until part of the masking blew away in high winds.

As early as 1914, the British zoologist John Graham Kerr had experimented with forms of camouflage inspired by his observations of the animal world. In a letter to First Lord of the Admiralty Winston Churchill, Kerr explained his goals were to confuse rather than to conceal, by employing patterns much like those of the giraffe, the zebra, or the jaguar. Irregular bands could be used to

The Canadian Pacific liner *Empress of Russia*, in the fore-
ground, was among the ships painted in so-called dazzle
patterns to confuse the enemy. AUTHOR'S COLLECTION

disrupt the easily recognizable vertical lines of ships' funnels and masts. Guns could be painted
in shades of colour from grey above to white below, so as to make them disappear against a grey
background.

Several ships, including the British warship HMS *Implacable*, were painted in Kerr's imagi-
native paint schemes during the Allied campaign in the Dardanelles in 1915, which was noted by
some of the officers involved to "increase the difficulty of accurate range finding," but following the
disastrous offensive and Churchill's subsequent ignominious departure from the Admiralty, the
Royal Navy reverted to plain grey paint schemes.

By 1917, however, the Allies were more than ready to take another look at various camouflage
strategies; and this time it was a marine artist and Royal naval volunteer reserve officer by the name
of Norman Wilkinson who lead the charge toward painting ships in even more radical fashion than
had been advocated by Kerr.

"Empress of Asia"

The *Empress of Asia* was sent to war in another variation
of dazzle paint. AUTHOR'S COLLECTION

Wilkinson's treatments, described as *dazzle camouflage* in Britain and *razzle-dazzle* in the United States, employed bold stripes and broken lines "to distort the external shape by violent colour contrasts." The British gave Wilkinson a full team of creative people—artists, painters, and set designers—whose job it was to make it more difficult for submarine commanders to estimate a ship's type, size, speed, and heading and thereby take up the wrong position to fire a fatal torpedo.

Black-and-white patterns were effective, as were those that employed various shades of blue and green, cutting a ship's profile into pieces. Contradictory patterns on a ship's superstructure and funnels were used to confuse the enemy as to what heading it was on. A painted curve on the bow could give the impression of a large bow wave, creating a misimpression about a ship's speed.

More than four thousand British merchant ships and four hundred naval vessels were painted in a variety of dazzle schemes worked up by Wilkinson's team. A young Franklin Roosevelt, then assistant to the secretary of the US navy, discussed the work with Wilkinson, which led to a number of American vessels undergoing dazzle treatments. In 1918, the Admiralty analysed shipping losses and concluded that, while dazzle painting had not prevented attacks on the treated vessels, it had made it more difficult to sink them. US data confirmed the findings. The strategy was also credited by many ships' captains for raising morale among the crews on board, as well as those being transported during the war.

Canadian Pacific steamships *Empress of Asia* and *Empress of Russia* had both been requisitioned as armed merchant cruisers by the British Admiralty in 1914. Later, while in service as troop transports on the North Atlantic, these speedy vessels were painted in vivid dazzle paint schemes designed by Wilkinson's team to make them less vulnerable to submarine attack.

After the First World War, the British Admiralty established a commission to determine who should receive compensation for the invention of dazzle painting on ships. Speaking out for Wilkinson's case were Royal Navy Admiral Sir Lewis Bayly, Commodore Hayes of the White Star Line, and Captain Kendall of Canadian Pacific Steamships. Kendall had served during the war as a commodore of convoys on a ship camouflaged with an early scheme in the years before Wilkinson's ideas were adopted.

"And did you regard it as a successful camouflage?" one of the commissioners asked Kendall.

"No, I did not," Kendall replied.

"I feel sure the members of the Commission will be interested to hear your reasons for this," said the commissioner, as Wilkinson remembered in later years that Kendall had been prompted to explain during his testimony.

"Well, she was sunk on the first voyage," said the CP captain.

Sometime after the laughter died down, the commission awarded Wilkinson two thousand pounds for his contribution to the successful prosecution of the Allied war effort. Despite rival claims from Kerr and others—Picasso insisted that Cubists like himself had invented the most abstract forms of camouflage painting—Wilkinson's innovations and applications were deemed unique and were judged to have been the most effective strategy for dazzling the enemy.

Norman Wilkinson went on to become a well-known and respected marine painter and advertising artist, who, among many such assignments, did a lot of contract work for Canadian Pacific between the two world wars. His realistic renderings of company steamships in action were not only used in tourist pamphlets and on immigration posters, but on many occasions also graced the walls in the executive suites. ⊹

THE NORTH ATLANTIC WAS A MARINE GRAVEYARD

During the Second World War, Canadian Pacific made an unprecedented contribution to the Battle of the Atlantic, turning twenty-two ships over to the British Admiralty to be used as troop ships and armed merchant cruisers, while releasing more than six thousand officers and sailors from company service to man them. By war's end, 71 of the men would be decorated by the British and Canadian governments for conspicuous service; 236 would be dead. Only five of the CPR liners would return to their peacetime sailings. The North Atlantic would exact most of the deadly toll.

The ships steamed more than two million miles in active duty through enemy-infested waters, carrying hundreds of thousands of soldiers to the overheated theatres of war and evacuating civilian refugees and Arabian kings from trouble spots around the globe to more secure locations. More than 59,000 German and Italian prisoners of war would also be escorted to confinement camps aboard CPR vessels before the end of the conflict.

Above all, though, CPR ships sailed back and forth in secret convoys across the North Atlantic, ferrying troops of the Canadian Expeditionary Force, along with millions of tons of food and war materiel. As early as the summer of 1940, in the dark days following the evacuation of Dunkirk, the company's *Duchess of Atholl* would return to Canada with eight hundred British children seeking a safe home for the duration of the war. Thousands more would follow, just before the crossing became perilous.

The *Beaverburn*, one of CPR's fast freighters launched in the late 1920s, was an early victim of a submarine torpedo, while executing a zigzag course across the Atlantic in 1940. The following year, Hitler's wolf pack would claim sister ship *Beaverdale* when a shell from a submarine on the surface struck five hundred tons of TNT in the forward hold, propelling pieces of the ship more than two thousand feet in the air. Just a month before, enemy aircraft had sent the *Beaverbrae* to the bottom in sheets of flame.

The largest merchant vessel to be sunk during the war—CPR's magnificent *Empress of Britain*, which had made eight world cruises and acted as a 42,000-ton regal yacht during the Royal Tour to Canada of King George VI and Queen Elizabeth. It met its end off the northwest coast of Ireland in grim, grey war paint, set on fire by German planes and finished off by submarine U-32. The thousands who had sailed aboard her, or had followed her short but storied career, mourned the loss of the famous and popular liner. Prominent newspapers around the world printed glowing epitaphs.

After CPR's flagship *Empress of Britain* was crippled by a German bomber, an attempt was made to tow her to port. Before the stricken ship could reach safety, however, two torpedoes from U-32 sent her to the bottom.
IMPERIAL WAR MUSEUM

Among them, the *New York Times* reported that she was "indeed an Empress, with pride and grace and dignity in every inch of her."

Canadian Pacific's merchant liner *Montrose* had been commissioned to serve as an armed escort and patrol ship in the dangerous waters of the North Atlantic. Renamed *Forfar* to serve in that role, her main armaments were eight 6-inch guns and a few anti-aircraft weapons. On December 2, 1940, while proceeding to Halifax to join a convoy back to the UK, *Forfar* fell prey to a Nazi submarine. After daybreak the next morning, destroyers HMS *Viscount* and HMCS *St. Laurent* picked up survivors, clinging to rafts and bits of floating wreckage. Thirteen other ships were sunk by the voracious enemy U-boats that same night.

Duchess of Bedford—one of CPR's popular cabin steamers and one of the largest ships to sail up the St. Lawrence as far as Montreal—no doubt would have also presented a tempting target for the marauding U-boats on the North Atlantic. But the merchantman turned the tables on the enemy when a patrolling German submarine surfaced a bit too close to the liner for its own good. The *Bedford* was steaming from Liverpool to Boston in a heavy sea. Closing to within a hundred yards, the ship's captain ordered its gunners to open fire on the raider, destroying the U-boat's conning tower in a terrible explosion. The submarine sank before her crew had any time to react. The *Bedford*'s crew spotted the periscope of a second U-boat about a mile away, but three rounds from the ship's guns were enough to drive off the threat. The plucky little liner was one of the few lucky ones to survive the war. ⚓

DOUGHTY SHIP DID NOT DISGRACE THE SERVICE

S etting sail from Halifax for Liverpool, just after nightfall on October 28, 1940, none of the men aboard the thirty-eight ships in Convoy HX-84 was under the illusion that the voyage would be without considerable risk. Although a strict code of secrecy about the precise details of such movements was vigorously maintained, Halifax was a wide-open natural harbour and enemy spies were everywhere.

Among those in command that night was Captain Hugh Pettigrew, a sixty-year-old veteran of Canadian Pacific Steamships service, standing on the bridge of the *Beaverford*, a ten-thousand-ton fast freighter that had been requisitioned from CPSS by the British Admiralty to ferry food, general cargo, and a large consignment of mail to Great Britain. Prior to the sailing, Pettigrew had changed the venue of his traditional bon-voyage meal with friends from the ship's dining room to an uptown restaurant. "I have a feeling this will be our last lunch together, so I thought a change would be good," he told them, with more than a little foreboding.

As the convoy steamed eastward at eight knots, the ships formed nine columns about six hundred yards apart with four hundred yards from stern to bow. The *Beaverford* was the middle ship in the seventh column. Most of the other vessels were unarmed cargo ships and tankers, but the *Beaverford* had been fitted with a four-inch, low-angle gun on a platform over the wheelhouse, a three-inch, high-angle gun on the foreside of the bridge and two First World War–era Lewis machine guns. Along with the modest armaments came a small detachment of DEMS (Defensively Equipped Merchant Ships) gunners.

The Canadian destroyers *Columbia* and *St. Francis* would accompany the convoy for the first two or three days to protect it from predatory German U-boats, or surface raiders. At the western approaches to the United Kingdom, a British anti-submarine escort would take up the task. The armed merchant cruiser *Jervis Bay* from the Royal Navy Dockyard in Bermuda would accompany them for the entire voyage.

For the first seven days, the ships maintained radio silence along the convoy's secret route across the North Atlantic. On the morning of November 5, an ominous shadow from an unidentified airplane passed over the flotilla. A few days earlier, unbeknownst to the British Admiralty and allied intelligence services, the German warship *Admiral Scheer* had slipped out of its anchorage at Gotenhafen—a Polish port on the south coast of the Baltic Sea, renamed from Gdynia by the conquering Germans—and was now on the prowl for enemy shipping. Worse still, the *Admiral Scheer*'s commander, Captain Theodor Krancke, knew when HX-84 had sailed, and one of the German reconnaissance planes had just discovered the convoy's location.

The *Admiral Scheer* and its sister ships *Lutzow* and *Graf Spee* were heavy cruisers, sometimes referred to as pocket battleships, equipped with six 11-inch, high-angle guns and torpedoes, along with radar, range-finding equipment, and gun-control systems. Proud members of Nazi Germany's Kriegsmarine, the deadly ships that could achieve an impressive speed of twenty-eight knots were designed to outgun any cruiser fast enough to catch them.

That fateful day, before the *Admiral Sheer* had been alerted to the position of the vulnerable convoy, the warship had sunk the British fast freighter *Mopan* and took its survivors on board. At 3:45 PM, the Allied ships spotted smoke on the horizon to the northeast, and an hour later the enemy raider had been identified. It was Guy Fawkes Day, and the sailors with HX-84 were about to witness more fireworks than they ever hoped to see on that auspicious occasion or otherwise.

Reacting quickly to the looming threat, Admiral M.B. Maltby—commodore of the hunted convoy, aboard cargo ship *Cornish City*—immediately ordered a forty-degree turn to starboard for all of the ships, while the unarmoured and severely outgunned *Jervis Bay* hoisted the signal for "prepare to scatter" and steamed toward the German raider to draw its fire.

In a flash, the whole might of the *Admiral Scheer*'s far heavier armaments was concentrated on the gallant defender. Guns boomed, shells shrieked toward their target, and great blooms of water erupted all around. A sailor with the convoy later reported that the *Jervis Bay* sailed straight into the maw of the German warship, "the White Ensign aflutter, guns belching their impotent fire, British tars meeting the old challenge." Aboard the plucky armed merchant cruiser, Captain Edward Fogarty Fegan and his brave crew did not hesitate; but after a short, valiant battle, during which the German cruiser stayed out of range of her opponent, the *Jervis Bay* was sent to the bottom in flames, after direct hits to her forward gun and her control room.

By the time the challenger met her doom, only three ships of the convoy were still in range of the enemy's guns. To obscure the trail of the fleeing vessels, the *Beaverford* and her nearest neighbour in the formation had rolled smoke canisters from their sterns. Now, using her reserve of engine power and the expert seamanship of her crew to evade the enemy's salvoes, the *Beaverford* turned toward the raider with all hands at their action stations.

For more than four hours, the intrepid little freighter evaded destruction, as the rest of the convoy fanned out into the gloom. As darkness fell, the *Admiral Scheer* filled the sky with star shells

The *Beaverford*'s vastly outgunned, but valiant sea battle against the pocket battleship *Admiral Scheer* has been largely forgotten.

CRHA/EXPORAIL CANADIAN PACIFIC RAILWAY FONDS P170-GR-372

to light the position of the *Beaverford*, while firing twelve rounds from her main armament and seventy-one from her secondary guns. Three shells from the big barrels scored direct hits, while the smaller guns found their mark another sixteen times. Still, the besieged vessel would not sink. With all of her lifeboats and life-saving apparatus smashed or ablaze, flames engulfing her bridge, death sweeping her decks, and sea water pouring through the gaping wounds in her sides, a torpedo from the *Admiral Scheer* tore through her hull. This time there would be no respite for any of the hunted vessel's crewmembers and all hands went down with the ship.

Later in one of the most understated epitaphs in the annals of war, a captain with the convoy, who had watched the gallant ship fight and saw her finish, stated for posterity: "The *Beaverford* did not disgrace the British Merchant Service."

In the aftermath of the sea battle, the *Admiral Scheer* was able to catch one more straggler from Convoy HX-84, adding the unfortunate ship to its tally of kills for the day. Within hours, the crew of the Swedish ship *Stureholm* rescued sixty-eight survivors from the *Jervis Bay* in various states of distress. Three of the injured would later die from their wounds. Allied media outlets broadcast details around the world of the armed merchant cruiser's epic encounter with the Nazi surface raider. Soon enough, her captain was awarded posthumously with a well-deserved Victoria Cross for his actions.

However, it wasn't until more than three years later that a Glasgow newspaper carried the story of the *Beaverford*'s heroic but tragic demise, and her unsung captain and crew came to the public's attention for the first time. They never received official recognition for their sacrifices. In the wake of the attention paid to the *Jervis Bay* and her survivors, the fate of Canadian Pacific's *Beaverford*, and the brave sailors who fought against impossible odds to protect Convoy HX-84, has largely been forgotten. ⁜

BOMBERS BY AIRMAIL

I t was Britain's darkest hour. France had fallen to the enemy, and Hitler's armies were massing for the invasion of England. The German Wehrmacht had an iron hold on Fortress Europe, while the Luftwaffe swept the skies of all opposition. Endless defeats in virtually every theatre of war had stretched the Allies' resources to their breaking point and, more alarmingly, there was now a critical shortage of fighter and bomber aircraft.

In early 1940, the United States was not yet officially at war with anybody, but military airplanes were nevertheless rolling steadily off assembly lines across the country. Many of the aircraft were immediately disassembled and shipped by rail and sea to Britain, a process that could take several weeks or months before the fighters and bombers saw any combat action.

The long logistics chain needed to deliver a North American warplane to the front lines in Europe ate up resources; and the journey across the North Atlantic was subject to the very real threat of marauding wolf packs—deadly German U-boats that had already sent hundreds of thousands of tons of Allied shipping to the ocean floor.

In desperate straits, Britain's Lord Beaverbrook, Winston Churchill's newly appointed minister of aircraft production, put forward an audacious plan.

Transatlantic aviation was still in its infancy, and many viewed winter crossings as too unpredictable and unacceptably risky. Nevertheless, Beaverbrook proposed that the Allies establish an all-weather, all-season staging route for flying military aircraft, primarily bombers, across the Atlantic. The planes would be delivered promptly, reliably—and secretly.

Because of its pre-eminence in world transportation and its vast experience in international logistics, Canadian Pacific was approached to organize the aircraft ferry service, together with the Royal Air Force, senior officers of Imperial Airways, and the British ministry of aircraft production.

"British Overseas Airlines offer cooperation with you in arranging pilot personnel and will provide any technical assistance, also such management as you may require from us here and there," wrote Morris Wilson—president of the Bank of Canada and Beaverbrook's representative in Canada and the US—to Edward Beatty, chairman and president of CPR.

The Lockheed Company of Burbank, California, had already agreed to deliver a certain number of its Hudson bombers between August and October, so the fulfillment of this

Canadian Pacific pioneered the bomber ferry service between North America and the United Kingdom, as an early component of FDR's Lend-Lease arrangement with Churchill. NICHOLAS MORANT PHOTO, AUTHOR'S COLLECTION

contract was a good opportunity to test the feasibility of a regular Atlantic bomber delivery system.

The contract between CPR and the British Government called for the establishment of Canadian Pacific Air Services (CPAS) as a department of the railway with a large administrative network from which to draw. Beatty was the chairman of the company's new air wing; George Woods-Humphrey, the former managing director of Imperial Airways, took the vice-chairman seat; and British Colonel Henry Burchall ran the day-to-day operations as general manager.

Together they combed the world for the more than one thousand pilots, co-pilots, astro-navigators, and other specialists they would need to operate the ferry service.

To overcome the shortage of experienced multi-engine pilots, a transatlantic ferry pilot school was established in Montreal in November 1940. The nucleus of the program, initially, was a pool of twenty-five experienced pilots from British Overseas Airways. While in town for training, the boys supplemented their instruction with a party or two at the Mount Royal Hotel, where the realities of war ensured the women always outnumbered the men.

The first transatlantic bomber delivery took place on November 11, 1940. Seven Hudson bombers, in formation, left Gander and successfully completed their flight to Prestwick Airport in less than ten hours. CP Air Services had opened a whole new chapter of aviation history.

At its peak, more than a thousand planes were flown to Britain each month. They flew across the continent from the factories to receiving bases on the East Coast at St. Hubert Airport, in Montreal, and Gander, Newfoundland, before crossing about seventeen hundred miles of ocean. In the impromptu air service were veterans of the First World War, men who had flown or fought in the skies above France, Germany, Spain, Czechoslovakia, China, Ethiopia, and Australia. They were mostly bush pilots who had flown the pioneer routes in Canada's far North.

The busiest crewmembers were the astro-navigators. With the help of some sophisticated instruments and—hopefully—with a clear look at the stars, a good navigator would always know the position of his aircraft within about five miles. To save valuable time and fuel, it was essential to maintain an accurate flight path.

For most of the distance, the planes would fly three or four miles above the weather. Usually the flights were uneventful, but the ride was not a cushy one. Warplanes weren't built for comfort. Each member had his own station, but each sat on a hard metal seat in the cold and cramped confines of his unheated, airborne fighting machine. With little space to stretch and relieve tired muscles, these men sat alert at their posts for ten to twenty hours at a time. The wireless operators stayed glued to their headsets but could only send a message in dire need, so as not to reveal their position to the enemy.

Before takeoff, the crewmembers slipped into soft flying suits that enveloped their bodies, on top of which they donned windproof and waterproof jumpers and a life jacket.

The new CP Air Services department engaged and paid all personnel, made arrangements for fuel acquisition and delivery, as well as other necessary supplies, and supervised the entire operation. Transportation, security, claims, insurance, and legal details were all handled through established CPR departments.

At first it was difficult to recruit radio operators in the United States, as wireless telegraphy was rarely used in commercial aviation, but Canadian Pacific Air Services secured the services of many Canadians who had worked with the Canadian Marconi Company or the Radio Division of the Department of Transport, in radio posts scattered across the country.

Arrangements were made in Montreal for additional space to house radio instruction and training for navigators. CPAS set up new operational headquarters in the Railway Exchange Building and expanded its storage capacity with the acquisition of a hangar at St. Hubert Airport, on loan from the Royal Canadian Air Force. In Newfoundland, CPR stationed a number of sleeping cars beside the airfield to house plane crews waiting to make the overseas hop.

By January 1941, the Battle of the Atlantic was raging, and the gravity of the war called for even greater volumes of aircraft to be ferried across the ocean. To handle the expanded workload, C.H. "Punch" Dickens was appointed vice-chairman of the Air Services department. Dickens flew for both the Royal Flying Corp and the RAF during the First World War, and was one of Canada's most outstanding commercial pilots, winning considerable fame for his pioneer work in the country's western and northern hinterlands. For the last five years, Dickens had been general superintendent of Canadian Airways Limited of Winnipeg.

Under Dickens, Canadian Pacific Air Services increased its operations and its personnel, almost daily. Aircraft deliveries reached record levels. Plans were made for bigger facilities in Gander and in Bermuda, while test flights of military aircraft were conducted from California across the Pacific to Manila, where they were turned over to the Royal Australian Air Force.

With the increasing importance of the aircraft ferry service, and the myriad international political and military considerations, came the growing realization among war planners that overall control should be directly in the hands of the British Government.

On May 27, 1941, Wilson informed Beatty:

The exigencies of the war have made it necessary that this service be operated in future by the British Ministry of Aircraft Production in close collaboration with the Governments of United States and Canada. I take this opportunity of expressing on behalf of the Ministry of Aircraft Production and myself, personally, deep appreciation of the valuable services rendered by your company in inaugurating these activities. The services performed by your company have been a notable contribution to the war effort.

An interim organization dubbed Atfero—for Atlantic Ferry Organization—was set up to assume control, and largely managed daily operations from March 1941 onward. Five months later, when the RAF Ferry Command took over the Atlantic ferry organization from Atfero, about forty Canadian Pacific administrative officers and employees were still handling much of the administrative work. Most of them stayed on with Ferry Command, providing a valuable link with the organization's birth and thorough familiarity with its growth and operations. ✢

GOLDEN AIRCRAFT FUND

More than fifteen thousand Canadian Pacific employees signed up for the armed forces and headed overseas to serve on the front lines of the Second World War. Those who remained on the job found a number of other ways to make a contribution to the Allied war effort, among them purchasing stamps or victory bonds, rationing strategic commodities, attending military dances and other morale boosting events, or contributing directly to any number of fundraising campaigns.

One of the most audacious of these boosters was Miss Gladys Gowlland of CPR's treasury department, who launched an ambitious campaign to raise enough money to finance the purchase of a bomber—in all likelihood a Lancaster—for the Royal Canadian Air Force (RCAF). Described as one of the most sophisticated models of military aircraft, it came with a price tag of $100,000.

Because cash was in short supply for most people and the fundraiser would have to compete with dozens of other initiatives, including a similar one by CPR employees in Montreal to supply the Canadian Armed Forces with two ambulances for wounded soldiers, this effort would focus largely on getting workers and their families to look for "old gold" they were willing to part with, however reluctantly.

By November 1940, despite the large numbers who had enlisted, there were still more than 45,000 CPR employees and pensioners around the world to answer the call for donations. And answer they did. By Christmas, five thousand separate contributions had made their way into the treasury department vault at Montreal's Windsor Station: wedding rings, watch chains, cuff links, brooches, pen nibs, medals, and coins.

Shining brightly among the accumulated treasures, like purloined possessions in a dragon's hoard, were Knights of Columbus rings; three heavy golden emblems of Masonry; medals from football, cricket, curling, golf, billiards, swimming, and shooting championships; cuff links made from Boer War–era South African half-sovereigns on which were engraved the head of Paul Kruger; and gold nuggets brought back from the Klondike gold rush of 1898 by the grandfather of a Sudbury clerk.

CPR president Edward Beatty personally donated twelve sovereigns, four half-sovereigns, a match case, two business cases, four pencils, five knives, a ring, two watch fobs, two key rings,

two watch chains, and a gold souvenir invitation to the opening of Sydney's Harbour Bridge. The campaign was now being called the Golden Bomber Fund by the company's publicity department.

As the fundraising efforts heated up, CPR's employees in the West, in particular, built upon the initial concept and dreamed up all kinds of schemes that went well beyond the numerous bake sales, teas, bridge parties, and social evenings that were scheduled. Two movie showings at the Palliser Hotel featured film footage of the 1939 Royal Tour to Canada, the battle of the River Plate, and the heroic evacuation of Dunkirk. Each drew more than five hundred paying audience members. Raffles in Edmonton and Calgary vied with the various successful efforts to raise funds organized by Canadian Pacific's US workers in Seattle, Portland, Tacoma, and San Francisco. Dances in Red Deer and Calgary were widely attended. Comedy motion pictures and newsreels from the front that were screened on several occasions in the Winnipeg depot received an impressive response.

Employees in the company's eastern region were hard pressed to keep up with their western counterparts, but a grand musicale was staged in the Alouette dining room at Windsor Station, featuring a lengthy lineup of employee talent, from singers and songwriters to concert pianists, violinists, and horn players.

Throughout 1941, a wide array of golden valuables continued to somehow emerge from the woodwork and make its way into the Golden Bomber Fund. A gold shamrock brooch that caught the attention of the campaign committee had an inset of an owl with emerald eyes and a new moon made up of pearls. A bag of gold, silver, and copper coins included one dating back to Julius Caesar. One of the donated medals had been awarded to a competitor during the Open Violin Championship of 1928. A gold swastika tiepin—somebody's good luck piece, which predated the rise of the Nazis—would "help to defeat Germany's black swastika," said a committee member.

As the year wound down, the campaign organizers acknowledged that $100,000 would be too ambitious a target to meet that year. A little more than half that amount had been raised, and badly needed fighter planes could be built for about a quarter of the cost of a bomber. In the face of the new reality, the campaign name was changed to the Golden Aircraft Fund, and plans were made to finance two Spitfires, the newest version of the highly rated Allied fighter that had played such a vital role in the successful outcome of the Battle of Britain the previous summer.

In support of the Allied war effort, the employee campaign aimed to pay for a bomber but ended up funding the manufacture of two Spitfire fighter planes. AUTHOR'S COLLECTION

On November 26, a public ceremony was held in the Windsor Station concourse to formally hand over $50,000 to the RCAF. The CBC broadcast the proceedings into the living rooms of Canadians across the country, while representatives from the army, navy, and air force came to attention, and Montreal mayor Adhémar Raynault beamed his approval. Air Vice-Marshall Johnson accepted the cheque on behalf of the RCAF and stated that "the personnel of the Force and the people of Canada will value the gift most highly, because it is not from a large and monied corporation, but is the combined efforts of the employees themselves."

Within months, two fighter planes rolled out of a factory in Britain with the designation Canadian Pacific I and Canadian Pacific II painted on their sides. The first of these Spitfires, of the Mark IX type, would soon be piloted by Flight Lieutenant G.B. "Scotty" Murray of Halifax, Nova Scotia, who would go on to win the Distinguished Flying Cross for one confirmed downing of an enemy aircraft and two probables, as well as damaging nine others. ⁜

FORCED GUESTS OF THE JAPANESE

The Second World War started early for Canadian Pacific employees in the Far East.

Ever since the Russians had been humiliated militarily on both land and sea during the Russo–Japanese War of 1904–5, the Japanese had been slowly expanding their empire at the expense of neighbouring countries. Korea was named a protectorate of Japan in 1905 and unofficially annexed five years later. In 1931, the Japanese seized Manchuria from Chinese control and set up the puppet state of Manchukuo. Throughout the 1930s, escalating acts of aggression by ships of the Japanese navy and small detachments of the emperor's marines along the coast of China and in the Philippines warned of worse to come.

Under the threat of the looming storm, many westerners in non-essential positions in the Far East left for home or were transferred to safer assignments elsewhere. By 1937, Canadian Pacific was scaling back its workforce in Chinese port cities and evacuating hundreds of beleaguered men, women, and children from the International Settlement in Shanghai to the more secure British colony in Hong Kong.

When the Japanese launched a surprise aerial assault on the American naval base at Hawaii's Pearl Harbor, on December 7, 1941, the battle lines had been irrevocably drawn. Six hours later, the Japanese pounced on Hong Kong and other Western settlements along the Chinese coast, revealing their ultimate goal for complete hegemony in the region.

Within days, several Canadian Pacific employees, who had just recently signed up as volunteers with the British Hong Kong Garrison, were killed in action. John Fairly, a former telegrapher with the company's Kettle Valley Railway; P.G. Halley, a CPR section man from Quebec's Eastern Townships; and A. Cunningham, a clerk with CP Steamships freight department, all fell defending the main island community.

At first, the Japanese concentrated on bombing and attacking military objectives, resulting in low civilian casualties; but inevitably, rapes, murders, and other atrocities occurred. Immediately after the capitulation of the Hong Kong Garrison, Charles Edwin "Ted" Ross, an assistant in the island's freight department who was serving with the British Ministry of Information, made a break for freedom with fifteen other civilians and a small group of pro-Chongqing Chinese guerillas. Barefoot and clad only in underwear soaked in oil from swimming across the harbour,

Ross trekked more than eighty-five miles through the Japanese lines, mostly travelling at night to avoid detection. When he reached free China, he was able to contact the Canadian ambassador in Chongqing, who sent a plane for him and his companions.

Most of Canadian Pacific's people who were still employed in commercial activities were herded into prisoner of war camps at North Point, close to the power station in Victoria Harbour. Others were taken to a prison at Stanley, on the south side of Hong Kong Island. Some from CPR steamship offices around the South China Sea were also interned at Hong Kong. Shanghai company agents Mr. and Mrs. A.J. Parkhill joined one of their clerks, A.M. Parker, in captivity. Accountant D.P. Ross and his twin brother, W.L. Ross, were both on leave from Canadian Pacific and were serving with the Royal Volunteer Naval Reserve as acting sub-lieutenants when they were forced to surrender.

The Japanese had also invaded the Philippines within hours of their sneak attack at Pearl Harbor. They gained full control there, after American forces were defeated at the battles of Bataan and Corregidor, in 1942. David Miller, CP's agent in Manila, was interned early that year, along with thousands of others. He spent three years in a prisoner of war camp, in the company of steamship office worker Basil G. Ryan.

US Navy lieutenant Ben Stearns had been a CP passenger agent in Manila before signing up for military duty. Now he was a guest of the Japanese armed forces, while his wife was sent to a civilian internment camp. J.H. Mancollis, who had served as CP freight agent in Yokohama, had managed to escape to Manila when the company closed its offices there more than a year earlier. Now, he was taken prisoner, as well.

During 1942, CP ships were busy evacuating civilians from several hot spots in the area. The *Duchess of Bedford* was bombed and strafed by gunfire while delivering 875 refugees, including company personnel, from Singapore to Batavia in the Dutch East Indies. Within a month, the *Empress of Scotland* had boarded fifteen hundred more evacuees. Many of these people were then carried safely to Britain by the *Empress of Australia*, which had arrived in Batavia in early February with more than two thousand British airmen and soldiers to reinforce Dutch forces fighting the Japanese.

In 1937, Canadian Pacific dropped both China and Japan from its steamship itineraries and closed its agency in Yokohama, shown here, shortly thereafter. While the company's Western employees in Japan had the opportunity to leave before the outbreak of war, others in China were not so lucky. AUTHOR'S COLLECTION

David Drummond, whose title was "CP Oriental Manager," lived with his family in their home on the south side of Hong Kong's Victoria Peak. Somehow, he managed to avoid being interned until March 15, 1942, more than three months after the Japanese invasion. He joined general passenger agent G.E. Costello, along with their accountant and two other agents in Stanley Prison.

Many of the company's employees were fortunate enough to survive the war. Some returned to Canadian Pacific offices in the East, after taking time to recover their health. Others were not so lucky. Among them, Private Tony Grimson, formerly a bellboy at the Empress Hotel in Victoria, BC, died of disease. Thomas Monaghan, an assistant manager of the Chateau Frontenac Hotel, in Quebec, before becoming catering superintendent for CP Steamships in Hong Kong, did not survive the war. John Ray Shaw, a former Montreal employee who had retired as a CPSS agent in Manila, also died in captivity. ✢

THE AERODROME OF DEMOCRACY

T he formation of an airline company, in January 1942, added a whole new dimension to Canadian Pacific's wartime involvements—on the land, on the sea, and now, in the air. By virtue of Canadian Pacific Air Lines' acquisition of several winged pioneer freighting and bush operations, the fledgling enterprise also took over six air observation schools and one elementary flying training school.

In support of Britain, France, and the Allied forces fighting against Nazi Germany, Canada had declared war on September 9, 1939. Seventeen days later, the authorities in the United Kingdom made plans for a British Commonwealth Air Training Program. By December, Canada, Australia, and New Zealand had signed an agreement with Britain to train the men who were urgently needed to climb aboard the fighters and bombers that were the last bulwark against the rising storm.

Because it was beyond the range of enemy aircraft, Canada was considered an ideal location for training pilots. The country had immediate access to the American industrial heartland, and it enjoyed an excellent climate for flying. To seal the deal, Canadian prime minister William Lyon Mackenzie King had insisted on three conditions: the Royal Canadian Air Force would be in charge of the scheme, the majority of the graduates would be attached to Royal Canadian Air Force (RCAF) squadrons, and the RCAF would remain a distinct entity under Allied command and would not be subsumed by the British Royal Air Force.

The birth of civil aviation in Canada had come during the latter part of the 1920s, with the advent of aerial prospecting and aerial freight services, largely in the north. Flying clubs were not only encouraged by the federal government but were supported with the loan of two de Havilland Tiger Moths per club and a subsidy of one hundred dollars for each registered student.

Beginning in May 1940, with the critical aid of those clubs and businesses, the first training schools were opened. More were added every month. At its peak, the British Commonwealth Air Training Program was operating more than a hundred schools that together produced an estimated 131,500 pilots, navigators, air gunners, wireless operators, flight engineers, and bomb aimers. Fifty-five percent of the graduates were Canadians. The rest were mostly from Britain, Australia, and New Zealand, with a smattering of trainees from France, Czechoslovakia, Luxembourg, Norway, South Africa, the United States, and elsewhere.

The Canadian Department of Transport selected the various sites for the schools. The Department of Munitions and Supply provided the aircraft and engines from factories in Canada, the United States, and the UK. While the RCAF was directly responsible for the instructors and the overall training program, the twenty-six Canadian flying clubs in existence by 1939 turned their expertise to elementary flight. The pioneer airline companies were given the task of organizing and staffing the air observation schools.

Among thirty-six civilian-operated flying schools, one elementary flying training school (EFTS) and six air observation schools (AOSs) were operated on a non-profit basis by airlines taken over by Canadian Pacific. The EFTS was located at Cap de la Madeleine, Quebec, and was run by Canadian Airways Limited. Dominion Skyways operated two of the AOSs, at Malton, Ontario, and St. Johns, Quebec. Single flying schools were also operated by Wings Limited, in Winnipeg; Yukon Southern, in Portage la Prairie, Manitoba; Quebec Airways, in Quebec City; and Canadian Airways, in Edmonton.

Training manuals at the schools hoped to instill pride in the students who flocked to their airfields and build respect for their instructors:

You'll find men who flew and fought in the Great War, men who have traversed Canada's Northland when the only navigation aids were the seat of their pants and a piece of string tied to a strut; men who have grown up with aviation in all its hundred and one ramifications.

An Air Observer was a man of many functions, chief among which were to guide his aircraft to its objective, bomb the target, and return the aircraft safely home again. As the war progressed and these functions became more complex, the schools created two new categories of graduate: the air navigator and the air bomber. A typical AOS could have as many as five or six hundred pupils at any one time.

When Canadian Pacific Air Lines took over the operations of the schools it inherited, it created a new administrative structure with one of the pioneers of Canadian civilian air operations in charge. Charles Roy "Peter" Troup was appointed general supervisor, flying schools and aircraft

Graduates of No. 9 Air Observation School at Saint-Jean-sur-Richelieu, Quebec, managed by Canadian Pacific personnel, pose with one of their trainer aircraft before heading off for the front lines in Europe. AUTHOR'S COLLECTION

The two daily CPR trains in the area were rerouted onto a passing siding, after track gangs spiked the switches at either end to ensure no mishaps. Two local families turned their cottages over to the president's party, but with the temperature falling off considerably at night, Roosevelt found it more comfortable to sleep aboard his railway car. As a result, the ice in the boxcar CPR had brought to the site for air-conditioning instead found its way into the cocktail glasses of the presidential entourage.

While four uniformed and two plainclothes RCMP officers guarded both ends of the president's train twenty-four hours a day, US naval boats secured the waters around Birch Island and the neighbouring, much larger Manitoulin Island.

Armed naval personnel and seventeen RCMP officers on rotating duty patrolled the woods around the site continuously. During daylight hours, they also arranged for air reconnaissance to fly above the planned fishing sites. A Coast Guard cutter, USS *Wilmette*, sat offshore during the visit, and provided speedboats and motor launches for the security patrols and fishing parties. Twice daily, military planes flew mail in from Washington.

Though the president's train included a dynamo car, outfitted with a full array of transmitting and receiving equipment, CPR also had a full-time telegrapher on duty at Birch Island. During the week, Roosevelt's party sent out more than two dozen messages relayed from CPR's telegraph office in nearby Little Current.

A couple of local fishermen had brief encounters with the president's fishing party, one exchanging pleasantries with Roosevelt himself about the catch of the day. Few others were aware of the visit until the *Sudbury Star* ran a story, by which time the secret train and all of its occupants had returned to the United States. It was later reported the American leader had very much enjoyed his Canadian sojourn, during which time he had caught a fair number of black bass and pickerel. In addition to having fattened up on locally sourced blueberry pie, Roosevelt was said to have acquired a healthy tan while spending many pleasant hours on the gleaming waters of Lake Huron.

On the same day FDR's vacation appeared in the Canadian press, Churchill was arriving in Halifax with his wife and daughter in tow, a week ahead of the Quebec Conference. He, too, would rely on Canadian Pacific to handle the logistics of his visit to Canada that summer. CPR had assembled a private train for Churchill's exclusive use, consisting of a baggage car; the dining car Arbuthnot,

Churchill and his daughter Mary stand on the back platform of CPR business car Mount Stephen, which was assigned to the family for their exclusive use during the British prime minister's visit to Canada. The ever-present Detective Inspector Walter Thompson watches over them from behind. IMPERIAL WAR MUSEUM H31958

METALLIC CONNECTOR

sleeping car Summerland; and three private cars: Mount Royal, Mount Stephen, and Strathcona. The British prime minister, who was somewhat of a railway buff, made himself right at home.

"See here, Mary, this is my bedroom," Churchill said to his daughter, as he strode down the corridor in the Mount Royal, the same railway car on which he had toured the Dominion in 1929. Not only did the prime minister remember every detail of his former home on wheels of fourteen years earlier, he also greeted business car steward George Grant by name. CPR was ready to place the entire train at his disposal, and it had assigned his former railway friend to accompany him for the duration.

Before returning across the Atlantic, Churchill would make good use of the resource, journeying 4,572 miles in his special CPR train. About a third of that time was spent in Canada and the rest travelling to Washington, D.C., and Hyde Park, New York, for meetings with Roosevelt, in advance of the summit.

Among topics of more serious import, the British leader took the time to brag to his American counterpart about the luxurious train CPR had assembled for him. "I wish I had time to go see that," FDR had replied. Within days, both of the leaders of the free world would make for Quebec City in their secret trains for the start of the conference.

Their travel itineraries were worked out to the minute, in complete secrecy. None of the details related to their movements or destinations would appear in writing until after the war. The leaders' specials were given priority over all other trains. All stops and meets with other rail traffic were precisely planned.

The CPR train crews had been selected after careful consideration of their service records and personal backgrounds. Maintenance of way men went over the routes with a fine-toothed comb. Railway roadmasters and constables were posted at every bridge, culvert, and switch. Every inch of track and every level crossing was secured. Throughout the visits, the railway kept spare engines under steam at strategic points along the line, in case they were required to replace any of the locomotives assigned to the special movements.

Following the Quebec Conference, Roosevelt once again boarded his train to head home to Washington. Churchill, for his part, wanted one more adventure aboard his own private land cruiser. The British prime minister imposed upon CPR to extend his North American tour for an additional six days of fishing at Lac des Neiges, in Quebec's Montmorency Forest. He was later reported to have been quite adept at making long fly casts, and demonstrating dexterity moving about in a canoe. On this leg of his trip, he didn't just have his favourite business car steward with him; he had also managed to secure his favourite chef from the Chateau Frontenac, to boot. ⚜

VALENTINE GREETINGS FOR HITLER

T he veracity of a seventy-four-year-old's memory was confirmed in the summer of 1990, when a vintage Second World War tank was pulled from its swampy resting place by six straining tractors and two power winches—right where the elderly Ukrainian villager remembered it to have disappeared more than forty years earlier. On its builder's plate, in clear, bold letters, was the inscription:

VALENTINE VII-A, VICKERS ARMSTRONG DESIGN,
BUILT BY CANADIAN PACIFIC RAILWAY

The perfectly preserved fighting machine was one of 1,420 Valentine tanks manufactured by CPR from 1941 to 1943, all but thirty of which were shipped to the Soviet Union under a lend-lease agreement with the Canadian government. The railway's massive locomotive facility at its Montreal Angus Shops had been converted for this purpose at the request of the federal Department of Munitions and Supply to help re-arm the Red Army in the wake of Hitler's surprise invasion of the Russian industrial heartland and the subsequent loss of vast numbers of Soviet military weapons and vehicles.

On January 25, 1944, during a day of intense fighting near the village of Telepino, about 112 miles south of Kiev, Valentine tank No. 838 had been involved in the long counter-offensive that would ultimately doom the German Wehrmacht in Eastern Europe. The 57th Regiment of the Soviet 5th Guards Tank Army had suffered immense destruction of both men and machinery during the decisive Battle of Kursk in the summer of 1943, but the Red Army had turned the tide in its war against Nazi Germany. The added loss of tank 838, while the Soviets pursued the retreating Germans across a partly frozen, swampy river the following winter, would be a relatively small one for the 57th, but one that would remain etched in the consciousness of the villager who witnessed the Valentine's demise.

All three of the tank's crewmembers escaped before it submerged.

Forty-six years later, after the armoured vehicle had been wrenched from its internment seven metres below the surface of the bog, two CPR pensioners were on hand for the unveiling of a

Shop workers who normally built steam locomotives quickly
turned their skills to the business of manufacturing war
machines. AUTHOR'S COLLECTION

perfectly preserved Valentine tank. At the invitation of the Ukrainian government, Jack Sharpley (77), who had been a draftsman in the Angus Shops tank department, and Andre St. Pierre (67), a former CPR machine apprentice on the wartime assembly line, made the trip in the company of CPR assistant chief mechanical officer Andre Langlois. When the rescued tank had been subjected to close inspection, all of its lubricants were found to be intact and its fuel clean—a testament to the solidity of its design and the expertise of its builders.

The Valentine was a modest fighting machine, overshadowed early in the Second World War by the larger, more heavily armoured tanks fielded by both the Allied and Axis powers. However, the relative ease of the tank's manufacture and the performance of the Valentine on the battlefield in the early stages of the war helped the Red Army survive its darkest hour.

The tank's name is said to have originated from the date its developers presented preliminary drawings to the British War Office: February 14, 1940. CPR's professional, experienced engineering staff made a number of design changes to the vehicle's Vickers-Armstrong engineering, notably the one-piece casting of its turrets and noses, a technique that was later widely adopted by other tank manufacturers.

Valentine tank No. 838 was presented to the Canadian War Museum in 1992. Surrounded by museum officials and members of the Canadian-Ukrainian community, CPR chief mechanical officer George Bartley thanked Ambassador, His Excellency Lecko Loukinecko for his country's gift and spoke about the role Canadians and CPR had played in the sturdy little tank's construction.

"This was an adventurous risk," he said, "because Canadians were untried in the logistics and manufacture of so complicated a product in such quantities with such short notice."

The initial order for three hundred tanks had been a desperate plea from a besieged British government following the disaster at Dunkirk, as well as a vote of confidence in CPR from a Canadian government anxious to do its bit for the Allied war effort. Production and supply efficiencies overseen by the railway allowed Valentines to take the field forty-five minutes after landing at a port in the Soviet Union, complete with fuel supply, spare parts, and full operating and maintenance instructions in Russian. On completion of the contract, Major-General I.A. Elyaev, chairman of the Soviet Government Purchasing Commission in the United States, wired H.B. Bowen, chief of motive power and rolling stock for CPR: "Congratulations to you and to all your associates and employees on the occasion of fulfillment of your plan of tank production."

Apart from their service in the Soviet Union, Canadian tanks, particularly the Valentine VII, showed good results in combat action near the Town of Bou Arada in Tunisia. The Supply Ministry in London commented that the tracks and steering gear on the Valentines stood up splendidly on hard ground and in extreme weather conditions. And the judgment of our ally on the Eastern Front was unequivocal: "After proof in battle, we consider the Canadian-built Valentine tank the best tank we have received from any of our allies." This from no less an authority than the Soviet general in charge of procurement in North America. ⚓

The sturdy little tanks would soon see action in the Soviet Union, as the Red Army struggled to turn back the onslaught of Hitler's rampaging Panzer divisions.
AUTHOR'S COLLECTION

4

URBAN CASTLES AND RUSTIC RESORTS

THE FIRST CPR HOTELS—MODEST CHALETS LOCATED BESIDE the tracks at Field, Glacier, and North Bend, in British Columbia—served the company's immediate need to accommodate railway workers between shifts, while providing a venue for feeding railway passengers, thereby eliminating the need to haul heavy, expensive dining cars through the mountains. Attracting tourists to view Canada's scenic wonders and linger to enjoy the country's wilderness playgrounds would come with time.

As the railway's public relations men developed a sophisticated strategy for keeping all of the tourist dollars in house, Canadian Pacific built substantial mountain hostelries and rounded out its holiday and sporting offerings with a network of bungalow camps, tea houses, and riding paths to suit the travelling public, from serious mountaineers to more casual hikers, nature lovers, and camera bugs. Fishing gear, trail guides, and horse were optional.

The cityscapes in all of the nation's major centres would also be subject to the lofty ambitions of Canadian Pacific planners, and the emerging urban chateau style favoured by CPR architects.

At one end of the rail line, taking an afternoon cup of tea in Victoria's Empress Hotel would epitomize Canada's connections to the old country, and at the other end, disembarking from a CP steamship below Quebec City's Chateau Frontenac would give visitors a lasting impression of the country's majesty.

Travellers around the world seeing pictures of the great Canadian Pacific landmark hotels in Montreal, Toronto, Winnipeg, Regina, Calgary, and Vancouver—in travel brochures, in newsreels, or in person—would come to view those impressive edifices as synonymous with the country itself.

THE MIRACULOUS WATERS OF CALEDONIA

Canada has grown with the value of its natural resources. Oil, gas and coal, timber and wood products, zinc, uranium, gold, nickel, and aluminum have fuelled industries around the globe. The country's prodigious output of agricultural products—wheat, barley, corn, and canola, as well as the enormous quantities of potash used for fertilizer, has helped to feed the world. Ultimately, though, the most valuable natural resource of all may prove to be Canada's abundant supply of water, as drought, human activity, and pollution make untainted supplies ever scarcer.

Long before Canada's fresh water became such a highly valued commodity, Canada—and CPR—were finding ready markets for what were believed to be the medicinal waters to be found in the village of Caledonia Springs, about five miles from the Ottawa River, in Ontario's Prescott County. Between 1835 and 1915, the country's most important spa was located in Caledonia Springs. Tourists and health enthusiasts came by the thousands to "take the waters," internally and externally. In its heyday, Canadian Pacific was the proprietor.

There were three natural springs in the area. One that was carbonated by hydrogen gas came to be known as the Gas Spring, another with heavy salt content became the Saline Spring, and a third was dubbed the White Sulphur Spring. Early on, water from the Gas Spring was sold to the public mostly for refreshment, under the brand names Caledonia Water and Caledonia Seltzer. The Sulphur Springs were said to do wonders for the relief of rheumatic and other ailments, while the waters from the Saline Springs were credited with restoring the health of many of the afflicted during the terrible cholera epidemic of 1836–37.

Tradition has it that the springs were already well known to the local Indigenous People when a newly arrived settler "discovered" them in the early 1800s. This man has been identified in some sources as a deer hunter named Kellogg. Others have suggested, more specifically, that he was beaver trapper Alexander Grant. In either case, the intrepid settler is said to have come across the waters by chance and became convinced of their curative qualities. The site soon had a small shanty on it and was attracting the sick and invalid for miles around.

By 1838, the popularity of what had by then become a full-blown spa had encouraged others to build a post office, church, schoolhouse, and several stores nearby. It would soon have a large hotel. At this point, the township of Caledonia Springs had a population of about six hundred.

Around the same time, an eminent New York physician and chemist, Dr. James R. Chilton, published a full report on the efficacy of the springs' therapeutic qualities.

The water, although unpleasant to the taste, is extremely bracing, and in much request. The most extraordinary cures which have been performed have been in the cases of rheumatism, diseases of the liver, dropsy, dyspepsia, scrofulous affections of every description [tuberculosis], fever and ague, jaundice, etc.

He also mentioned that the "superhuman cures" in cases of syphilis "cannot be too forcibly impressed upon the public."

In an 1843 edition of the village newspaper *Life of the Springs*, a writer described the less aquatic goings-on in the Caledonia Springs Hotel:

Here, every visitor can enjoy his own peculiar taste, independent of the most social and agreeable conversation . . . There is in the ladies drawing room a good piano, and violin music, accompanied by the most delightful singing.

In 1874, two new partners acquired the property around the springs, renovated and refurbished the existing accommodations, and reopened the main building as the Grand Hotel. Two outstanding features of the Victorian-style hostelry were the new billiard room and a miniature steam-powered train, which gave rides around the site to the Grand's clientele.

The spa and resort also included a more elaborate bottling plant that marketed Magi Water, a beverage said to "exercise a most beneficial influence." A seltzer, named Duncan Water, after one of the early proprietors of the springs, took top prize in its category at the 1893 Chicago World's Fair. The spa's most popular product, Adanac Dry Ginger Ale, which the company claimed to be both "sparkling" and "healthful," got its name from spelling Canada backwards.

The product Dr. Chilton a half century earlier had deemed "unpleasant to the taste" had been miraculously transformed into something a thirsty public found quite palatable.

Before the CPR was built through Caledonia Springs in 1898, tourists came by rail only as far as Calumet. There they crossed the Ottawa River by ferry, to a dock just outside the little Quebec village of L'Orignal and travelled the rest of the way to the resort by horse and buggy.

Presumably, somebody at the railway company took notice of the untapped potential of the springs as, less than a decade after the railway arrived in town, CPR bought the Grand Hotel,

The elaborate, gingerbread-encrusted hostelry at Caledonia Springs joined Canadian Pacific's hotel chain alongside the more well-known city landmarks and mountain resorts. AUTHOR'S COLLECTION

the bottling plant, and the entire surrounding property. Reverting to its old name, the Caledonia Springs Hotel became a new Eastern link in the railway's transcontinental hotel chain.

The hotel and spa prospered under CPR management. A tennis court and full-size gymnasium were added to the attractions, and one of Canada's first golf courses was opened on an adjoining property.

But the First World War, and the growing inclination of people to favour pills over mineral water to treat their various ailments, led to declining profits at Caledonia Springs. The railway closed the hotel's doors for the last time in 1915, salvaging many of the fixtures and ornate furnishings for use in other CPR hotels.

Canadian Pacific did, however, maintain a financial interest in the bottling plant and its products. Prohibition, which gained most of its public support during the 1920s, was a godsend to the soft drink market. In Canada, the sale of alcohol was never totally outlawed the way it was in the United States, but there were enough provincial restrictions in place to inhibit its wide consumption. Quebec

The many refreshing beverages bottled by the Caledonia Springs Company were particularly appreciated during the years of Prohibition, though restrictions on alcohol were much more lenient in Canada than they were south of the border.
AUTHOR'S COLLECTION

was the only jurisdiction to reject prohibition entirely.

At a CPR conference and banquet, in 1919, one of the speakers joked about how the company had become a good friend of the temperance movement with its foray into the soda pop business:

When the people were deprived of their seductive scotch and soda, and the merry-making martini and Manhattan, and the genial gin fizzes were banished into utter oblivion, the CPR would timely come to the rescue. And though there might be no mornings after the night before, there would be the rare vintages of Magi Water, the effervescing Adanac Ginger Ale, the delectable cream soda—the delight of the hardened drinker—sparkling Cola Champagne, whatever that might be, to assuage the imperishable thirst, and to revive one's drooping spirits, and these with a bumper or two of that justly celebrated and far-famed Duncan water, would make every day a Sunday in the sweet bye and bye.

In 1927, CPR sold the bottling company to J.J. McLaughlin Limited, licensing the new owners to use the Adanac trademark a few years later, and relinquished complete control to the pioneer soft drink company on February 29, 1940. McLaughlin flipped the letters of the popular brand and took its product to the world under a new corporate name: The Canada Dry Ginger Ale Company. ⁺

CROSSROADS OF EMPIRE

The Canadian Pacific Railway opened the doors of its first Vancouver hotel on May 16, 1887, the same year the railway was extended from Port Moody to a new Pacific terminus on English Bay. From all reports, it was a bit of a workaday affair, the hotel being described in one contemporary newspaper as "a glorified farmhouse." Nevertheless, it was an imposing structure, located on the bluff at the corner of Georgia and Granville. A new and essential centre of activity, it would continue the westward shift of the town's social and commercial life, away from Water Street and Gastown, where most of the citizenry still resided.

The railway company had selected the site, in part, for very practical reasons. As they approached the inner harbour, vessels sailing for the CPR docks sighted natural features on the bluff to judge when to make a necessary turn in deep water. The ships' officers were able to use the hotel as a prominent, added marker to ease navigation.

Across the street, in front of the hotel was the CPR Park, complete with bandstand, croquet lawns, and wooden tennis courts. The grounds proved a valuable asset for hotel guests, who could view the goings-on on the sports fields and enjoy the strains of the military bands that played in the evenings. On Dominion Day 1900, it served as a campsite for a visiting army regiment from Victoria. On another occasion, it was used to dry a large quantity of tea salvaged from a sunken steamship.

Vancouver grew rapidly. Soon the Hotel Vancouver was extended along Granville Street. Within ten years, Francis Rattenbury, the renowned architect of the British Columbia Parliament Buildings and CPR's Empress Hotel, had added a major new wing to what would become Vancouver's most popular corner at which to meet and socialize. The veranda in front of the expanded hotel proved to be a very popular spot for the locals to enjoy a beverage or two, while placing bets on the horseraces that raised the dust on Howe Street. And in quieter moments, the socialites could listen to the melodious sounds emanating from the bandstand across Georgia.

In 1910, the architect Walter Paynter added yet another wing along Howe Street. He also built a separate annex beside it, at the corner of Robson. A passage was constructed across the lane to connect the two sections of the hotel, but it was removed in 1918 when the annex was sold to new owners and rebranded as the York Hotel.

CPR's landmark hotel in Vancouver was for many years among the city's most fashionable social centres. IMAGE C-06508 COURTESY OF THE ROYAL BC MUSEUM AND ARCHIVES

Within another two years, the city had grown sufficiently to render this piecemeal approach redundant. The original structure was razed, along with the subsequent additions.

Six million dollars later, Vancouver's most storied and prestigious hostelry stood at what trade publications of the day described, in laudatory terms, as the "Crossroads of Empire." Encompassing the entire block bounded by Granville, Georgia, and Howe, the new and spacious railway hotel incorporated a grocery, butcher shop, poultry store, fish shop, bakery, and huge kitchens with what was said to be "the biggest cooking range in the world." It had its own power plant to keep the whole thing humming.

The new landmark hotel had 560 rooms, all but 100 with private baths, requiring a staff of 520 to meet the needs of the more than 115,000 guests who walked through the doors every year. The kitchen staff served an annual half million meals to keep its clients sated.

Celebrities such as Will Rogers, John Barrymore, Sarah Bernhardt, Edgar Rice Burroughs, Mary Pickford, and Douglas Fairbanks strolled the hotel's hallways and grounds, keeping the gossip columnists busy. Sir Rudyard Kipling, in the midst of a well-publicized tour of British possessions, was reported to have been regaled by a drunken fan at the hotel's front door with a spirited recitation of "Gunga Din."

The Prince of Wales—later to be crowned Edward VIII, if only briefly—sent many hearts aflutter on his frequent visits to the famed Rooftop Garden, where local bigwigs rubbed shoulders with visiting notables. Winston Churchill once gave one of his cigars to the doorman.

The second Hotel Vancouver was noted for its afternoon teas, its supper dances, and its epic New Year's Eve parties. But like its predecessor, the grand old dame fell out of favour with the travelling public, as new, more modern, more fashionable hostelries arose throughout the city. On May 17, 1939, the Vancouver Board of Trade hosted a farewell luncheon, before the hotel doors were closed to business.

A mere eight days later, a third Hotel Vancouver, jointly owned and operated by Canadian Pacific and Canadian National, welcomed its first guests. Rising one block west of where its forerunner still stood, the replacement hotel was, in part, a fulfillment of a promise made by Canadian Northern Railway builders, Mackenzie and Mann. The *other* transcontinental railway, the Canadian

The tramway ferried both passengers and baggage from the railway station at Laggan (later Lake Louise) to the famous hotel in Banff National Park, below Victoria Glacier. PHOTO BY BYRON HARMON, WHYTE MUSEUM OF THE CANADIAN ROCKIES, BYRON HARMON FONDS V263/NA-4864

the two gasoline-powered, open-sided, twenty-eight-foot vehicles with automobile engines and transmissions were designed to transport up to thirty-five passengers at a time from station to hotel. Two other cars were intended to carry the baggage in tow.

The railway had built a 42-inch gauge piece of track at Montreal's Angus Shops to test the vehicles, as opposed to the usual track width of 56.5 inches on which the vast majority of North American trains and transit cars operated. The six-cylinder touring automobile engines with which they were fitted were expected to generate sixty horsepower to propel the tramcars up the 4 percent grade, and over the 3.61 miles from the trackside turntable at Lake Louise to the covered platform and loop on the hotel grounds 1,000 feet above. The tramcars groaned and struggled with their mountain duties that first year but were made equal to the task when their underpowered engines were replaced with sixty-six-horsepower Pierce-Arrow motors the following year. Shortly after, one of the baggage cars was converted to passenger use to meet the increased demand.

Chateau Lake Louise suffered a devastating fire in 1924, which destroyed most of the older wooden structure. For the next two years, Winnipeg contractor Carter, Hall & Aldinger used a small donkey engine (a steam-powered winch typically used in logging) and several flatcars to bring construction materials from the railway to the lakefront, where the imposing Chateau we know today arose in all its grandeur.

At the same time, two new, larger, close-sided tramcars were built at Angus to complement the hotel's more modern appearance and accommodate a growing number of guests. Equipped with 150-horsepower Sterling Seabull engines, the sleek and shiny vehicles could each seat forty-three passengers comfortably, though on one occasion sixty-eight persons and their luggage were squeezed onto a single car.

The Lake Louise Tramway—as the cars were lettered in latter years—operated continuously during the hotel's operating months, during the summer seasons from May to September, until 1930. During that time, the agent at the CPR station used the telephone link to inform the hotel staff of the imminent arrival of up to thirty parties of guests each day. ⚜

SWISS CHEESE IN THE CANADIAN ROCKIES

Canadian Pacific's legendary builder, William Cornelius Van Horne, famously said: "If we can't export the scenery, we'll import the tourists."

One of the strategies he employed to keep them coming was to lay claim to the most prominent and majestic features of the Canadian West—what he and the CPR would characterize in publicity campaigns as the Canadian Pacific Rockies. Exaggerated artistic renderings, hyperbolic promotional musings and the catchphrase "Fifty Switzerlands in One" would soon propel the company's propaganda machine in a direction even P.T. Barnum would have been proud of.

When famed American mountaineer Philip Stanley Abbot fell to his death on Mount Lefroy in the summer of 1896, there had been calls from many quarters to ban climbing in the Rocky and Selkirk Mountains. But CPR was not about to lose one of its more compelling attractions. Before the decade was out, Canadian Pacific brought two professional Swiss guides, Edouard Feuz and Christian Hasler, to work at the company's mountain hotel at Glacier House in Rogers Pass. During the next fifty years, a virtual parade of guides would be imported from Switzerland, mostly from the Interlaken District, to teach safe climbing techniques to thousands of CPR hotel guests and others.

All of the travel arrangements for the guides were handled by Archer Baker, CPR's European manager, who garnered some addition publicity by having the hired mountaineers pose for photographers in full climbing gear on the roof of the company's Trafalgar Square offices in London. By the time the guides arrived in Montreal, the stunt had been refined to include a staged demonstration at a local quarry, the actors decked out in the appropriate occupational ties and hats, with distinctive pipes and alpenstocks in hand. After the men were ensconced in their CPR mountain retreats, they were expected to show up in full regalia to schmooze with railway passengers at the CPR stations.

Most of the guides who came to Canada in the first few years were well known in Europe and the United States for their expertise and accomplishments. Even the great English climber and conqueror of the Matterhorn, Edward Whymper, was recruited by CPR for the advertising campaign, despite the fact that he made few actual climbs in Canada and was looked down upon by his Swiss counterparts as nothing more than an overbearing and overrated drunk.

The ersatz Swiss village of Edelweiss, built on a hillside above the town of Golden, BC, was thoroughly impractical—but it looked good for the tourists. GLENBOW ARCHIVES, ARCHIVES AND SPECIAL COLLECTIONS, UNIVERSITY OF CALGARY NA-3799-4

At Field, the guides were asked to take care of a big, black bear that was kept on a chain in the village to amuse the tourists. They had soon taken it upon themselves to add a friendlier mascot to their growing entourage. Hasler somehow convinced Feuz's son, Edouard Jr., to dress all in white, lie under the body of a female goat he had shot, and grab the mother's baby when it came to feed. They proceeded to give the captured prize a bath, fed and brushed her, and put a ribbon in the curls on her head. When the transcontinental trains rolled in, the prissy mountain goat joined the alpine circus on the station platform, leading to many a discussion about all of the animals to be found in the mountain playground.

One day, a tourist from Philadelphia took a particular liking to the shaggy, four-legged ambassador, insisting that the city park in his hometown could really use a goat of its own. The guides were soon splitting the sale's fee of $500 between them and congratulated themselves, no doubt, on their business acumen.

By 1909, Canadian Pacific was bringing several guides to its hotels in Lake Louise, Field, and Glacier each year for the climbing season, which corresponded with the months the mountain hotels stayed open for business, between early May and the end of September. In light of the considerable costs involved in transporting the guides back and forth to Switzerland, as well as arranging food and board while the men were in Canada, CPR passenger manager R.A. Kerr was spurred to propose a possible solution that would bring even more attention to the railway's colourful promotional campaign.

The company should build a colony, or village, not farther west than Revelstoke, in British Columbia, Kerr advised CPR land manager J.S. Dennis. It would be "built after the plan of the little Swiss cottages in the Alps" and would allow the guides to raise chickens and goats, provide them with vegetables, and possibly even inspire them to grow flowers for the railway's dining cars. They might, Karr suggested, call the village Edelweiss.

Two years later, Canadian Pacific began to implement the plan on a hillside at Golden, BC, reasonably close to Field and Lake Louise, and offering easy access to the Columbia Icefields. The location would also allow the village to be seen by CPR passengers from the local railway station. The initial plan called for half a dozen six-room chalets to be built on the slope of the hill, with several ten-acre ready-made farms established at the base of the property. Edelweiss was about to become a reality, of sorts.

Getting the guides to live there was another matter entirely.

CPR's contract with the men stipulated that each would receive a cow, two sows, ten Plymouth Rock hens, and a rooster. The men would have to be married to take up residence in one of the chalets, and they could be dismissed at any time for drunkenness or disobedience (presumably to their CPR bosses and not to their wives).

When they arrived in Golden in the spring of 1912, they were dismayed to find the buildings still under construction, and the front entrances difficult for their families to access, being precariously perched at the top of lengthy staircases. The signs above the front doors of the brightly painted homes read *Lebe Wohl* (farewell) rather than *Willkommen* (welcome), as had been intended. This misstep may have contributed to the guides' misgivings.

The six chalets built by George Stanley Rees of Wilson & Rees, Calgary, were a North American's ersatz vision of what a Swiss chalet should look like. They had multiple storeys, large balconies, and gingerbread trim, and were resplendent with Union Jacks and Swiss flags flying above them. More discerning eyes would deem them to be "unlike the size, pitch, and construction" of the authentic item overseas.

Four of the guides—Edouard Feuz, Ernest Feuz, Christian Hasler, and Rudolph Aemmer—each occupied one of the chalets with their families that first season. They were asked to help the company find Swiss colonists to settle on the farms below.

Several of the guides would cycle through the unwieldy village over the next few decades. The land at the base of the hill would eventually be sold to local residents. Edouard Feuz Sr.—one of the original CPR mountaineers—would refuse to have anything to do with Edelweiss. He soon moved back to Switzerland for good, leaving his son to manage the group's future relationship with CPR. Ultimately, Canadian Pacific sold the entire village and the land on which it sat to the youngest Feuz brother, Walter.

Still, the rather bizarre saga had yet to run its course. During the 1920s, three of the Swiss guides—Rudolph Aemmer, Edmond Petrig, and Bruno Engler—took their careers as photogenic CPR salesmen to a whole new level, with short stints as Hollywood movie stuntmen. On leave from the railway, Rudolph appeared on the silver screen in the film *Eternal Love*, as a double for film star John Barrymore. Aemmer had a good time hamming it up with the actor for promotional shots and garnering even more publicity for his team of intrepid mountain guides.

Swiss guides Edward Feuz and Christian Hasler pose for a publicity shot in full mountain climbing regalia.
GLENBOW ARCHIVES, ARCHIVES AND SPECIAL COLLECTIONS, UNIVERSITY OF CALGARY NA-841-153

Despite CPR's somewhat hackneyed and exploitative promotional initiatives, the Swiss guides made an enormous contribution to the sport of mountaineering in Canada. Among other achievements, the men led numerous teams of climbers, professional and amateur alike, on more than 250 first ascents in the Rocky and Selkirk Mountains, safely and memorably, right up until the end of their employment with CPR in 1954. The legacy of their long, successful careers and, indeed, the ongoing efforts of their Canadian descendants, helped Canada to develop modern mountain rescue, professional avalanche control, and accessible heli-skiing.

In later years Edouard Feuz Jr. recalled:

Up to the beginning of the thirties, there were days when I went shine, or rain or anything, climbing for two months steady every day in the summer season. Every guided party that left Glacier House was issued a bottle of wine per client, a pleasant and rewarding custom that may have been helpful in gaining repeat customers.

Over the years, the guides had posed for thousands of campy photographs with CPR guests and broke open innumerable picnic lunches supplied by the railway's hotel kitchen staff. And what goes better with cheese than wine, eh? ✧

FOUR ENGLISH WOMEN FISH FOR TOURISTS

n the late nineteenth century, Canadian Pacific took full advantage of the latest fashion in tourism, marrying the exploitation of the wilderness vistas provided by the new rail line with a more genteel version of the frontier experience.

To set the scene, railway builder and general manager William Van Horne had sketched a design for a charming log station to be built at Banff, in Rocky Mountains National Park (now Banff National Park), the first such preserve in the country. Other rustic log stations were also constructed by the promoters of the new transcontinental at Laggan (now Lake Louise), Field, and Glacier.

In keeping with the frontier theme, CPR also built a small log chalet on the shores of Lake Louise, in 1901, and two years later erected a larger square-log structure at Emerald Lake. Around the same time, the Northern Pacific Railroad in the United States was pursuing a similar strategy by constructing the Old Faithful Inn in Yellowstone Park. It, too, combined rustic charm with contemporary comfort.

Meanwhile, CPR's publicity men were hiring local cowboys and trackers to cut a network of bridle trails through the bush, connecting their growing chain of tourist hotels with various relatively unknown local lakes and unconquered mountains. The new trails offered the railway's patrons opportunities to explore the backcountry by foot or on horseback, in the company of old-style mountain men. Visitors would be among the first to ascend the spectacular peaks that dominated the landscape, under the guidance of archetypal mountain guides from Switzerland, imported by the CPR for that express purpose.

In the early years before the First World War, men such as Tom Wilson, who held the title of official CPR guide, would often overnight with groups of railway travellers at scenic locations in the mountains that the outdoorsmen had themselves discovered, and to which they had recently opened access for the new breed of wilderness tourist.

Many of these wilderness locations would begin as seasonal tent camps, occasionally warranting the construction of a small teahouse to offer trail riders and hikers the most basic shelter and a bit of refreshment in the bush. In later years, CPR developed some of the more pristine spots into full-time bungalow camps for the burgeoning number of vacationers looking for a rustic getaway. Leading the trend toward permanence in the wilds of the Canadian Rockies was an improbable partnership of four Englishwomen with a well-honed sense of adventure.

Eileen Strick had, by her own account, done a great deal of camping in Wales, before coming to Western Canada in 1913 with her companions, Barbara Dodds and Marjorie Danks. According to Miss Strick at the time:

> When we came to [Lake] Louise and took the drive out here [to Moraine Lake], the idea of a camp came into our minds. For we saw an opportunity of running one to meet a pressing need. Scores of visitors came daily from [Lake] Louise to see Lake Moraine and the Ten Peaks, and it seemed a good idea to establish a camp to cater to them.

The official name of the attraction they established was the Moraine Lake Fishing Camp, about nine miles from what by then was being referred to as the CPR's Lake Louise Hotel. The camp catered mostly to those who found the company's more traditional hostelry prevented them from being on the water in the early morning or in the evening, when the fish were most likely to bite.

The railway had already built a rough teahouse at Moraine Lake the previous year, which gave the women a venue from which to offer lunch for sixty-five cents per person, and tea for $0.50. The rate for a full day at their camp, with tent accommodation and refreshments, was $2.50. The enterprising women also rented out fishing rods, tackle, and rubber boots.

Within the year, they were joined by a fourth Englishwoman, Miss Marie Benet, who helped with the cooking, washing, and general maintenance of the camp.

For the railway's part, Hayter Reed, CPR's manager in chief for hotels, authorized Miss Strick and her associates to draw upon the Lake Louise Hotel for provisions at cost and loaned them several tents to live in and rent out.

"Of course," wrote Miss Strick in the camp's first advertising pamphlet, "visitors must not expect electric light and such modern conveniences, but we do everything to make our

The camp's canvas accommodations soon gave way to more substantial log cabins. WHYTE MUSEUM OF THE CANADIAN ROCKIES, V653/NA-1199

guests comfortable in the camp . . . The CPR have been most kind to us, and have helped us in every way."

In 1922 and 1923, the CPR erected several sleeping cabins at Moraine Lake, creating one of the first of a string of bungalow camps the railway would build in the mountains during the postwar tourist boom, along with a new, enlarged teahouse at the same location. The original pioneering fishing enterprise had become a thing of the past: but two of the four adventurous Englishwomen who had started the business stayed on as the new attraction's first managers. ⊹

A NOSE FOR WINNIPEG GOLDEYE

For those who travelled long-distance on the CPR, part of the allure was the siren song of the dinner bell and the opportunity to visit the dining car. The delicate rose bowl floating on a whiter-than-white linen tablecloth, the impeccably laid out Limoges plates and mono-grammed silverware, the finger bowl with fragrant lemon-water with which to freshen up before coffee and dessert, all conspired to create an atmosphere of elegance and refinement.

Generally, the meals themselves consisted of standard fare—hardy, nutritious, and tasty enough, though somewhat restricted in their variety by the limited storage, refrigeration, and cooking space available in these rolling restaurants. However, when opportunity presented itself, there were exceptions to this rule, and seasoned travellers soon learned what special dishes to request.

Regular members of the railway kitchen staff were keenly aware which parts of the country were likely to provide particular meats, vegetables, and fruits, depending on the time of year. Accordingly, they would often make arrangements for local delicacies to be delivered trackside, coinciding with the arrival of the passenger trains.

One of these specialty items was Winnipeg goldeye, a prairie treat that was long a favourite with Canadian and American sportsmen in the know. Its reputation had grown over the years, fuelled by the enthusiasm of those who encountered this species of fish in the course of their travels.

Some of the goldeye's early chroniclers had initially been less than enthusiastic. In the late nineteenth century, renowned artist Paul Kane stopped sketching his North American subjects long enough to pen a few derogatory words in his diary about the storied fish.

"The goldeye is a peculiar species of fish," he commented, "like the herring, though larger, thicker, and not worth catching."

Not a ringing endorsement, nor one that was likely to land goldeye on CPR dining car tables any time soon, particularly when coupled with the assessment of Kane's travelling companions that "they eat like mud."

Unfortunately for Kane, he had not been aware of the hidden properties of the fish that could be brought out by smoking one's catch over a willow-wood fire, a procedure routinely practiced by local Cree. The smoking imparted a reddish gold colour to the goldeye and gave the fish the delicious flavour that could only be achieved in this manner.

The railway offered local delicacies such as Winnipeg goldeye in its hotel dining rooms and aboard its transcontinental trains as they traversed the country. AUTHOR'S COLLECTION

Before 1900, it was not uncommon to find goldeye on the market for a cent a pound, or less. Its main commercial uses were as dog food and fertilizer.

Tradition has it that a certain Mr. Bendit of Gimli, Manitoba, learned of the Cree cooking method in his backyard smokehouse. The rest is culinary history.

As people began to smoke the previously maligned fish before eating it, the fame of goldeye spread throughout Canada and the United States. Robert Firth, an immigrant to Winnipeg from Hull, England, is credited with making goldeye commercially available on a regular basis. Though supplies were limited, one could always obtain some in the area around Winnipeg and, of course, on the transcontinental passenger trains that ran through the so-called Gateway to the West.

By 1910, despite Kane's negative evaluation, goldeye had become a fashionable gourmet dish, espoused by such luminaries as Woodrow Wilson and the Prince of Wales. Sportsmen actively sought to increase their catch, and fishmongers were eager to sell it.

In its natural habitat, goldeye varied in colour from dark blue to blue-green, with silvery sides and white underbelly. Invariably, however, the irises of its eyes were yellow to gold—which, of course, is how the fish got its name.

At first, the entire catch came from Lake Winnipeg and the river and streams that fed into it, but soon Lake Winnipegosis was yielding a fair amount of goldeye, as well. Eventually the industry discovered goldeye in Lake Manitoba, Red Lake, and Lake Athabasca. Even Quebec's Lake Temiskaming gave up a few goldeye, although the quantities were small. Unexpectedly, some of the meatiest and most edible catches in Manitoba were pulled from the Saskatchewan River and the adjoining Carrot River.

The 1920s were the peak years for goldeye consumption. In both 1926 and 1929, more than a million pounds were marketed. The yield tapered off after that. Rarely was there a sufficient supply for export, although a few enterprising Americans managed to bring home their catch to appreciative diners in the US.

Not surprisingly, goldeye became a staple at CPR's Royal Alexandra Hotel in Winnipeg. Lucien Shickele, many years after serving as a chef in the Alex, could still remember his introduction to the local fish:

As I opened the Hotel Royal Alexandra, in 1906, I made out my a la carte menus. Having done so, I met with the manager of the Winnipeg Fish Company to find out what sort of different fish he had for the bill-of-fares. So he showed me, among other fish, the goldeye. And so I asked him then to smoke me some, which he did very satisfactorily; hence I called it the smoked Winnipeg Goldeye, as then they were only obtainable from Lake Winnipeg.

Soon there was a shortage of willow for smoking large quantities of fish, so oak and maple were often substituted with the same fine results as to flavour, though the appealing reddish colour could not be achieved. (A little red aniline dye solved that problem.)

The association of this singular fish with Winnipeg was cemented in the 1950s, when the local minor league baseball team was named the Goldeyes. A modern team, resurrected in 1993, still plays under that name. For his part, Shickele attested to the goldeye's growth in popularity, in the kitchen as well as on the ball diamond, in a way that was certainly understated: "I may say as time went on during my thirty-four years of service, the demand for them increased."

And that's no fish story. ✤

LITTLE CABINS IN THE WOODS

Before the First World War, CPR had very little competition for tourist business in the Canadian wilderness, particularly in the national parks where automobiles were largely banned from operating. Shortly after the end of the hostilities, however, that monopoly was increasingly threatened by the growing network of roadways and the competitive pressures from newly formed Canadian National Railway and that company's ambitions to create a resort system to rival that of the first transcontinental.

In 1911, the Dominion government had erected a small lodge of unpeeled logs at Lake O'Hara, BC, southwest of the CPR station at Hector, Alberta. The builders were local men, Fred Pepper and Bert McCorkle. In 1920, CPR erected a second, larger building nearby, with materials brought to the site by Claude Brewster. Around the new cabin, the railway hired workers to put up a cluster of basic, canvas-roofed structures for hikers and trail riders to camp overnight. The next year, CPR hired local men to begin building small clusters of proper log cabins at Lake O'Hara and at Lake Windermere, farther to the south. The era of the tourist bungalow camp had begun.

Bungalow camps were a logical extension of the railway's strategy for developing the tourist potential of the region, which earlier had seen CPR set up tent camps along the rough trails that had been cut through the bush around and between the company's various stations and resorts in the mountains.

Two men, in particular, embraced the camp concept: John Murray Gibbon, the railway's chief publicity man; and Basil Gardom, its superintendent of construction for western hotels. For Gibbon, the little cabins in the woods were just one more lure for the growing numbers of mountaineers, hikers, and trail riders he was bringing into CPR's vacation playgrounds. For Gardom, the quaint and comfortable groups of lodgings were a challenge for his engineering expertise that would require all of the logs, stones, cut lumber, doors, and windows to be either judiciously acquired on site or packed into the remote areas by packhorse.

"Behind the Bungalow Camp idea is an impelling thought," CPR publicists wrote in the company's 1923 advertising brochure, *Bungalow Camps in Canada*, "that of taking men and women close to the real heart of nature and providing for them at modest cost physical and mental recreation amid beautiful scenery, not otherwise so easily accessible."

Company brochures emphasized creature comforts along with rustic charm. CRHA/EXPORAIL CANADIAN PACIFIC RAILWAY FONDS P170-5955

CN followed basically the same formula as CPR for a network of rustic getaways, beginning with the establishment of a bungalow camp at Lac Beauvert, three miles outside the Jasper, Alberta, town site, where they also built the renowned Jasper Park Lodge.

All of the buildings at the CPR camps were one-storey bungalows of a rustic design and built of wood or log construction. At the centre of each group of cabins was a community building, which typically included a large, stone fireplace and an open wraparound veranda. The camps were much less formal than CPR's large resort hotels and were preferred by vacationers who wanted to stay in a quiet location where old clothes were perfectly acceptable at all times.

With customer rates not much more than $5.50 a day, or $35 a week, the camps were "leased at a seasonal rental to reliable, capable and responsible persons," CPR promotional materials maintained, "who operate them under the general supervision of the Company."

During the 1920s, CPR built bungalow camps in a number of locations in Banff National Park, as well as in Yoho and Kootenay Parks. The expansion of the system was very much aided by the development of a viable road network and the increased use of the automobile as a pleasure vehicle favoured by the middle class.

In 1920, the highway from Calgary reached Lake Louise. Six years later, it had arrived in Field, BC. The most significant roadway development, however, was the opening of the Banff–Windermere Highway in 1923, a 110-mile link in what was known as the Grand Circle Route, looping down to Portland, Oregon, through sixteen national parks in the United States and back up to the Canadian border south of Cranbrook, BC.

The new highway facilitated access to three new CPR bungalow camps: Storm Mountain, Vermilion River, and Radium Hot Springs (later renamed Sinclair Hot Springs), joining camps previously established at Moraine Lake and Wapta Lake, in Alberta, and at Emerald Lake and Yoho Valley, in British Columbia.

The last of the CPR bungalow camps to be built was Mount Assiniboine Bungalow Camp, located within Mount Assiniboine Provincial Park, near Lake Magog, about twenty miles south of Banff. The CPR built it during 1927 and the early part of 1928, on a fifty-acre site leased from the BC government. All of the railway's bungalow camps were now accessible by car, except for the high, remote location at Lake O'Hara, which required its clients to hike or ski to the site.

Interior of Cabin

Storm Mountain Bungalow Camp

Storm Mountain Bungalow Camp
Banff~Windermere Highway

The Camp

Recreate in the Canadian Pacific Rockies

Dining and Living Room

The bungalow camp at Lake O'Hara was only accessible by foot or on horseback. AUTHOR'S COLLECTION

In 1929, CPR was forced to close the camp at Vermilion Lake due to the lack of a safe water supply. Some of the other sites expanded during the Depression of the 1930s, as a result of the relatively inexpensive vacations they could provide. The camps at Lake O'Hara, Emerald Lake Yoho, and Wapta did especially well. Over time, the smaller bungalow camps were sold off to independent operators, or simply closed down by the railway.

By the 1950s, CPR had divested itself of virtually all of its remaining backcountry facilities, in response to changing tastes and lodging preferences. However, a few of the bungalow camps sold to willing entrepreneurs are still in their original locations, waiting to be rediscovered by those seeking a more rustic wilderness vacation. ✛

AN ALPINE HUT ON DEATH TRAP COL

During the early years of mountaineering at Lake Louise, the CPR's Swiss guides would often have to shepherd their clients through two or three hours of bushwhacking between the hotel and the base of their intended conquests, before they could begin the assault on the peaks themselves. It could be a tiring process, and it took away from the pleasure of ascending above the treetops to the ultimate goal. Rudolph Aemmer and Edward Feuz, Jr., two of the most storied climbers in the railway's employ, came up with a solution to this problem, one inspired by their homeland.

In the early 1920s, there were more than a hundred alpine huts at high elevations in Switzerland, in which climbers could rest before beginning the serious business of a mountain ascent. Aemmer and Feuz suggested to the CPR's superintendent of construction that they build such a structure for the benefit of hotel guests at Lake Louise. The superintendent, Basil Gardom, was in charge of all building and repairs associated with the CPR's hotels in the mountains. He had already supervised the construction of several bungalow camps for Canadian Pacific, with which the company's Swiss guides had been extremely helpful. He was open to this interesting proposal.

Working with the Alpine Club of Canada, the guides chose a location at an elevation of around 9,612 feet, between Mount Lefroy and Mount Victoria. The route over the low point in the ridge between the two peaks was named Abbot Pass after Philip Stanley Abbot, who lost his life while climbing there in 1896, the first such fatality in North America. Unofficially, the worst part of the passage was known as Death Trap Col, largely because of its exposure to avalanches. The safer approach was from Lake O'Hara, in the south.

The first Canadian alpine hut, perched on the Continental Divide between Alberta and British Columbia, would be called Abbot Pass Hut. At the time of its construction, the sturdy little haven was the highest permanent, habitable structure in Canada. It would not be for the faint of heart. To this day, the building is exceeded in elevation only by the Neil Colgan Hut, which is nestled thirty metres higher, in the Valley of the Ten Peaks. Both of the huts are within the boundaries of Banff National Park.

Throughout 1922, the three CPR men and a number of local labourers moved all of the materials up the mountainside that they would need to construct the stone structure. Where possible, horses were used at the lower elevations to haul heavy items across Victoria Glacier. The innovative construction crew built a system of pulleys and ropes to winch loads up steep slopes. They used wooden ladders to bridge the crevasses that blocked the route to the rising alpine hut. The Swiss guides themselves carried up an estimated two tons of supplies of their backs.

The finished building was nothing if not impressive. It was built with stones gathered in the pass and finished with a wooden interior. The hut featured a big kitchen for dining, ladies' and gentlemen's rooms that could each sleep six, and a large attic for storing supplies, which in a pinch could also accommodate as many as twenty cots for extra sleeping space.

In 1923, twenty-two members of the Appalachian Club came up from the United States to officially open the Abbot Pass Hut, under the leadership of Professor Dean Peabody Jr. Fittingly, the CPR guides were also in attendance. More than a hundred people registered as guests in the little alpine lodge that first season, most of whom arrived for the night in the secure company of the veteran Swiss mountaineers.

When they came inside, what they found in the common area was a large cook stove and, remarkably, a full-size organ. There was nothing to burn above the treeline, so the Swiss guides would cut bundles of wood below, on the Plain of Six Glaciers, and sell them for $0.50 apiece to the climbers, who carried them up to the hut.

The year after the Abbot Pass Hut inauguration, CPR opened a teahouse on the Plain of Six Glaciers as a rest stop on the way to the hut from Chateau Lake Louise. During the summer months, the wife and two daughters of senior mountain guide Edward Feuz worked there serving tea and light snacks to CPR guests.

For fifty years, Feuz was responsible for the Swiss guides and, above all, for ensuring the safety of climbers in their charge while climbing in the Rockies and Selkirks. During that time, there were a few accidents but, notably, no deaths.

The Abbot Pass Hut is still as solid as ever and is maintained and operated by the Alpine Club of Canada. ✠

When the Abbot Pass Hut was constructed on its lofty perch, it was the highest permanent structure in Canada. WHYTE MUSEUM OF THE CANADIAN ROCKIES, ROLLIN T. CHAMBERLIN FONDS, V22/NA66-2409

GIBBON'S TRAIL RIDERS SADDLE UP

There they were on Wolverine Plateau, in the midst of a Rocky Mountain snowstorm, in July 1923. CPR's chief publicity agent, John Murray Gibbon, had organized a fishing trip for a group of outdoorsmen and wildlife aficionados, while networking on behalf of the railway. They had been unexpectedly socked in for the night.

Among the stranded companions were such luminaries as Reginald Townsend, editor of *Country Life in America*; Henry Beach Clow, president of Rand McNally & Company; Byron Harmon, a mountain photographer often employed by the Alpine Club of Canada; and Reinhold Heinrich Palenske, noted Chicago painter.

As they waited out the storm, Gibbon, Townsend, and Palenske—clearly enjoying each other's company, as well as the exquisite beauty of their shared detainment—decided they should form a club of like-minded individuals to camp out together in the mountains every year, exploring and enjoying the backcountry on horseback, just as they were currently doing, but perhaps with a few more provisions. Thus was born the Order of the Trail Riders of the Canadian Rockies.

Their enthusiasm was so contagious that the following year the first official outing of the new organization attracted more than two hundred riders from Canada, the United States, and Europe. Clow and Harmon had readily answered the call to saddle up with the three founders, undeterred by their snowy initiation the year before. Joining them were Carl Rungius, painter of international fame; Walter Painter, architect; Harry Pollard, photographer; the superintendent of Banff National Park; and various representatives of the Canadian Historical Association, the Alpine Club of Canada, and the New York Zoological Society.

This was becoming a big tent organization for everybody with a love for the Rocky Mountains and, as Gibbon had hoped, a boon for tourism in Canadian Pacific's wilderness playground. Among them were "scientists, authors, artists, photographers and mountain enthusiasts," reported the *Calgary Herald*, "from many branches of the world's professional and leisure classes."

The largest gathering ever seen in Yoho Valley rendezvoused at the Canadian Pacific bungalow camp at the foot of Takakkaw Falls. CPR erected twenty teepees to supplement the limited cabin space, and a group of Nakoda (or "Stoney") people, under the supervision of Chief Walks-in-the-Road, set up a huge Sundance lodge in the centre of the field to serve as camp headquarters.

With Dr. Charles E. Walcott, secretary of the Smithsonian Institute in Washington, D.C., presiding, the members unveiled a bronze tablet memorializing the pioneering work of Tom Wilson, the earliest guide in the Canadian Rockies, and the first white man to lay eyes on Lake Louise. Wilson attended the ceremony, joined the Order of Trail Riders, and became one of its most loyal adherents.

That first ride established a pattern for the organization that would benefit CPR, typically beginning and ending at one of the company's mountain hotels or bungalow camps. Along the way, the riders would negotiate mountain passes, glaciers, and backwoods trails, in and around the most spectacular scenic destinations in the Rockies. Official membership in the order was open to all, "irrespective of sex, age, race, creed, profession or colour," who had ridden more than fifty miles on horseback through the mountains. Various levels of lapel pins were awarded to those who ventured in the saddle for distances of fifty, one hundred, five hundred, one thousand, and twenty-five hundred miles.

Members shared an avowed reverence for the majesty and beauty of nature. The aims of the organization were to encourage travel on

Members ride in Banff National Park through Gibbon Pass, named for the CPR publicity man who founded their club. WHYTE MUSEUM OF THE CANADIAN ROCKIES, JOHN MURRAY GIBBON FONDS, V226/NA66-2409

horseback, promote good fellowship among those who visit and live in the mountains, encourage conservation and love of outdoor life, and create an interest in Indigenous customs and traditions.

The cost of participating in the annual ride was modest, ranging from $7 to $10 per day in the 1920s. Riders supplied their own blankets and sleeping bags and stayed overnight in CPR cabins or tents, initially supplemented by addition mountain shelters built by the order and in later years as authorized by the Canadian Commissioner of Parks.

The Brewster Transportation Company, a long-time supplier of transit and supply services to Canadian Pacific, handled many of the logistical considerations of organizing trail rider events. President Jim Brewster was an avid supporter of the riding club, for many years offering two weekly mountain trips every July and August, during which participants could spend enough time on horseback to qualify for their fifty-mile button. Perhaps the most famous of the aspirants were the king and queen of Siam, who proudly earned their silver (hundred-mile) and bronze (fifty-mile) buttons respectively, in 1931, while visiting Canada in an official capacity.

The Order of Trail Riders developed a tradition of congenial gatherings each night before turning in, as well as organizing what they termed a "grand pow-wow" at the end of their annual rides. Wilf Carter, an aspiring cowboy singer who later went on to make a name for himself, was an early member and frequent entertainer. Chief Buffalo Child Long Lance—a CPR publicist, magazine writer, and pseudo-Indigenous figure—was sometimes called upon to showcase First Nations–style song and dance.

Perhaps the most welcome presence at many of the gatherings was the portable harmonium donated to the order by Harold Eustace Key, musical director of CPR's hotel department. For many years, the trusty keyboard set the tone for the members' enthusiastic singsongs, until being hurled over a precipice, in 1944, by packers fed up with the task of hauling the unwieldy instrument along precarious mountain trails. ⚜

NEW CLUB CROSSES THE SKYLINE ON FOOT

A decade after John Murray Gibbon had established the Order of Trail Riders of the Canadian Rockies, it was an unquestionable success as was evidenced by the growing list of members from multiple nationalities and all walks of life. But there were those who wished to take part in the mountain exploits without having to do so on horseback; and CPR president Edward Beatty apparently was one of them. As a result, Gibbon took the only logical option open to him: he created a sister organization known as the Skyline Trail Hikers of the Canadian Rockies. Beatty was named honorary president.

The new group was organized with the help of a committee consisting largely of members from the Trail Riders of the Canadian Rockies and the Alpine Club of Canada.

The goals of the organization were similar to those of the trail riders, but above all the group of intrepid trekkers aimed to, simply enough, "encourage walking on foot over the trails through the Canadian Rockies." As with the older organization, CPR's publicity department centred the activities of the trail hikers on the railway's tourist properties. For the first few years, beginning in 1933, the annual excursion of alpine wanderers moved from one company lodge to another, through the most scenic mountain passes, across spectacular glaciers and alongside mighty rivers. Members were encouraged to carry alpenstocks, the traditional walking stick of the mountaineer. A Kodak moment awaited the adventurers around every corner.

In 1936, CPR began to set up "teepee camps" at strategic locations, to supplement the limited space in its remote cabins. Shadow Lake and Egypt Lake were two such sites, as were the lush meadows at the foot of Takkakaw Falls and Twin Falls.

Carl Rungius and Reinhold Palenske, avid members of the hiking association, made quick pencil sketches from which they would later produce painted works at their leisure. Fellow artist Gordon Gillespie, who also earned an official membership with the group by walking the required twenty-five miles on the mountain trails—not necessarily on consecutive days, or in any one year— found inspiration in the vicinity of Lake Duchesnay and Laughing Falls.

Not surprisingly, two of CPR's most faithful mountain guides, Rudolph Aemmer and Ernest Feuz, signed up with the trail hikers, sharing their encyclopedic knowledge of the network of remote trails, and adding a welcome emphasis on safety to the growing entourage of less experienced

Good sturdy walking boots and an alpenstock were essential gear for the mountain trails. AUTHOR'S COLLECTION

members. Cowboy singer Wilf Carter, already a familiar figure with the horseback set, did double duty with those who preferred to hoof it without the four-legged conveyance.

By 1961, Canadian Pacific had decided that the time it took their publicity and hotel staff to arrange the annual activities of the Skyline Hikers had become onerous. In addition, the whole operation was no longer showing the same payoff in tourist dollars it once had. Accordingly, the company announced that the equipment owned by the organization—teepees, other tents, cooking equipment and such—would be auctioned off to the highest bidder. To ease the somewhat outraged reaction from club members, CPR president N.R. "Buck" Crump sold the whole kit to the group, which went independent, for $1. ✣

LOG SEIGNEURY ON THE OTTAWA RIVER

The arrival of a railway construction gang in the spring of 1930, and the spiking down of a 3,697-foot spur from the CPR tracks to a verdant site on the north bank of the Ottawa River, was enough to pique the curiosity of the citizens in the sleepy nearby hamlet of Montebello, Quebec.

For some time, there had been rumours about developing the land around the old Papineau family manor, which dated back more than a century to when the famous Quebec patriot and seigneur Louis-Joseph Papineau had lived there. The locals could scarcely have imagined that such talk would lead to the frenetic activity soon to take place on that property, particularly as the Great Depression had recently set in. Hubert Saddlemire, a Swiss-American millionaire who had recently bought the property, was about to develop the property in a manner few could have envisioned.

By early March, workers had erected several bunkhouses on the site and established construction camps in Montebello and the neighbouring village of Fassett, Quebec. When fourteen CPR colonist cars were positioned at the end of the rail spur to accommodate even more workers, it was evident that whatever project Saddlemire had in mind would be a substantial one.

Guided by the elaborate drawings and exacting specifications of Montreal architect Harold Lawson and supervised closely by Finnish master log builder Victor Mymark, more than 3,500 men were soon at work on a private members' club and a resort to be known as Lucerne-in-Quebec. Initially, it would be owned by the railway company, but leased to the private Seigneury Club.

At the time, the road system in the area was quite rudimentary, and simply not up to the task of ferrying large quantities of supplies in and out. As a result, all of the necessary materials were hauled to the construction site by rail.

The preliminary layout of the grounds called for three main structures: an enormous, four-storey chateau; a single-level, horseshoe-shaped garage; and a two-storey staff residence, to be named Cedar Hall. All were to be constructed of massive logs, cedar shakes, and stone. With the CPR and the intended resort operators planning for a grand opening of the resort on July 1, 1930, the delivery schedule for materials was a demanding one.

In all, more than twelve hundred carloads arrived by rail at the site, consisting primarily of cement and rubble stone for the foundations, as well as lumber and rough-hewn logs for the facades.

The resort's main hotel building was the largest log structure in the world.
AUTHOR'S COLLECTION

opposite: This view of one of the lodge's bedroom wings shows the stone foundation and
signature notched-log construction that characterized the resort. AUTHOR'S COLLECTION

A Log Lodge Bedroom Wing, showing notched log construction.

The main entry to the log lodge included a driveway where automobiles could pull up to the front door. AUTHOR'S COLLECTION

More than ten thousand trees were hewn from the forests of British Columbia. Seventeen freight cars were required to transport the half million western red cedar shakes that would be used for the roofs of the three buildings.

Excavation work began on March 15, 1930, and the first logs were set on the finished foundations three months later. All of the logs were sorted by length and diameter and arranged on skids, where they would stay clean and be readily accessible to the workers. Construction manager Harold Landry Furst organized the work with precision. With the help of eight hundred professional builders from Europe, the logs were cut, grooved, and scribed,

Attendees at the 1981 G7 summit included, from left: Gaston Thorn, president of the European Commission; Zenko Suzuki, prime minister of Japan; Helmut Schmidt, chancellor of Germany; Ronald Regan, president of the United States; Pierre Trudeau, prime minister of Canada; François Mitterrand, president of France; Margaret Thatcher, prime minister of the United Kingdom; and Giovanni Spadolini, prime minister of Italy.

PHOTO BY RICK ROBINSON, RICK ROBINSON COLLECTION

using the same methods that had been employed in Russia and Scandinavian countries for centuries.

As the interior work progressed, more than fifty-three miles of plumbing and heating pipes, 843 toilet fixtures and 700 radiators went into the buildings. Upwards of seven thousand sprinkler heads were installed to protect the massive wooden structures.

With the aid of electric lighting, the crews were able to work in continuous shifts throughout the day and night. The Catholic Church did not approve of the men working on the Sabbath, but by remarkable coincidence, when the local priest was sent off to Rome for nearly two months, the project proceeded with alacrity. Within four months, the buildings had been constructed and furnished, the grounds cleared and landscaped, and the doors of the new hotel and private club opened for business.

The remaining logs would be used to construct an arch over the entranceway and build a railway station in the community of Montebello that would be aesthetically compatible with the resort.

Three days after the official opening, on July 1, 1930, Saddlemire and his new resort management team staged a magnificent costume party, attended by the Governor General of Canada, CPR executives, officers from several national banks, and a host of other local notables. It was just a taste of the high-class clientele that would grace the hotel and grounds in the years to come.

Over the next four decades, Lucerne-in-Quebec thrived. So, too, did the private Seigneury Club, whose elite membership met in the old Papineau manor house on the grounds of the resort.

Foreign dignitaries and royalty walked through the doors, alongside Canadian prime ministers and governors general. Harry Truman, Prince Akihito of Japan, Prince Rainier and Princess Grace of Monaco, Perry Como, Bing Crosby, Bette Davis, and Joan Crawford all came to experience the charms of the largest log structure in the world.

But it was not until Canadian Pacific Hotels acquired the property, in 1971, that the luxury resort—inconspicuously located in small-town Quebec—would achieve worldwide recognition. Notably, it would be the scene of several international gatherings and conferences, culminating with the meeting of the G7 industrialized nations in the summer of 1981. While Ronald Reagan, François Mitterrand, Margaret Thatcher, and other luminaries discussed the state of the world with Canada's own Pierre Elliot Trudeau, the rustic but elegant setting was locked down tight. A small army of international police, and the most advanced array of security devices known to man, kept a close eye on everything that moved through the woods and on the roads and river in the vicinity.

Now owned by Fairmont Hotels, Le Chateau Montebello's popularity has grown apace. The resort's wealth of distractions—swimming pools, an eighteen-hole golf course, volleyball, badminton, tennis, hiking, and biking, to name but a few—have enhanced the resort's status as a vacation destination, honeymoon hideaway, sportsman's paradise and unequalled convention centre.

Unexpectedly, though, it was and still is primarily the lure of the expansive dining room and the popularity of the hotel's famed Sunday buffet brunch that keeps its clientele coming back for more. ⊹

5

IN THE AIR, ON THE SEA, AND BY LAND

THE MEN WHO HELPED FINANCE AND BUILD the Canadian Pacific Railway may not have envisioned it would grow to be the multimodal transportation and resource powerhouse it became; but a crucial decision by CPR's legendary general manager, William Van Horne, set the company on an early road to greatness. "Why should we take the milk, and leave the cream to others?" he is reported to have said.

Many North American railroads attended to their core business, while allowing other entrepreneurs to build, own, and operate ancillary infrastructure such as locomotives and rail cars, telegraph poles and wires, hotels, steamships, and express trucks. CPR management chose to create all of these assets in house and manage them as departments of the parent corporation, all under the centralized control of one board of directors. The efficiencies and savings inherent in such an administrative arrangement, and the synergies achieved through coordinated marketing, financing, and operations, allowed the company to claim "Canadian Pacific Spans the World."

To strengthen that claim, the company operated an airline that served five continents, and flew its red-and-white checkered house flag in ports around the world. Its global agencies produced and distributed tens of thousands of pamphlets and brochures, in dozens of languages. Its Exhibits

Branch and graphics production team produced a decades-long run of commercial posters that was unprecedented anywhere in the world. And its photography department shot and maintained an image bank of several hundred thousand views for the use of its legal, insurance, and investigative departments—and, most memorably, to publicize and promote the "World's Greatest Travel System."

EXPRESS GOES OFF THE RAILS

With the advent of efficient railway services in connection with river and canal routes, it was only a matter of time before some astute entrepreneur would introduce express package delivery to speed the rapidly accelerating pace of commerce.

Tradition has it that William Harnden was that worthy man. In 1839, he told merchants in Boston and New York that he could quickly deliver parcels along the rail and water routes between those two cities within the secure confines of his trusty carpet bag. One of Harnden's helpers at Albany, New York, a young man named Henry Wells, would soon branch out for himself with partner William Fargo, forming famed pioneer express company Wells Fargo & Company.

In Canada, CPR was quick to see the benefits of adding an express parcel service to its expanding suite of transportation services. In 1882, while rail construction was still proceeding west from Winnipeg, the railway company acquired Dominion Express, a prosperous company that had been chartered by a group of Toronto businessmen in 1873.

At the same time, CPR took over a small enterprise in Winnipeg that, in an era less concerned than ours with brand exclusivity and protection, had already set up operations as the Canadian Pacific Express Company. CPR combined the two companies under the Dominion Express banner in a new Winnipeg headquarters building.

A story is told about CPR general manager William Van Horne's choice for the man who would serve as the first superintendent of CPR's express arm. The American W.S. Stout, a recruit from south of the border who, reportedly, was in fact rather slender, was escorted into Van Horne's office.

"Who are you?" demanded the chief.

"I'm Stout."

"Well, you don't look it," the notoriously crusty rail boss replied, and thus the relationship was cemented.

Stout began his career at the age of seventeen with the United States Express Company in Havana, Illinois, as an office boy and messenger. As the head of express operations for Canadian Pacific, he organized an efficient service between Rat Portage (now Kenora) and Oak Lake, Manitoba, from a modest, two-storey wooden building in Winnipeg, with the aid of six employees, one horse, and a second-hand wagon.

In its first full month of operations in August 1882, the CPR-controlled express company grossed just over $1,000 in receipts from those two points, as well as from agencies in Brandon, Broadview, Carberry, Portage la Prairie, Selkirk, Stonewall, Virden, and Whitemouth.

Within a year, Dominion Express had set up a joint traffic route in partnership with Vickers Express Company between Toronto and Owen Sound, in connection with the Toronto, Grey & Bruce Railway, and steamboat service to Prince Arthur's Landing on Lake Superior.

The company's reach expanded with the completion of the CPR transcontinental rail line a few years later. Horse-drawn wagons and stagecoaches were used to service areas remote from railway lines. During the 1890s, Dominion Express crossed the ocean to China, Japan, Australia, and New Zealand, after the railway inaugurated a trans-Pacific steamship service. By 1905, CP was operating an overseas department for express services out of London, Liverpool, and Glasgow.

Dominion Express was among the early proponents of cash-on-delivery (COD) service around the turn of the twentieth century, along with being among the first to introduce express money orders. Travellers cheques soon followed.

Dominion Express and Canadian Pacific took delivery of their first motor vehicles in 1912, at Montreal's Windsor Station. More than 250 horses in use at the time would be put out to pasture in favour of the speedier and more efficient trucks, which were soon ubiquitous at railway platforms and steamship docks across the country.

In 1925, the railway company incorporated Canadian Pacific Transport to operate a suburban and interurban bus service between Preston and Galt, complementing the electric Grand River Railway service it was already running between the two Ontario towns.

The following year, a special act of Parliament changed the name of CP's expedited parcel service from the Dominion Express Company to a reborn Canadian Pacific Express, while CP Transport was buying up road freight carriers in Saskatchewan, Alberta, and British Columbia. The company's new transport company would effectively take over all of Canadian Pacific's long-haul highway licences.

In 1928, the first air transport services were integrated with Canadian Pacific's rail, highway, and steamship operations, when government mail and express packages were rushed by truck to

The horse-drawn vehicle standing behind this new motor-ized conveyance at Montreal's Windsor Station would soon be put out of business. AUTHOR'S COLLECTION

CP Express trucks provided the link between fast trains and even faster airplanes. GLENBOW ARCHIVES, ARCHIVES AND SPECIAL COLLECTIONS, UNIVERSITY OF CALGARY ND-3-4350(B)

Toronto's airfield and flown to Montreal. There, another truck received the shipments and delivered them directly to a plane heading for Rimouski, Quebec, where they were loaded aboard the company steamship *Empress of Scotland* bound for the United Kingdom. The Canadian Pacific Express Company had contracted with Canadian Transcontinental Airways Limited and Canadian Airways Limited to take to the skies.

The growth of CPR's highway services continued apace, going into high gear after the Second World War. During 1947 and 1948, the company acquired a series of carriers in Western Canada, notably Dinsdale Cartage and Storage Limited of Manitoba, Audette of Saskatchewan, and Hodges Freighter of both those Prairie provinces.

In 1959, a new corporate entity, Canadian Pacific Merchandise Services, was created to handle all express, less-than-carload railway freight and truck traffic, including all the business of the former CP Transport Company. The move was followed immediately by the acquisition of the Canadian operations of Smith Transport, at the time the British Commonwealth's largest trucking company. By 1967, Canadian Pacific was operating highway services that comprised close to nine thousand miles of routes, mostly in Western Canada.

Along with the tens of thousands of parcels quietly shuttled back and forth across the Canadian Pacific system, the company's public relations people touted the express company's expertise at handling more exotic and fragile shipments.

Pigeons, parrots, swans, canaries, and other songbirds were trusted to the freight carrier. Monkeys and minks, dogs and cats, rabbits, foxes, bears, and snakes all came aboard company vehicles for a trip down the road, from their old homes to new ones.

Perishable goods such as eggs, butter, fruit, fish, and poultry products shared trailer space with precious stones, valuable documents, and priceless works of art. There were even a few occasions before, during, and after the Second World War, when the company's express services moved large quantities of gold and silver bullion for the British, Ethiopian, and Canadian governments.

Special railway cars were designed and operated for ventilating and refrigerating the perishable goods, while armoured trains and highly trained guards watched over the transport of the more valuable commodities.

By the 1980s, CPR's expedited parcel service reached its zenith with the formation of a new umbrella company, Canadian Pacific Express & Transport Limited. Sub-departments, CP Transport and CP Express, had already been revived as recognizable members of the CPR's transportation empire, but few industry observers realized the extent of the new freight carrier's reach. Among its more obscure but not insignificant components were Canpar, Express Airborne, Bulk Systems, Highland Transport, Moffatt Brothers, and Deluxe Moving & Storage. ✢

BRASS POUNDERS AND MERCURIES

anadian Pacific's charter from 1881 included the right to "construct, maintain, and work a continuous telegraph line and telephone lines throughout and along the whole line of the CPR." Seeing that right translated into a viable commercial venture was very much in line with general manager Van Horne's philosophy of keeping all of the railway's peripheral ventures in house.

As early as 1883, CPR opened a telegraph office in Winnipeg and, along with using its own wires to conduct business, began to transmit commercial messages eastward to Port Arthur and westward to Medicine Hat. At the time, the initiative was not well received by those already engaged in capitalizing on Samuel F.B. Morse's revolutionary invention. A Toronto official of the Great North Western Telegraph Company, in an interview with the trade publication *Electric World of New York*, put a voice to the disapproving establishment:

> I believe the Canadian Pacific is about to try a business for which it is unqualified. They cannot make it pay, they will simply be throwing away piles of money in erecting and running lines exclusively for themselves.

CPR's arrangements with the US Postal Telegraph Company and the Baltimore & Ohio Telegraph Company to extend its service into the United States and, soon afterward, with the Commercial Cable company for transatlantic and trans-Pacific connections, ensured this particular industry spokesman was very much mistaken.

In 1886, Canadian Pacific had taken over all of the federal government's telegraph lines in British Columbia, as well as the underwater cable to Victoria, and was leasing two wires from Western Union between Toronto and Niagara Falls. By 1902, the Pacific Cable had been completed between Canada and Australia. CPR then entered into an exclusive contract with the Canadian Cable Board to serve the governments of Great Britain, Canada, Australia, and New Zealand.

The telegraph business grew rapidly and soon "spanned the world," as the CPR's well-known slogan proudly proclaimed for its entire suite of multi-modal services. The fourteen thousand miles of telegraph wire, hung during the railway's construction years, were able to accommodate more than half a million public messages in 1886 alone, the first year the company offered country-wide commercial service. By 1923, the company's expanded telegraph infrastructure and negotiated connections to all points across the globe handled ten times that volume.

The expansive network required a small army of linesmen to keep the messages flowing smoothly. The workers maintained the poles and wires from weather, rockslides, and general wear and tear, along with replacing glass insulators that were subject to the unwarranted attention of random target shooters and rock throwers. But the system was surprisingly resilient.

On one occasion in the early years, C.R. Hosmer, CPR's first telegraph manager, sent a message to Van Horne informing him that a bear had damaged two wires in the BC interior, temporarily disrupting the westward flow of messages. When the boss fired back an immediate query about how he knew a bear was the cause of the problem, Hosmer explained:

> No wind prevailed at the time, but there were marks of the bear climbing the pole next to where the wire had been . . . Humming in the pole, due to the tension in the wire, caused Bruin to think there was a nest of bees.

A line of CP Telegraph messenger boys in full uniform stand proudly beside their delivery vehicles. Behind them are four wannabes in training. GLENBOW ARCHIVES, ARCHIVES AND SPECIAL COLLECTIONS, UNIVERSITY OF CALGARY ND-3-2322

The telegraphers, or brass pounders, named for the brass telegraph keys with which they tapped out the Morse-coded messages, were the most visible members of the system. The youthful messengers who delivered paper copies of the telegrams to the doors of recipients, on foot or by bicycle, were sometimes called Mercuries, after the messenger-god of classical mythology.

The telegraphers were not confined to sending messages from the station agents' desks in CPR stations. As telegraph service proliferated and penetrated all areas of society, the key operators set up shop in newspaper offices and brokerages. The brass pounders tapped out the results of championship boxing matches and World Series baseball games and informed the voting public about election returns. Often the telegraphers would work in pairs, so they could keep copy flowing without the need for a break. Some operators were able to send as many as 2,500 words per hour out over the wire.

There were times when up to a dozen telegraphers would be working an important hockey game at the same time. Jack Raymond, a stalwart figure in CPR's Montreal communications department, missed his first national hockey match-up in 1937, after sending out messages during 598 consecutive games

By the 1930s, CPR's telegraph lines were filling the gaps in the commercial trans-Canada telephone service. In 1932, Canadian Pacific secured the contact, jointly with Canadian National, to provide the national wire network over which the Canadian Radio Commission (later the Canadian Broadcasting Corporation) would transmit its programs across the country.

One and a half million words and more than two hundred photographs were transmitted over CP telegraph lines just to cover the 1939 royal tour of Canada by King George VI and Queen Elizabeth.

Increasingly, the two railways cooperated in providing telegraph services. In the early 1960s, CP and CN built a three-thousand-mile microwave-messaging network between Montreal and Vancouver that would soon be the basis for a new company called CNCP Telecommunications. Ultimately, it would usher in a complete change in the way information was transmitted. Broadband messages, faxes, emails, and telephone texting would follow one another in quick succession to make communications technology virtually unrecognizable to the men and women who once tapped out Morse-code messages.

The railway's telegraph business has morphed continuously and changed hands several times in recent decades. Nobody sits at a brass key to send out coded messages anymore, and few people remember the incessant clacking noise at the receiving end in a busy telegraph office. Nevertheless, if you are so inclined, you can still fire off an old-fashioned telegram through one of the CPR Telegraph Company's successors with a click of a button on the internet. ⁜

HOLLYWOOD NORTH

Canadian Pacific was quick to recognize the power of the silver screen to draw attention to the potential of the land it had to sell, the resources it had to exploit, and the facilities it had to offer, all of which could be maximized by putting them at the service of those who worked in, around, and for the motion picture industry.

As early as the turn of the twentieth century, CPR commissioned a series of films to promote immigration to Canada, following on the heels of the federal government's efforts in that area. The railway soon supplanted the latter's role as the major cheerleader for settlement of the "Golden Northwest."

By 1915, the government's superintendent of immigration, W.D. Scott, was telling enquirers that "the department does not collect or distribute films . . . and does not intend to go into the motion picture business." He did, however, advise the letter writer to contact Canadian Pacific, as "the interests of the railway and the Dominion are similar." For the next fifty years, CPR would use film to promote its many varied interests and those of the country as a whole.

Among the first films ever shown at sea were the short promotional pieces presented to the passengers aboard the CPR steamships *Empress of Britain* and *Empress of Ireland*, as they crossed the North Atlantic on the way to fulfill their passengers' New World dreams. Until the introduction of non-flammable films in the 1920s, the movies were shown on deck for reasons of safety. The operators of the cinematographic outfits would run the hand-cranked projectors with one hand while maintaining focus with the other.

Shortly after the First World War, CPR founded the film-producing and processing firm, Associated Screen News. Initially its main purpose was to promote Canadian immigration, settlement, and investment opportunities, but in short order there were few major industrial enterprises in the country not making use of the company's motion pictures, in connection with some aspect of their business. In 1924, camera operator John Alexander was the first man Canadian Pacific named to promote its cruise ships. That first assignment saw him boarding the *Empress of Britain* for the West Indies and South America. Two years later, he was heading for the Mediterranean on the *Empress of France*, this time with five assistants in tow. Newsreels produced by Associated Screen News would show the wonders the moviemakers captured in film houses around the world.

A film crew working outside the railway's Mount Stephen House at Field, BC, shoots details for a film by the Edison Company, in 1910. AUTHOR'S COLLECTION

opposite: This movie, produced by 20th Century Fox, was even more ridiculous than the usual ham-fisted historical dramas presented to a jaded North American audience. LIBRARY AND ARCHIVES CANADA MIKAN 3931146

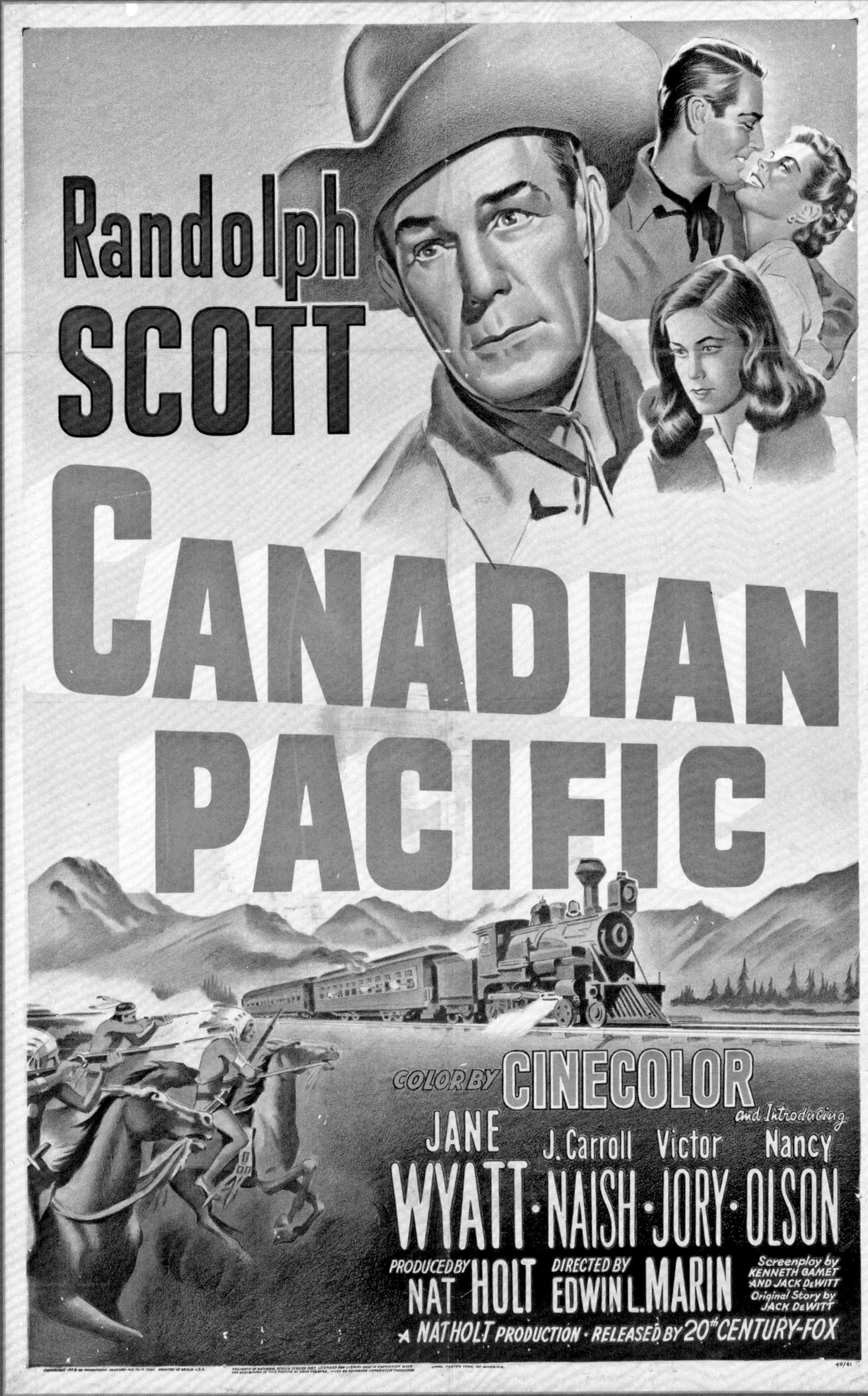
Randolph
SCOTT
CANADIAN
PACIFIC
COLOR BY CINECOLOR
and Introducing
JANE WYATT · J. Carroll NAISH · Victor JORY · Nancy OLSON
PRODUCED BY NAT HOLT
DIRECTED BY EDWIN L. MARIN
Screenplay by KENNETH GAMET AND JACK DeWITT
Original Story by JACK DeWITT
A NAT HOLT PRODUCTION · RELEASED BY 20th CENTURY-FOX
49/41

CPR photographer Nicholas Morant was a technical advisor during the shooting of action scenes such as this one from the movie *Silver Streak*. PHOTO BY NICHOLAS MORANT, OMER LAVALLÉE COLLECTION

CPR's expansive advertising campaigns shone a spotlight on the many attractions that Canada and the "World's Greatest Travel System," as the company styled itself, had to offer. Inevitably, that led to film crews from other countries, notably the United States, descending on the CPR's turf to share in the visual exploitation of the vast Canadian wilderness. The company's mountain hotels were particularly well situated to accommodate the needs of large film production teams, none more so than the Banff Springs Hotel, located as it is in the country's first and arguably most spectacular national park.

The hotel's guest list over the years reads like a who's who of Hollywood stardom down through the decades, from John Barrymore, Burt Lancaster, Jack Lemmon, Lee Marvin, Robert Mitchum, Laurence Olivier, Gregory Peck, Randolph Scott, and Jimmy Stewart to Charles Bronson, Gene Hackman, Dustin Hoffman, Alan Ladd, Paul Newman, and Shelley Winters. The movies shot in the vicinity of CPR's most storied hostelry ran the gamut from the acclaimed drama *Doctor Zhivago* to the wild west action film *Buffalo Bill and the Indians* and the low-budget *Ski Lift to Death*.

In 1943, the Banff Springs welcomed its first canine star on the premises, when scenes for *Lassie Come Home* were shot nearby. In 1954, Marilyn Monroe created a publicity storm while filming *River of No Return* by breaking her leg during filming at the back of the hotel and appearing on crutches for the rest of her working visit.

Literally dozens of movies have been filmed in and around CPR properties. However, none are remembered as well as those that used railway equipment on loan from the railway. One that was a big feature film back in the day—though all but forgotten now—was called, appropriately enough, *Canadian Pacific*. The Nat Holt production, filmed in Cinecolor, told the story of a two-fisted surveyor played by Randolph Scott, as he drove the construction of the railway through the mountains of British Columbia. The plot included every hackneyed ingredient for a good western tale, from murder to romance, with a requisite attack on the heroic entrepreneurs from a group of "Indians" shooting flaming arrows. The storyline strayed nearly as far as possible from the historical record but landed as if from the action-packed pages of a boy's annual.

By the 1970s, things had gotten a little more sophisticated. In 1976, Twentieth Century Fox managed to borrow no less than two diesel units and eight stainless steel passenger cars from the CPR to star in its production of the *Silver Streak*. The movie, starring Gene Wilder—of *Blazing*

Saddles and *Young Frankenstein* fame—featured action scenes with stuntmen hanging from the sides and the roofs of the cars as the train negotiated a hair-raising piece of track above a two-hundred-foot gorge. Several CPR locomotive engineers and other operating crewmembers were also on loan from the railway, and CPR supervisory staff oversaw safety concerns during the filming. Many of the scenes looked highly dangerous but were shot while the railway equipment moved at slow speeds and were enhanced afterward by speeding up the film.

And speaking of danger, CPR put at risk all of the safety messages the railway brings to school children and adults across the country, when a teenager with otherworldly powers jumped in front of a moving train during the filming of the 1978 *Superman* movie, starring Christopher Reeve and partly filmed on CPR tracks between Crowsnest Pass and Lethbridge.

In that scene, a young Clark Kent on his way to school in the countryside near Barons, Alberta—substituting for a rural site in Kansas—uses his superpowers to race a train to a level crossing. At the last moment, he leaps over the tracks in front of the locomotive and continues on his way to school with a smile on his face. It was a great action sequence for the movies, kids, but not something you want to try on your own. ⚜

THE RUSSIAN CONNECTION

n 1858, when Russia and China signed the Treaty of Aigun, borders were formally established between the two countries that effectively handed the Russian Empire vast new territories in eastern Siberia. Significantly, the area ceded by representatives of the weakened Chinese Qing Dynasty gave expansionist Russia a coveted all-year port on the Pacific Ocean, at Vladivostok.

At the time, the population of Vladivostok comprised but a handful of Chinese and Koreans. The challenge for the Russians was to develop the port, while establishing firm connections with its main commercial centres thousands of miles to the west—a mirror image of the scenario faced by Canadians.

In the latter case, the building of the Canadian Pacific Railway provided a necessary economic lifeline between the far reaches of the country and stimulated the growth of Vancouver as the nation's gateway to the Pacific.

Thus it was not surprising that the CPR figured prominently in the debate among Russian authorities on the merits of building their own national transcontinental railway. A permanent rail link would make the desired commercial connection, while helping to settle eastern Siberia with Russian peasants. At the same time, the line would work to prevent any plans China might have to reacquire territory in the Russian hinterland.

The Russians were impressed by the role CPR had played in settling the Canadian West. And, tellingly, they noted the value of the railway in quelling the Riel Rebellion, and in stifling American ambitions to annex the sparsely populated land north of the 49th parallel.

By 1891, work had begun on the Trans-Siberian Railway. It was largely completed within a decade, revolutionizing Russia's trade with the East. While Siberia's northern extremes were largely inhospitable, its vast expanse also included much more temperate, fertile belts. It was a land of prairie and forest, rich in agricultural and mining possibilities, not unlike Canada; and along with the new rail line came a tide of settlers relocating from the more crowded European territories of the Czar.

For the directors of CPR, the primary attraction of the Trans-Siberian was the new, highly efficient world-girdling route that it could offer in connection with the Canadian company's own formidable transportation network. Accordingly, CPR vice-president William Whyte was dispatched

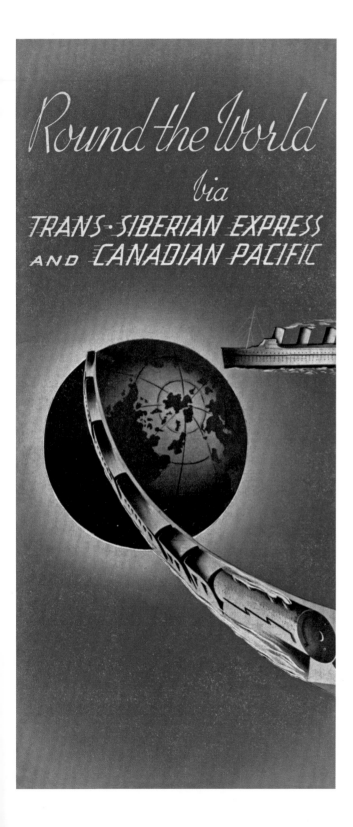

A promotional brochure heralds the round-the-world connections of the Canadian Pacific Railway and steamship lines in connection with the Trans-Siberian Railway. AUTHOR'S COLLECTION

to St. Petersburg, in 1901, to explore the possibility of establishing a steamship connection between Vancouver and Vladivostok.

Though Whyte and CPR ultimately deemed it premature to invest in a dedicated service directly to the Russian port, they secured agreements with various steamship lines and with the Trans-Siberian Railway that allowed Canadian Pacific to offer around-the-world ticketing. In the years before the First World War, these connections were perfected to the point where a US newspaper reporter was able to circumnavigate the globe in thirty-five days, twenty-one hours, and thirty minutes—the fastest time on record for such a journey.

John Henry Mears, of the *New York Sun*, left New York City for London, on July 2, 1913, by the Cunard steamship *Mauretania*. A coordinated series of steamship and railway connections whisked Mears through Paris and Berlin to St. Petersburg, where he boarded the Trans-Siberian. By July 24, he had arrived by ferry in Yokohama to catch CPR's *Empress of Russia* for the Trans-Pacific arm of his trip.

A smooth transition to the company's crack passenger train, the Imperial Limited, and a seamless US railway connection delivered the intrepid Mr. Mears back safely to his hometown with more than twenty-one thousand miles of travel under his belt.

The Sun ran a list of world-girdlers and the record times they set. It compared Mears's feat favourably with such famous trips as Magellan's historic three-year voyage, from 1519 to 1522, and the circumnavigation of Jules Verne's fictional hero Phileas Fogg, from *Around the World in Eighty Days*.

Both the Canadian and the Russian railway networks were strained to capacity during the First World War, moving men and materiel toward the various theatres of engagement. In early 1917, in the midst of the conflict, CPR vice-president George Bury was invited by British Premier Lloyd George to visit Russia as a member of a special British commission, charged with inspecting the railway system and presenting a report to the War Cabinet.

Conveyed by a fast Canadian navy destroyer to Bergen, Norway, Bury arrived by rail in Petrograd (formerly St. Petersburg), where he witnessed massive demonstrations and the chaos of the February Revolution that preceded the abdication of Nicholas II and the ascendency of the Bolsheviks and the Red Army.

"Canada has ten times more railway mileage per unit of population than has Russia," Bury determined, while travelling from Lapland to the Caucusus in the company of Russian government officials. "Had Russia been equipped with railway transportation, say as in Canada, she would have been able to have played a much greater part in the war," he told his CPR bosses.

For several years, the Red Army fought to overthrow the Russian White Guard and the Allied armies of intervention that held the port of Vladivostok and large tracts of land in the East. By the early 1920s, the revolutionary Soviet government had consolidated its hold in most of Siberia and was formally recognized by the Western powers.

Canadian Pacific had been quick to open an agency in Moscow as soon as the civil war ended, but a decision by the Canadian federal government to refuse entry to several "undesirable" Russian trade commissioners into Canada led to retaliatory measures. The CP office was closed. It would be a few more years before normal commercial arrangements were re-established, though the Trans-Siberian was showing the adverse effects of war and revolution.

"The shocking state of the railway track in many places and of the rolling stock has caused some [accidents]," said one traveller in a letter to the *Times* of London, on October 14, 1925.

Others have been brought about by removal of bolts and pins of rails by (1) Counter-Revolutionary soldiers who have wished to rid Soviet Russia of various individuals who were supposed to be travelling in certain trains, and (2) by bandits.

About half way between Baikal and Irkutsk, bandits had interfered with the permanent way so that a freight train was derailed, and ten hours later we travelled slowly on the second set of rails and passed eight freight cars either upside down or piled on the top of each other and smashed like matchwood. One of the bandits had tried to ascertain from one of the railway track guards the time our train was expected, and as he (the guard) said he did not know, he was shot dead on the spot. The stoker of the freight engine was scorched to death and the engine driver badly damaged.

Three years later, conditions had improved so dramatically that leading Danish newspaper *Politiken* was prepared to challenge the round-the-world record set before the war. By then, CPR's network of travel agencies spanned most of the world, and Canadian Pacific representatives were authorized to book travellers with dozens of domestic and foreign railway and steamship companies, in connection with CPR's own extensive transportation system.

Danish newspaper contest winner, Palle Huld, left Copenhagen on March 1, 1928. Sailing from Greenock, Scotland, on the CP liner SS *Montcalm*, he reached Montreal on March 12. Three days later, he made the connection between CPR's Trans-Canada Limited and the company's flagship, *Empress of Canada*, to sail to Yokohama.

All of the arrangements for his further trip to Korea, China, Soviet Russia, and back to Copenhagen had been in the hands of CPR. The fifteen-year-old Danish globe-circler had completed his circumnavigation in just forty-three days. ✣

THE MOUNTAIN THAT WALKS

Battle-hardened Crow and Blackfoot warriors refused to camp near its base because they said it had the habit of moving, slowly like a turtle. Nevertheless, at 4:10 on the morning of April 29, 1903, Turtle Mountain moved with terrifying speed as it sent sixty-six million tons of rock crashing down on CPR's Crowsnest railway line, burying a large portion of the sleeping town of Frank, Alberta (then still part of the Northwest Territories).

A CPR freight train had whistled through the mountain community not long before. Its crew-members were busy switching cars west of the town, near a small trestle over the Crowsnest River. The men later reported hearing an enormous roar and, looking back, seeing a vast cloud of dust billowing through the valley. So close did the rockslide chase after their moving train that the last set of wheels on the caboose was derailed by the onslaught.

Confusion reigned up and down the line. The first messages were sent by telegraph not more than fifteen minutes after the event, from the railway agent at Donald, BC, to company officials in Calgary and Macleod, Alberta. At first, the cause was cited as an earthquake or a volcanic eruption. But as the air cleared, it became apparent that an enormous chunk of "the mountain that walks" had broken away and barrelled down on the Town of Frank. More than two square miles of the valley floor and the steep slopes on either side of the railway line had been buried in rock and debris to a depth of over one hundred feet.

When the slide occurred, the conductor of the nearby CPR work train, Henri Pettit, quickly assessed the situation and, recognizing the potential danger to other movements on the railway line, quickly sent his brakeman, the now-celebrated Sid Choquette, clamouring over the rock-slide, through the dust and confusion, to flag down the approaching westbound passenger train. Choquette would become a local hero for having done so.

The train he stopped was CPR westbound No. 31 en route from Medicine Hat, Alberta, to Kootenay Landing, at the south end of Kootenay Lake, in British Columbia. In later years, some newspaper and magazine articles referred to the train as the Spokane Flyer, but Canadian Pacific never ran a train with that official name. At the time of the slide, CPR passengers bound for Spokane would have had to make a connection with a Great Northern train at Morrissey, Creston, or Nelson.

Immediately upon receiving the news of the blocked line at Frank, Charlie Fyfe, the agent and operator at the CPR station in Macleod, sent a telegraph to all points announcing that westbound trains would be stopped in his town. Fyfe then set to work assembling a special auxiliary train and called for all available local doctors and nurses to climb aboard on a relief mission. They were soon joined by a handful of police, newspaper reporters, and mine inspectors from the town and vicinity.

In Calgary, William Pearce, superintendent of mines and former chief inspector of surveys for the federal government, was instructed by the Deputy Minister of the Interior to make for the scene of the rockslide as soon as possible. A CPR train left the following evening with Pearce onboard. North-West Mounted Police inspector Douglas, along with ten of his officers from Calgary, accompanied him. On the way, NWMP Inspector Davidson joined them with a sergeant and constable from Pincher Creek. Inspector P.C. Primrose with twenty-five more officers from Macleod rounded out the passenger list. Sometime between 2:00 and 3:00 AM the next day, they arrived at the east end of the blockage and "we did the most foolish thing that any sane man would be guilty of," said Pearce several years later in a report to the CPR.

> We climbed over the broken rock with the aid of a lantern for between three and four miles into Frank. Why we did not break our necks, as the rock was covered with fine dust, is something I have never quite understood. We reached Frank when it was just getting light, slightly after four in the morning, and I think I am safe in saying that there were not fifty people in the town in bed and of those awake there were not three percent sober.

Soon thereafter, Pearce related, CPR chief engineer A. McHenry had arrived on the scene and organized a westward evacuation of many of the local workers and others to Fernie, Michel, and other points on the Crowsnest line. On his instructions, the railway backed two long trains of boxcars into Frank to move both people and household goods out of the half-buried town.

Of around six hundred people, many of whom were railway personnel or miners, Frank had lost about eighty of its citizens. (Reports varied from sixty-six to as many as a hundred people dead.) Twelve bodies were recovered from the rubble. By great good fortune, much of Frank's

The first through train passes over the rebuilt line after the slide debris was cleared from the right of way.
GLENBOW ARCHIVES, ARCHIVES AND SPECIAL COLLECTIONS, UNIVERSITY OF CALGARY NA-1784-3

business section, as well as parts of its main residential area, had remained intact or the toll in human lives might have been much higher.

There was much conjecture in the ensuing months about the root cause or causes of the disaster, and many fingers were pointed at the mining activity carried out by the Canadian-American Coal Company that had burrowed deep within Turtle Mountain, since beginning its mining operations more than two years earlier. For the mine's opening extravaganza on September 10, 1901, attended by most everybody in town, CPR had brought in some heavyweight dignitaries, among them company president H.L. Butte, of Montana, Fred Haultain, premier of the Northwest Territories, and Clifford Sifton, minister of the interior in Canadian prime minister Wilfred Laurier's cabinet.

A commission set up by the federal government, upon determining that the great mining chambers cut under the foot of the mountain had played a role in the disaster, initially shut down all diggings. In addition, its investigations concluded the already unstable base of Turtle Mountain, consisting of limestone, shale, sandstone, and coal beds, had been further compromised in the days leading up to the massive slide by unusually heavy rains, alternately freezing and thawing in the water-filled fissures caused by the mining activity. However, the mine was allowed to reopen several months later, and continued operating until 1913.

It was many months before CPR managed to clear the seven thousand feet of track that had been buried by the massive hunks of rock that came down with the slide, some bigger than the houses that were crushed underneath. Regular train operations then resumed through a ruined landscape of giant boulders that to this day still inspire awe. A smaller slide, two years later, came down near Frank and struck a westbound CPR train, killing the fireman. Since then there have been no further movements of the restive mountain.

Conductor Pettit and brakeman Choquette were each given letters of commendation from Canadian Pacific and were awarded with $25 bonuses for their quick thinking, attention to duty, and valourous lifesaving actions. Choquette later went on to work in the US for the Illinois Central Railroad, but he has remained a folk hero to the people of Frank and stands tall in the legends of the Crowsnest Pass. ⊹

UP, UP, AND AWAY

anadian Pacific's foray into Canada's air transport industry, in 1942, consolidated ten fledgling companies into a comprehensive north–south network that complemented the existing east–west transcontinental air route established by its rival, government-owned Canadian National, five years earlier.

The two national railway systems had become actively associated with air development as early as 1930, when both had invested in small northern operator Canadian Airways, with a view to expanding that company's reach across the country together. Ultimately, CPR declined to participate in the joint effort when the federal government had determined that the privately owned railway would have to put up one-half of the start-up capital for the airline, but would receive only one-third of the company's voting power. The government and Canadian National went on on to launch Trans-Canada Air Lines without the CPR in 1937.

At the beginning of the Second World War, the country's commercial airlines were in chaos. Canadian Pacific's proposed amalgamation of various floundering commercial air companies was designed to eliminate unnecessary route duplication, propel borderline operations to profitability, and release redundant personnel for the war effort.

In 1939, Canadian Pacific obtained permission from the Dominion government to purchase some of the independent bush airlines operating in the north. Within three years, it had acquired Yukon South Air Transport, operating out of Vancouver and Edmonton; Ginger Coote Airways of Vancouver; Mackenzie Air Service of Edmonton; Prairie Airways of Moose Jaw; Arrow Airways of Le Pas, Manitoba; Wings Limited of Winnipeg; Starratt Airways of Hudson, Ontario; and Quebec Airways and Dominion Skyways, both headquartered in Montreal, to add to its already substantial holdings in Montreal's Canadian Airways.

Canada was uniquely suited to the development of the commercial airlines industry, being a country of remote and disparate communities separated by vast distances and devoid of significant ground transport infrastructure. Many northern Indigenous People, trappers, prospectors, and miners became seasoned airline travellers before they developed any familiarity with trains, automobiles, or streetcars.

An early acquisition to the Canadian Pacific fleet is lettered for the company's new Airlines. The Edmonton hangar is still painted with the original designation, Canadian Pacific Air Lines. AUTHOR'S COLLECTION

opposite: Canadian Pacific took to the sky in completion with government-owned Trans-Canada Air Lines. AUTHOR'S COLLECTION

Canadian Airways, in particular, had built a reputation for steady service between Winnipeg and the Rocky Mountains, laying the foundation for a transcontinental airmail route. In the fifteen-year period between 1927 and 1941, the pioneer line had carried a record eighty million pounds of air cargo and eight million pounds of airmail, in addition to its 250,000 passengers.

Another key acquisition was Yukon South Transport, the airline organized by Grant McConachie, who would go on to become president of Canadian Pacific Air Lines and an industry legend. Before 1942, when CPAL was formed, McConachie had already mapped out an air route from Canada to the Far East that crossed only 40 miles of open water between

LINKING NORTH AND SOUTH
BY AIR!

CANADIAN PACIFIC AIR LINES

756-A

Canadian Pacific
AIR LINES

THE *Wings* OF
THE WORLD'S GREATEST TRAVEL SYSTEM

the two continents, while chopping more than 4,500 miles from the southern route across the Pacific.

Yukon Southern provided mail and passenger services from Vancouver and Edmonton to Whitehorse and Dawson City, Yukon. Trailblazing work by this company, in the way of developing airfields and landing strips, aided greatly in the development of the Alaska Highway, which was completed during the war, around the same time Canadian Pacific was taking to the skies.

The seventy-seven small planes from among the fourteen varieties that CPAL initially acquired proceeded to carry upwards of fifty thousand pounds of airmail per month. They also delivered an undisclosed amount of war materiel to US Army camps along the Alaska Highway.

The formation of Canadian Pacific Air Lines succeeded in providing the more remote regions of the country with an efficient, uniform service. It helped to stabilize rates and ended the cutthroat competition that had been ruinous to the independent bush airlines. It also reaffirmed Canadian Pacific's claim to the world's greatest travel system and proved to be the first step in establishing a top-of-the-world air route across the Arctic.

Famed Arctic explorer Richard Finnie said at the time:

The ultimate Northwest Passage is an aerial one. The short cut from New York to Tokyo is via Hudson Bay, the barren lands of the Northwest Territories and Alaska. The shortest distance from Chicago to Calcutta is straight north. If you want to fly from Calgary or Edmonton to Moscow, your quickest way is across the Canadian Arctic Archipelago. If you are in a hurry to get from Los Angeles or San Francisco or Vancouver to London or Paris, your shortest route is over Baffin Island, Greenland and Iceland.

With the cessation of hostilities and a rapid expansion of airline services around the world, all of this would come to be.

Canadian Pacific Air Lines was winging its way into history. ⁜

POSTWAR RETURN TO THE ATLANTIC

The ravages of the Second World War, including the loss of the company's flagship *Empress of Britain* to enemy action, left Canadian Pacific with a greatly reduced ocean steamship fleet. Only five of the seventeen passenger liners, which had been requisitioned by the British Admiralty for war duties, had the good fortune of returning to a more tranquil calling. Taking a hard look at postwar economic realities, management made the decision to abandon the company's pioneering Pacific runs and concentrate on revitalizing the transatlantic service.

The former cabin-class tourist liners *Duchess of Bedford* and *Duchess of Richmond* were upgraded to first-class status upon their release from war service. They were rechristened *Empress of France* and *Empress of Canada*, respectively, with all due ceremony.

Initially the *Bedford* was to have been renamed *Empress of India*, but before the ship was ready for postwar service, India had become a republic. Instead, the former Duchess liner was relaunched as *Empress of France.* On July 15, 1948, the newly resplendent steamship left Canadian Pacific's Liverpool dock to re-enter the North Atlantic passenger business. A postwar shortage of both materials and skilled labour held up the return of the *Empress of Canada.* By 1947, however, she set sail from Liverpool to Montreal in the wake of the enthusiastic welcome-back messages her supporters had sent to CPR.

The two reconditioned liners were painted in CP's traditional White Empress livery. In their refurbished and reconditioned state, they were both capable of achieving a quite-acceptable 18.5 knots for the Atlantic crossing, to Montreal in the summer season and to Saint John, New Brunswick, in winter. Each of the stately liners could accommodate four hundred first-class and three hundred tourist-class passengers. Third class had been eliminated in favour of providing more room for crewmembers and cargo.

Another survivor of the war was the *Empress of Scotland*, a veteran of the Pacific service since 1930, when it had been launched as the *Empress of Japan.* That ship had been renamed in light of Japan's attack on Pearl Harbor. It spent a large part of 1943–44 shuttling Allied soldiers between Newport News and New York on one side of the Atlantic, and Liverpool and Casablanca on the other.

As the formerly unbeaten racehorse on the Vancouver-to-Yokohama run, the *Empress of Scotland* was a welcome addition to CP's postwar Atlantic fleet, carrying as many as 458 first-class passengers and 250 tourists per crossing, at a speedy twenty-one knots. Gone were the accommo-

Two enthusiastic members of the 1959 world cruise on the *Empress of France* flaunt their connections with Cowtown. AUTHOR'S COLLECTION

dations for the more than 500 Asians who travelled in steerage on most of the ship's eastbound voyages in her early years.

The converted Duchesses were sufficiently comfortable for the postwar trade, but the *Empress of Scotland* went further in bringing some of the old-style elaborations from the glory days of the ocean liners. Connected by a long, windowed gallery, its first-class rooms included a glass-domed lounge, smoking room, and card room, as well as a palm court, the latter invoking all the exotic comforts of a tropical isle.

In 1951, a special suite of rooms onboard the *Empress of Scotland* was provided for Princess Elizabeth and Prince Phillip on their return voyage to Great Britain from a royal tour of Canada.

The one dark note in Canadian Pacific's return to the Atlantic occurred at the Gladstone Dock in Liverpool, while the *Empress of Canada* was undergoing a general overhaul, on January 25, 1953. A fire of unknown origin had broken out, while only a small security crew was onboard. By the time fire brigades were able to reach the dock, the ship was ablaze. The weight of the water poured from fire hoses onto the burning ship caused it to turn over on its side, leading to the complete loss of the liner, and a very lengthy and expensive salvage operation.

Fortunately, the steamship company was able to find a quick replacement for the ill-fated *Empress of Canada* with the acquisition of the French Line steamer *De Grasse*. Rechristened the *Empress of Australia*, the second CP ship to bear this name, the replacement vessel made the first transatlantic sailing for its new owners on April 28, 1953, at a modest sixteen knots.

The *Empress of Australia* would remain in service for only three years. By then, Canadian Pacific had come to the momentous decision to invest in three brand new, fully modern liners for the company's transatlantic service, completing its postwar rebirth on the sea as much as it had on land.

In 1971, the *Empress of Canada, Empress of Britain,* and *Empress of England* would be launched to much fanfare. Their days in the North Atlantic would be short-lived, but the elegant ocean-going yachts would go on to distinguished careers as cruise ships—particular in the Caribbean trade. ⊹

FALL OF A COMET

When the world's first jet airliner, the de Havilland Comet, rolled out of its hangar for test flights, it captured the imagination of Canadian Pacific Air Lines president Grant McConachie. In 1949, the pioneer airman had bigger things in mind than simply continuing to serve the bush plane routes that had been the stock and trade of the ten smaller regional companies that together comprised his fledging enterprise. If he had any say in the matter, the service on his airline, and the equipment on which its customers flew, would be second to none.

By May 2, 1952, when the Comet jetted from London to Johannesburg on its first commercial flight for British Overseas Airways Corporation (BOAC), CPAL had already set its sights on being a major player in the Pacific. The potential benefits of the exciting new technology were an easy sell for the ambitious McConachie. With a cruising speed of just under five hundred miles per hour and a range of 1,750 miles—twice the distance the experts had initially thought possible—the streamlined jetliner was just what CPAL needed for its Vancouver to Sydney service.

No longer would passengers be subjected to the numbing noise and vibration of the four 3,400-horsepower engines that typically powered conventional aircraft on long-haul routes. Flying above 35,000 feet, the Comet would envelop air travellers in what its manufacturer called a "cone of silence," while requiring less power and fuel to propel the aircraft through the thinner air.

This high-altitude strategy required the first pressurized cabin for a commercial airliner, but the resulting efficiencies meant that the four de Havilland Ghost engines—turbojets each capable of delivering five thousand pounds of thrust—could easily outperform the conventional propeller engines of the day.

The Comet had quickly logged one hundred million miles with the BOAC, carrying more than 28,000 passengers on its routes from the UK to the Far East and Africa. Along with Air France, British Commonwealth Pacific, France's Union Aéromaritime de Transport and Japan Air Lines, CPAL was among the first purchasers, placing an order for two Comet 1As for its south Pacific route between Sydney, Fiji, Canton Island, and Honolulu.

McConachie's plan was to continue to use the long-range, piston-powered Douglas Super DC-6B on the leg between Vancouver and Hawaii, while operating the Comet on the southern portion of the route, from Hawaii to Sydney. Maintenance of the new jetliner would be carried out

The de Havilland Comet was the first commercial jetliner in the world when it began operations with British Airways. CPAL was quick to see its potential. AUTHOR'S COLLECTION

at a facility de Havilland was planning to set up in Sydney and at CPAL's own shop in Vancouver, at what would become the world's first commercial jet base outside of the UK. When the Mark II model of the Comet came off the assembly line in 1954, its greater range would allow the jet to take over flying duties on the entire Vancouver to Sydney run.

CPAL's first Comet was dubbed the *Empress of Hawaii* as a salute to the stalwart Pacific Empress liners operated by Canadian Pacific Steamships in the years between the late 1880s and the Second World War. On March 1, 1953, CPAL Comet 1A CF-CUN *Empress of Hawaii* departed London airport for its flight to Australia, where it was to be placed in regular service on the Pacific.

Aboard the aircraft were six de Havilland jet technicians and five CPAL top crewmembers. Captain Charles Pentland, the forty-two-year-old director of the airline's overseas flight operations, and co-pilot Captain C. North Sawle were in charge of the assignment. Both had plenty of flying experience in piston-engine planes—Pentland with Imperial Airways and BOAC, and

Sawle as a bush pilot in the challenging Canadian North. The two captains had taken a short yet rigorous training course in flying the Comet at the de Havilland aerodrome in Hatfield, England, where they had endured the usual taunting to which all old-fashioned "windmill jockeys," or pilots of propeller-driven aircraft, were subjected.

Accompanying the captains on the flight were radio-navigator John Cooke, chief navigator Patrick Roy (a recipient of the Distinguished Flying Cross during the Second World War), and flight engineer James Smith, who was slated to become CPAL's chief maintenance man in Sydney.

At McConachie's insistence, their first service flight would be not just a milk run; it would establish a new air record of elapsed time between Britain and Australia, with refueling stops along the way. The decision would make the flight "bloody rough on us cockpit help," according to an understated quip from Pentland, who no doubt was fatigued and under considerable stress when the Comet prepared to take off from Karachi for Singapore at 3:00 AM on March 3. Within minutes, the *Empress of Hawaii* and all eleven of her passengers would perish in a ball of fire at the end of the runway.

The extensive investigations that followed in the wake of the Comet's tragic demise showed the

Company publicists jumped the gun when they printed posters featuring the jetliner that never went into revenue service for Canadian Pacific. AUTHOR'S COLLECTION

In the Air, on the Sea, and by Land

causes to have been partly a design flaw and partly human error. The Comet tended to be sluggish on initial acceleration, particularly when fully loaded with fuel. Accordingly, Pentland had set the brakes as he pushed forward the throttle to power up the jet's four Ghost engines, before releasing the brakes and beginning his roll down the runway at full bore. He had learned in training that both the wings of the plane and the shape of the Comet's air intakes created drag and diminished jet thrust in a nose-high position, but he did not follow textbook procedure.

As he pulled back on the control column to lift the nose wheel from the tarmac, Pentland should then have levelled the plane so that the wheel barely skimmed the surface, thus allowing the Comet to obtain sufficient speed for liftoff. Instead he continued to roll along the ground with the plane's nose too high to reach its 122-knot takeoff speed.

As the runway got shorter, Pentland panicked and pulled the nose up sharply, causing the Comet's tail to strike the ground. Recognizing his error, he made a desperate attempt to level the plane and build more ground speed.

Unfortunately, time had run out for both Pentland and the *Empress of Hawaii*. When the Comet hit the bank at the end of the runway, the explosion lit up the sky for miles around. The bodies of the eleven people on board were burnt beyond recognition and were later buried in a common grave in Karachi.

A number of other serious accidents occurred during Comet flights that year, but McConachie maintained his faith in the innovative jetliner. "Comets have logged fifty million engine miles without mechanical fault, a record never approached by any conventional aircraft," he said when CPAL placed an order for three Comet IIs, to be delivered in 1954.

McConachie's enthusiasm, however, was short lived. On January 10, 1954, a BOAC Comet en route from Rome's Ciampino Airport to London disintegrated at 26,000 feet, grounding all of the de Havilland jetliners for several months while an inconclusive inquiry was conducted. Two weeks and two days after the resumption of jet service, on April 8, another Comet flying from Rome to Cairo was lost. The ensuing investigation concluded that a rapid change in altitude had caused extreme stresses at the corners of the Comet's square windows, leading to metal fatigue and a bomb-like explosion that instantly depressurized the jet's cabin.

As a result of the tragic events, CPAL allowed its order for the later model of the Comet to lapse. For the foreseeable future, it would operate its Pacific routes and a new polar route to Amsterdam with the DC-6B's piston engine. ✢

FASTER THAN A RIFLE BULLET

By 1964, Canadian Pacific Air Lines (CPAL) was ready to go supersonic.

That was the year company chairman, Norris R. "Buck" Crump, and airline president, Grant W.G. McConachie, signed an agreement with the United States Federal Aviation Agency to get into the delivery line-up for three American supersonic aircraft. Boeing, Lockheed, and North American were all competing to build the airframe for the futuristic plane that would go head-to-head with the Anglo-French Concorde and take air transport to a whole new level.

CP had chosen to go with the American supersonic model because its specifications called for a longer-range capability, a consideration that was paramount for an airline company that was already serving some of the world's longest commercial routes. With a range of 4,500 miles, and a payload of 150 to 230 paying customers, the new supersonic transports (SSTs) were expected to cruise at 75,000 feet and travel through sub-space at an astonishing 1,800 to 2,000 miles per hour—more than three times the speed of sound.

Company executives estimated the supersonic jets would make the flight from Vancouver to Tokyo in four hours, about six hours faster than the airline's current fleet of DC-8s could. The popular Montreal-to-Rome route showed a similar promise of halving the scheduled eight-hour marathon trips regularly flown. CPAL's long routes were tailor made for supersonic jets. Under favourable conditions, Canadian Pacific could expect to put its first sound-breaking passenger airliners in operation by 1974. Each plane would come with a price tag of $25 million, but they would be well worth it.

The company that was the airborne arm of the Canadian Pacific Railway had through hard work and perseverance earned the right to fly to fifteen countries and on major routes across Canada.

In 1946, the American experimental plane X-1 had been the first aircraft to break the sound barrier. Two years later, it went on to fly one thousand miles per hour, and in 1954 sixteen hundred miles per hour. Now many in the airline industry were expecting their company's planes to fly routinely at supersonic speeds. In fact, some were already anticipating the next generation of *hyper*sonic jets that would knife through the atmosphere at speeds perhaps approaching seven or eight thousand miles per hour.

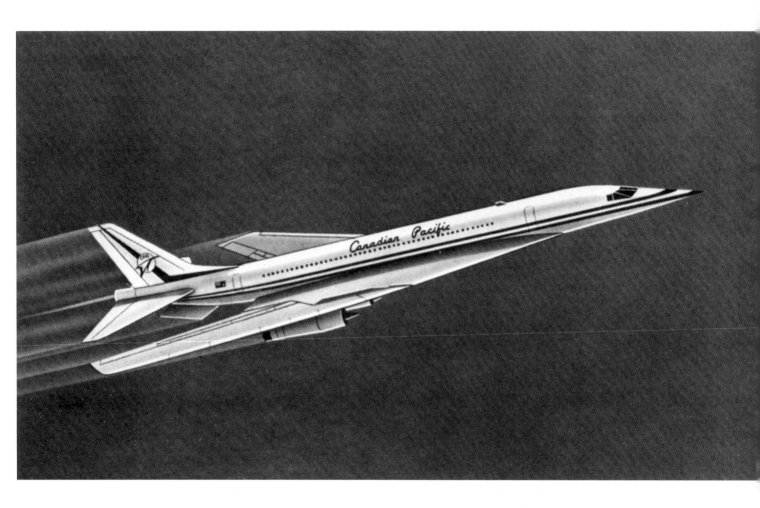

The SST was custom-made for CPAL's long routes across the Pacific, but the technology never took hold in North America. AUTHOR'S COLLECTION

While Curtiss-Wright, General Electric, and Pratt & Whitney were still vying for the contract to manufacture the engines that would double the power of anything then in the air, Boeing won the airframe competition. The original drawings called for titanium and stainless-steel construction to withstand the extremely high temperatures that would be experienced as a result of the air friction at supersonic speeds.

The initial designs also anticipated using a swing wing, which would appear similar to that of a tradition aircraft upon takeoff but would fold back into a more streamlined position at cruising speed. A subsequent, necessary move to a less complex delta wing would soon require a complete redesign and cause considerable delays.

Much hope was placed on the American supersonic. Even the British Overseas Airways Corporation and Air France, the main backers of the rival Concorde aircraft, each ordered six US planes to hedge their bets in the supersonic sweepstakes.

Accountants at Canadian Pacific Air Lines salivated at the prospect of grossing more than $63 million in the first year their three American supersonics would take to the air.

In 1967, CPAL president J.C. Gilmer announced that the company would build a $26-million overhaul and maintenance facility at Vancouver International Airport, one of the world's first bases for supersonic aircraft. It would also be able to accommodate the airline's current fleet, which included its dependable DC-8s and a few elongated Spacemaster DC-8s on order.

Before working prototypes of the Boeing plane—designated the 2707—were able to take to the sky, however, an avalanche of negative press centred on twin evils: the sonic boom caused by supersonic aircraft when they broke the sound barrier, and the perceived potential for destruction of the ozone layer, which supersonic flight presented. These fears took their toll on the endeavour, while cost overruns dealt the final blow.

In 1971, the US Senate refused to give any more funding to the supersonic development. In a desperate bid to keep the dream alive, aviation buffs across the world contributed more than a million dollars to save the American SST, to no avail. In quick succession, the US House of Representatives also voted to end funding. Left unfilled would be 122 orders from 26 airlines around the world, among them Alitalia, Delta Air Lines, Iberia, KLM, Northwest Airlines, World Airways, and CP Air Lines.

Massive layoffs at the Boeing plant in Seattle, where the aircraft of the future was to have been manufactured, were greeted with disappointment and cynicism in the industry, and with the media at large. The SST was labelled "the airplane that almost ate Seattle." Amid the rapid exodus of airline personnel, a billboard on the edge of town read: "Will the last person leaving Seattle turn out the lights."

In 1976, the Anglo-French Concorde made its inaugural flight. Fourteen SSTs of this type were built for commercial service across the Atlantic. They served dependably until being taken out of service in 2003, in the aftermath of an unfortunate crash of a supersonic a few years earlier, which killed all one hundred passengers and nine crewmembers. A commercial SST designed, built, and launched by the Soviet Union made only fifty-five passenger flights, before being grounded for technical reasons.

The operational tragedy of the Concorde, along with the accompanying loss of public confidence and rising cost of maintenance, brought the age of the SST to ground.

Canadian Pacific Air Lines had missed its chance to go supersonic. ✛

FILMING THE NATIONAL DREAM

Dozens of books have been written about the building of the Canadian Pacific Railway, and there have even been one or two full-length movies, notably the 1949 film *Canadian Pacific* starring Randolph Scott and Jane Wyatt. But none of these offerings managed to raise public awareness of the role the CPR has played in the birth and development of the nation of Canada as did the publication of Pierre Berton's companion volumes *The National Dream* (1970) and *The Last Spike* (1971) and, perhaps more importantly, the Canadian Broadcasting Corporation's dramatization of the stories in an eight-part series entitled *The National Dream: Building the Impossible Railway.*

The film series took full advantage of the popularity of Berton's two histories, which created a detailed Canadian mythology around the characters who were front and centre during the planning and construction of the transcontinental railway. While dramatizing the myriad political and physical obstacles that had to be overcome in building the line, the television series brought to the broad Canadian public Berton's vision of CPR as the main catalyst for turning the dream of a viable, coast-to-coast nation into a reality.

In 1973, while the CBC was still exploring where to film various scenes in its docudrama mini-series, the producers contacted CPR for help in accessing the availability of vintage railway equipment. The railway's official historian and archivist, Omer Lavallée, was immediately recruited as the railway's chief liaison to the production team.

Perhaps the most important mechanical actor in the drama would be one of the 1880s-era, standard CPR locomotives that were once so ubiquitous in the company's operations—but which were now extremely rare historical artifacts. Fortunately, one of the last such engines had been preserved by a Toronto lawyer and train buff named Neil McNish.

Together with members of the Ontario Rail Association, McNish agreed to not only put the locomotive in working order, give it a fresh paint job, and fit it out with a new wooden cab, but also to make certain cosmetic changes to help portray CPR's construction period accurately. In doing so, the volunteer engine builders ensured that, with a few quick changes to things like its number board and its style of smokestack, the locomotive could be made to represent several different iron horses, as necessary to the plot.

Pierre Berton's two-volume history of the building of the Canadian Pacific Railway, and the accompanying TV series that aired on CBC, sparked a renewed interest in Canada's first transcontinental railway. PHOTO BY BOB SMITH, AUTHOR'S COLLECTION

During the search for appropriate railway rolling stock, CPR's subsidiary Dominion Atlantic Railway contributed two open-platform boarding cars, which were once used as suburban coaches. At Winnipeg's Weston Shops, these cars were given an extensive external restoration, with new windows and such, and painted to represent period railway equipment.

The Alberta Pioneer Railway Association—with the good graces of Canadian National—offered a baggage car of the correct era from its collections. And the mechanical department folks on CPR's Alberta South Division located and repainted a wooden boxcar that was close enough to requirements, while fabricating a nonexistent, early flatcar from the remains of several pieces of scrapped cars around the yard.

Filming required Lavallée and the railway to identify two geographic locales with little or no revenue traffic on them. One was a flat, uncultivated prairie setting to shoot the progress of track-laying across the Northwest Territories (now Saskatchewan and Alberta) during the summers of 1882 and 1883. The other was a rugged setting meant to portray the construction of tunnels and trestles through the mountains of British Columbia.

For the tracklaying scenes, CPR assistant regional engineer Alex Price supervised the filming on the railway's Cassils Subdivision, which extends across arid grazing land a few miles west of Brooks, Alberta. Under Alex's guidance, the railway workers (fifty young men from nearby Brooks Composite School) carried the rails from the flatcars to the railhead with their bare hands, as had been the practice in the 1880s—and there were no hardhats or safety vests needed, either.

The mountain shots were filmed on CPR's Carmi Subdivision, through the Myra Canyon east of Okanagan Lake. About twenty miles of track were used to capture the right feel for various scenes. Partly dismantled wooden trestles on the subdivision stood in perfectly for partly constructed bridges on the original main line.

Pierre Berton himself was a consultant for the mini-series and appeared on camera at the start of each segment to set the stage for the dramatic re-enactments that followed.

The CBC aired the eight-part production over the months of March and April 1974. The audience for *The National Dream* was estimated at about three million viewers within Canada, a record for CBC in terms of dramatic programming. The series was later dubbed in French and broadcast on Radio-Canada and was afterward seen in modified form on BBC in the United Kingdom. ⁜

MORE THAN JUST A MEMORY

A tangible and vivid link to the past was severed when photographer Rick Robinson left CPR on early retirement, in 2009. Robinson was the last custodian of the railway's in-house image factory, where more than a century of dedicated lens men systematically viewed and recorded for posterity the growth of an institution and the emancipation of a nation.

CPR's involvement in the production and use of high-quality photographic images dates back to the company's roots in the 1880s. So numerous were the requests from photographers to record the building of the railway through the pristine wilderness of the Canadian West that they were regarded as somewhat of a nuisance or, as CPR general superintendent John Egan characterized them, "photographic fiends."

There were notable exceptions to Egan's broad condemnation, however, as CPR was quick to recognize the enormous publicity value of a well-chosen and well-produced image. Established practitioners such as Alexander Henderson, Oliver Buell, and William Notman & Sons were commissioned by the railway to enliven company pamphlets and brochures.

William McFarlane Notman—son of the elder William Notman, a highly regarded Montreal photographic entrepreneur—travelled west on CPR business as early as 1884. A year after regular transcontinental service was inaugurated in 1886, Notman was afforded the luxury of a private railway car, specially outfitted for his artistic endeavours. On seven trips across the CPR system from 1887 to 1909, Notman used his large-format view camera and flash-pan powder to record the wonders of the railway's scenic route on classic, glass-plate negatives, many of which would be used to attract prospective settlers and tourists to Canada.

A self-styled professor, Buell was an itinerant photographer, best known for his magic lantern, or stereopticon, slide shows, with which he entertained audiences in Canada, the United States, and overseas. He, too, was given access to the CPR photographers' car, after railway

CPR photographer James C. Bennett took great pains—and his tripod—to get spectacular panoramic views of the Rocky Mountains. GLENBOW ARCHIVES, ARCHIVES AND SPECIAL COLLECTIONS, UNIVERSITY OF CALGARY NA-5234-15

builder and second company president, William Van Horne, deemed Buell's work to be "of a very high order of merit."

Henderson was the first to be placed on a regular salary with the fledgling photographic department of the 1890s. A one-time assistant of Notman, Henderson was provided with his own understudy, regular use of the company's photographic car, and the express cooperation of the entire railway system, including personal assistance from a CPR sectionman to overcome physical obstacles to obtaining the best vantage points from which to ply his craft.

Concurrently, a number of independent photographers were also granted travel passes. The railway often purchased the resulting views for publicity purposes, as well as to illustrate a series of collectors' portfolios. Some of the better known of these specialists were Trueman & Caple and the Bailey Brothers of Vancouver, Boorne & May from Calgary, and Steele & Company of Winnipeg.

Although much of CPR's photographic work was carried out under the auspices of the passenger department, the engineering department also undertook an important visual survey of all the bridges, stations, and ancillary structures on the railway. Company engineer Joseph W. Heckman is credited with producing an invaluable photographic record of all of the structures extant between 1898 and 1915.

Another Notman protégé, James C. Bennett, joined CPR in 1902. Twelve years later, around the time of the outbreak of the First World War, Bennett was asked to reorganize all of the railway's photographic activities as a responsibility of its publicity department.

Canadian Pacific also had a keen interest in motion pictures and the production of newsreels for theatrical release. In 1920, its formation of Associated Screen News, producers of both still images and motion pictures, greatly added to CPR's photographic coverage of significant company and national events.

In the twenties and thirties, Associated Screen News photographer Harry Pollard was probably the most well-travelled cameraman in the world, cruising with CPR steamships on more than a dozen tours around the globe.

In 1929, Nick Morant walked through the doors at CPR's Winnipeg press bureau. Over the next fifty years, with only two brief interruptions in service, he earned the right to use the title CPR Special Photographer on his railway business card. Morant became legendary across Canada and around the world. His memorable Canadian images not only appeared in magazines such as *Time, Look, Life, Saturday Evening Post,* and *National Geographic* but were also etched into the plates used to print Canadian ten-, fifty- and hundred-dollar bills. A particularly scenic spot not far from Lake Louise, Alberta, where the famed cameraman liked to take publicity shots of CPR trains, is still officially known as Morant's Curve.

Nicholas Morant shot thousands of photographs for Canadian Pacific. Many of them became the iconic images that defined the railway's golden era. OMER LAVALLÉE COLLECTION

Bennett and his successor, Armand Lafrenière, continued to expand the company's operations throughout the 1930s and the war years. Lafrenière, himself, achieved a measure of fame when he was given the opportunity to record several of the key events at the historic Quebec Conference, attended by Churchill, Roosevelt, and Mackenzie King. The images were rushed to print and shown as news spots around the world.

In the Air, on the Sea, and by Land

Staff photographers James Bennett, seated at right,
and J. Armand Lafrenière work in one of the railway's
cars that was specially outfitted for their trade.
AUTHOR'S COLLECTION

By the early 1940s a suite of eleven rooms in Montreal's Windsor Station was devoted to the photography department. It included a portrait studio, dark room, finishing room, contact printing room, enlarging rooms, lantern-slide room, photostat room, file room, storeroom, and office.

During the Second World War, Morant was loaned to Canada's Wartime Information Board, where his keen eye produced the images that illuminated the country's contributions to the Allied war effort. At the same time, the CPR shutterbug was honing his skills in aerial reconnaissance with the Royal Canadian Air Force, afterward teaching classes in photography at the wartime air observer school in Portage la Prairie, Manitoba. One of his students, Mickey Potoroka, would go on to join the railway as a press representative in Winnipeg and in Toronto.

In the ensuing years, Norman Hull succeeded Lafrenière. Later, Arnold Harrington, a camera buff and hobbyist, took CPR's photographic activities to a new professional level. Under Harrington, the operation became truly state of the art, with a full studio, black-and-white and colour processing, mural-size mounting presses, and an eight-member staff that was among the best in the business.

Together they generated virtually thousands of images for books, magazines, and company promotional materials, and out shopped countless prints for office walls, museum exhibits, and home décor.

As an integral part of corporate communications and public affairs, CP's photographic services led the country in the field of industrial photography through the latter half of the twentieth century, winning numerous awards and systematically amassing the country's largest private photo collection. Along the way, the company's photographers created an incredible archive of every aspect of CPR's economic and historic involvements, nationally and internationally. Every railway occupation is represented; the activities and the faces of tens of thousands of employees captured for all time.

The last three stalwarts of the department were Maurice Quinn, Bob Kennell, and Rick Robinson, all of whom carried on the tradition of recording every important CPR milestone,

The last CPR photographer, Rick Robinson, takes a high-angle shot of restored steam locomotive 2816, as it rounds the bend at Morant's Curve in Banff National Park. PHOTO BY DAVID JONES, AUTHOR'S COLLECTION

including the company's centennial celebrations in 1981; the re-enactment of the driving of the last spike, one hundred years after that most famous of Canadian events; and the move of the railway's head office from Montreal to Calgary in 1996.

With CPR's relocation to Calgary, Robinson single-handedly continued the tradition, producing a steady stream of stills for company publications and websites, along with video footage for internal and external consumption. With his departure, the railway no longer has a full-time witness to the passage of time and the making of history. Only time will tell if freelance professionals and a public—awash in digital devices, generating transient images—will be able to continue the story for future generations. ⁜

ACKNOWLEDGEMENTS

Shortly after I began working for Canadian Pacific in 1974, I was asked to join a small group of people who were establishing a comprehensive corporate archive. The main functions of the department would be to aid with the retrieval of important legal papers and to preserve, for posterity, interesting and valuable historic and promotional materials, both documents and artifacts.

The day-to-day activities of acquiring, organizing, preserving, and sometimes displaying various parts of the collection that eventually grew to be the most diverse and historically significant company archive in Canada inspired me to complete a university degree in history and library studies. When I left the archives group to join Canadian Pacific's department of communications and public affairs, I felt an overwhelming urge to write about the many fascinating and inextricable links between the company's diverse activities and the overall settlement and development of the country itself.

In 2002, that ambition came to fruition with the publishing of *Tales of the CPR*, a series of short, anecdotal stories about some of the many transportation and resource-based involvements of Canadian Pacific. Eighteen years and several books later, I have managed to assemble this second offering of tales from a seemingly bottomless well, once again mostly drawing upon primary source materials from the Canadian Pacific Corporate Archives collection.

A few of the stories were also fleshed out by facts gleaned from some of the many published works about Canadian Pacific. Among these are "The Big Hill" and "Schwitzer's Railway Pretzel," from Graeme Pole's *The Spiral Tunnels and Big Hill*; "Phantom Train Presaged Disaster," from Ken Lidell's *I'll Take the Train*; "Van Horne's Garden of Eden," from *Minister's Island*; and "The Tragic BC Architect," from Terry Reksten's *Rattenbury*. The publishing details for all of these are listed in this volume's "Further Reading."

Most of the photographs from the author's collection were acquired over the years, either from the Canadian Pacific Corporate Archives or from Canadian Pacific Photographic Services, of which neither department still survives. Many of the images will still be available from the Archives Centre at Exporail, the Canadian Railway Museum, and the current custodian of the CP photography and archives collections, whose staff provided three of the images for Railway Nation.

In addition, I am grateful to the staff members at Glenbow Archives at the University of Calgary, the Royal BC Museum and Archives, Library and Archives Canada, the Imperial War Museum, and the Whyte Museum of the Canadian Rockies.

I am further indebted to Rick Robinson, a CP photographer and good friend with whom I worked for many years, who did a lot of the scanning for this volume and also provided a photograph of the G7 meeting in Montebello, Quebec; Philippe Beaudry, who gave me a portrait shot to accompany the story about himself and the *Empress of Ireland*; and Doug Phillips, a colleague from the National Dream Legacy Society, who contributed two images and often had to straighten me out on some small technicality of CPR operations, about which he is an incredible font of knowledge.

For help with the preparation of this edition, I thank the people at Heritage House Publishing, particularly editor Warren Layberry and editorial coordinator Nandini Thaker; former Glenbow archivist Doug Cass for graciously providing a foreword; and my wife, Erika Watters, for proofreading the manuscript and offering constructive suggestions.

FURTHER READING

Berton, Pierre. *The National Dream: The Great Railway 1871–1881.* Toronto: McClelland & Stewart, 1983.

———. *The Last Spike: The Great Railway 1871–1881.* Toronto: McClelland & Stewart, 1983.

Choko, Marc, and David Jones. *Canadian Pacific Posters: 1883–1963.* Montreal: Meridian Press, 1995.

Cruise, David, and Alison Griffiths. *Lords of the Line.* Markham, ON: Penguin Books, 1988.

Gibbon, John Murray. *Steel of Empire: The Romantic History of the Canadian Pacific Railway, the Northwest Passage of Today.* London: Rich & Cowan, 1935.

Ham, George H. *Reminiscences of a Raconteur.* Toronto: The Musson Book Co., 1921.

Hart, E. J. *The Selling of Canada: The CPR and the Beginnings of Canadian Tourism.* Banff, AB: Altitude Publishing, 1983.

Jones, David Laurence. *Famous Name Trains: Travelling in Style with the CPR.* Calgary: Fifth House, 2006.

———. *See This World before the Next: Cruising with CPR Steamships in the Twenties and Thirties.* Calgary: Fifth House, 2004.

———. *Tales of the CPR.* Calgary: Fifth House, 2002.

———. *The Railway Beat: A Century of Canadian Pacific Service.* Markham, ON: Fifth House, 2014.

Keith, Ronald A. *Bush Pilot with a Briefcase: The Happy-go-lucky Story of Grant McConachie.* Don Mills, ON: Paper Jacks, 1972.

Lamb, W. Kaye. *History of the Canadian Pacific Railway.* New York: MacMillan, 1977.

Lavallée, Omer. *Van Horne's Road: An Illustrated Account of the Construction and First Years of Operation of the Canadian Pacific Transcontinental Railway.* Toronto: A Railfare Book, 1981.

Lidell, Ken. *I'll Take the Train.* Saskatoon, SK: Modern Press, Prairie Books Service, 1966.

McKee, Bill, and Georgeen Klassen. *Trail of Iron: The CPR and the Birth of the West, 1880–1930.* Vancouver: Douglas & McIntyre, 1983.

Miller-Barstow, D.H. *Beatty of the CPR: A Biography.* Toronto: McClelland and Stewart, 1951.

Musk, George. *Canadian Pacific: The Story of the Famous Shipping Line.* London: David & Charles, 1981.

Pole, Graeme. *The Spiral Tunnels and the Big Hill on the Canadian Pacific Railway.* Hazelton, BC: Mountain Vision Publishing, 2009.

Reksten, Terry. *Rattenbury.* Winlaw, BC: Sono Niss Press, 1988.

Sullivan, David. *Minister's Island: Sir William Van Horne's Summer Home in St. Andrews.* St. Andrews, NB: Pendlebury Press, 2007.

INDEX

ABOUT THE AUTHOR

DAVID LAURENCE JONES is a long-time employee and former manager of internal communications at Canadian Pacific Railway. A graduate in history and library studies from Concordia University, he worked for fourteen years in the railway's corporate archives, organizing, cataloguing, and making records available to researchers, authors, and moviemakers. Along the way, he has collected stories and anecdotes about CPR's rich heritage, which can be found herein, as well as in his earlier works *Tales of the CPR, See This World before the Next, Famous Name Trains,* and *The Railway Beat*. Jones is a member of the Chinook Country Chapter of the Historical Society of Alberta and the National Dream Legacy Society. He is currently working on a comprehensive study of Canadian Pacific's extensive role in the settlement and development of the "Golden Northwest."